TWENTIETH-CENTURY AMERICAN WOMEN'S FICTION

Also by Guy Reynolds

WILLA CATHER IN CONTEXT

Twentieth-Century American Women's Fiction

A Critical Introduction

Guy Reynolds

St. Martin's Press
New York

TWENTIETH-CENTURY AMERICAN WOMEN'S FICTION

Copyright © 1999 by Guy Reynolds

St. Martin's Press, Scholarly and Reference Division,
175 Fifth Avenue, New York, N.Y. 10010

First published in the United States of America in 1999

This book is printed on paper suitable for recycling and made from fully managed and sustained forest sources.

Printed in Hong Kong

ISBN 0–312–22636–5 clothbound
ISBN 0–312–22637–3 paperback

Library of Congress Cataloging-in-Publication Data
Reynolds, Guy.
Twentieth-century American women's fiction : a critical introduction / Guy Reynolds.
p.   cm.
Includes bibliographical references and index.
ISBN 0–312–22636–5 (cloth). — ISBN 0–312–22637–3 (pbk.)
1. American fiction—Women authors—History and criticism.
2. Women and literature—United States—History—20th century.
3. American fiction—20th century—History and criticism.
I. Title.
PS374.W6R47   1999
813'.5099287—dc21   99–15611
                                                                     CIP

PS
374
· W6
R4 7
1999

For Isabel

Contents

Preface

This book sets out to provide readers with a reasonably comprehensive account of a range of novelists, all of whom were women and Americans (whether they have anything in common on account of their gender and nationality is one of the subjects of the book). It is, I hope, a sufficiently wide-ranging account to achieve the authority of a 'critical introduction' or 'survey'. But it is also, I again hope, argumentative enough to take on the flavour of a monograph. That the book is something of a critical hybrid is a testimony to its subject: fictions by American women have often shifted across idioms or conflated genres.

Another form of hybridity might be found in the imagined readerships for this book. Most authors find themselves predicating a reader; in my case, I have had to imagine a number of different, and perhaps competing, readers. Written in the UK, by an Englishman, for a British (and now German-owned) publisher, this is a work rooted in a European context. But it will also be published in New York, and I trust it will find an American audience. What is known to an American reader is not necessarily known to a European, and vice-versa; I found myself moving between the continents in terms of what can be expected to form a general body of received cultural knowledge. Thus, American readers might be slightly surprised at the emphasis on the particulars of their own national life. The book is written by an outsider, and the explication of historical detail is designed to help readers unfamiliar with American history. Equally, non-American readers will have to accept that, in some places, it seemed sensible to preserve US rather than British spellings of key terms: 'local color' fiction remains just that, 'local color'.

GUY REYNOLDS

Acknowledgements

The writing of this book has been greatly facilitated by the support, encouragement and, not least, money of two institutions: the University of Kent at Canterbury and the British Academy. The School of English at UKC granted me study leave to work on the project; the British Academy provided further support under the 'Research leave' scheme. Several colleagues have helped with suggestions, corrections and insights as I drafted the manuscript: Henry Claridge, Rod Edmond, David Herd and Lyn Innes. Thomas Docherty hosted a seminar where a valuable commentary about ideas of 'genealogy' evolved under his guidance. And the members of the Kent Centre for American Studies indirectly but significantly contributed, by turning my teaching towards the interplay of history and literature.

In the United States, I have had a regrettably intermittent but none the less important connection with members of the Willa Cather scholarly community, particularly with Susan Rosowski of the University of Nebraska. Becoming part of the wide circle of Cather scholars gave me the confidence to move into other areas of American literary studies. At the University of Tulsa, Oklahoma, the librarians of the McFarlin Special Collections helped me enormously, both with primary and secondary materials in the field of women's literature.

The production of the book was handled with characteristic smoothness by staff at Macmillan, notably Margaret Bartley. I must also add my thanks to the anonymous reader of the manuscript, whose perspicacious review helped me to clarify the direction of the final text.

Finally, a phalanx of family members from the Reynolds and Anton-Smith clans provided the reasonably calm conditions in which to write. Above all, Cal Anton-Smith kept the two little wolves from the door.

Introduction: the Genealogy of American Women's Narrative, 1892–1995

After nearly thirty years of canon-busting, critical revisionism and renewal, is it possible to generalise about American women's narratives produced during the past century? For American women's fiction (and associated forms of prose, such as autobiography and the diary), continual recoveries of lost works mean that the 'canon' has hardly come into being. As soon as a canon begins to take shape, the deconstructive turn of modern criticism undermines its foundational principles. Women's fiction, as a body of work *sui generis*, began to attract serious and sustained critical attention in the wake of the 1960s women's movement. Feminist critics attacked what they saw as the 'masculinist' bias of American literary criticism; the motifs, topics and themes celebrated by the masculinist critics were, it was now argued, highly gendered, and took little account of the contribution of American women to the national literature. Attacks on the male bias of literary scholarship went hand-in-hand with recoveries of lost female writers and marginalised traditions (the increased attention to nineteenth-century sensational and domestic writing dates from this phase in the early 1970s). Well-known writers such as Willa Cather or Edith Wharton continued to be read; but their work was increasingly seen as a distinctively *female* achievement. Earlier studies of Cather had tended to 'de-sex' her, but now gender and sexuality came to the fore; critics became fascinated by the lesbianism which informed, in complex and often covert ways, Cather's narrative strategies.[1]

None the less, while critics unpicked the motifs of masculinist canons, there were relatively few overarching 'stories' of American women's writing, few critical pathways through the maze of individual authors. The masculinist canon within

1

America was posited on powerful grand narratives which placed fiction within a story about the growth of a nation: R. W. B. Lewis's 'American Adam' (fiction as celebration of heroic, youthful individualism); Leo Marx's 'Machine in the Garden' (the primacy of geographical space; the contrast between industrialism and pastoralism); the obsession with the wilderness and the frontier, analysed in Henry Nash Smith's *Virgin Land* and Leslie Fiedler's *Love and Death in the American Novel*. Feminist criticism was partly committed to deconstructing these critical paradigms by revealing their masculine partiality and theoretical naivety. Having deconstructed the male biases of literary scholarship, exposing the covert ideologies of criticism, feminist scholars were understandably tentative about replacing one set of constructs with another. Instead, the critical drive was towards literary archaeology (recovery of lost texts or authors), or towards interpretative strategies focused on groups of writers within more localised schools (for instance, Southern writers, local colorists, or various ethnic groupings). Critics were keen to avoid a universalism which would simply see women's fiction as a set of unchanging, synchronic 'features', uninflected by the very large differences within women's culture (differences of race, class and sexuality, not to mention the aesthetic differences from one novel to the next).[2]

Would it be possible, in the aftermath of all this revisionism and re-discovery, to construct 'post-canonical' critical narratives: networks of continuity, inheritance and influence which tie together disparate texts across a spread of time? 'Post-canonical criticism' can be defined as the qualified recovery of a tradition of so-called minority writing – 'qualified' because the critic is cautious about positing overly synoptic or binding generalisations. Generalised aesthetics have often been subject to critical attack. Thus within feminist criticism of American women's writing, the folk arts of quilt-making and weaving, the patching and piecing of material, have come to stand for a womanly aesthetic. As Elaine Showalter summarises:

> Both theme and form in women's writing, piecing and patchwork have also become metaphors for a Female Aesthetic, for sisterhood, and for a politics of feminist survival. In the past two decades especially, they have been celebrated as essentially feminine art forms, modes of expression that emerge

naturally from womanly impulses of nurturance and thrift, and that constitute a women's language unintelligible to male audiences or readers.[3]

Given our uneven recovery of lost texts, and the hesitation fostered by the deconstruction of established canons, this suggestive model of literary communality seems more persuasive than a tightly argued thesis. But, as Showalter points out, there is also danger in the lack of historical specificity to the aesthetic of the patchwork (surely these domestic arts have changed through time?); and to couple women's writing to the home is to risk essentialism or triviality. The two great theoretical problems facing the identification of a distinctive female literary aesthetic in America are those of history and essentialism.

One solution might be to identify both thematic and formal features which have changed through time, but none the less consistently appear as basic motifs in women's fiction of the past century. Such motifs would suggest a synchronic consistency, but would also mutate diachronically. Some of these features might be shared by both men's and women's writings, even though they would have a very particular cast when they appear in the sisterly genealogy. The word 'genealogy' has a particular centrality in my argument. If the desire, even need, to construct a literary tradition repeatedly conflicts with a sense that 'tradition' is either too static or too monolithic a term, then one solution might be a pragmatic one: to replace tradition with a more flexible and light-footed term, but also to find a word that will carry the very real sense that many women writers have of the interconnections between them. 'Genealogy' carries with it resonant and useful associations; a genealogy suggests familial and dynastic relations, while allowing for evolutionary change through time. A genealogy is both stable, allowing us to identify its key members, and subtly changing as new beings are added to it. And, with every new addition, the established genealogy will look slightly different, as previously unperceived correspondences now reveal themselves. Furthermore, the word 'genealogy' carries with it the tang of a bracing Nietzschean interrogation. Whereas a 'tradition' remains coloured by its associations with T. S. Eliot's model of poetic tradition, a genealogy implies the possibility of irony and subversion – and subversive irony has often been central to women's encounters with their literary forebears.

A literary genealogy is founded on the recognition that all writing is intertextual. 'Intertextuality' is the term normally used to suggest the relationships between writers; authors are imagined as borrowing from, revisiting and revising earlier writers. Intertextuality, when used of women writers, also implies affection, kinship or homage across the generations. Many feminist critics have wanted to replace Harold Bloom's poetics of male rivalry with their own model of intertextuality as a process of communality. Bloom argued that male writers were caught up in an Oedipal struggle, an epic creative struggle as literary sons attempted to supplant their fathers. Feminists have wanted to replace the Bloomian 'agon' of literary rivalry with intertextual theories of collective sisterhood, thereby creating what Annette Kolodny calls a 'map for rereading'.[4] Thus the warmth of Alice Walker's 'Dedication' to the collection of pieces by Zora Neale Hurston which she published in 1979: 'We love Zora Neale Hurston for her work, first, and then again . . . we love her for herself.'[5]

However, for many women writers the relationship with a predecessor has been one of co-mingled rivalry and communality, an intertwined knot of allegiance and rivalry. Genealogy posits this relationship, with its broad sense of connectedness and its dynamic torque. Just as in a family the genealogical tie might encompass envy, rivalry, indifference, even hatred, so a writerly genealogy allows for a range of responses between writers. In place of rivalry (the Bloomian masculine model) or community (the feminist response) genealogy presents a dialogue between writers which is sometimes comradely and sometimes critical. The term allows for a more textured and nuanced sense of intertextuality than either of its predecessors. The very term 'genealogy' carries with it the notion of a multiplicity or diversity within a single entity; typically, we talk of a 'genealogical tree', imagining successive generations as proliferating branches off a single trunk.

Susan Sontag's play *Alice in Bed* (1993) can be read within a genealogical matrix. Her comic Beckettian piece focuses on Alice James, sister of Henry and William; it sketches Alice's brief life as invalid and writer *manquée* (my first chapter contains an account of her *Diary*, a major work recovered from the margins of the literary canon). The play pits the male relatives, with their imprecations about getting better and feeling better, against the relentlessly morbid and mordant Alice, a woman who sums up the female fate as 'sickbed deathbed birthbed'. Sontag certainly draws on Alice's status as one of the iconic lost women of American letters, but balances hagiography with a tougher tone of iconoclasm. Sontag rebukes Alice James for her retreat from broader social and political engagement. In one scene she has Alice encounter a working-class Cockney burglar, 'a representative of the world that does not have the bourgeois luxury of psychological invalidism'.[6] Elsewhere, a phantasmagoric tea party, based on the Madhatters' tea party in *Alice's Adventures in Wonderland*, sees Emily Dickinson speaking a language of mystic solipsism (most of the things she says are simply incomprehensible to her literary sisters). This is both a funnier and more sarcastic view of female intertextuality than we are accustomed to; it plays literary sisterhood off against the demands of political engagement. And in the jokes at the expense of Dickinson's sequestered speech, we see a sly dig at notions of 'female speech' – Dickinson's hermetically sealed discourse has, in Sontag's play, led only to isolation. Sontag both admires and chides her nineteenth-century predecessors, praising their imaginative achievements but chastising them for failure to reach beyond the 'victories of the imagination':

> A play, then, about the grief and anger of women; and, finally, a play about the imagination.
>   The reality of the mental prison. The triumphs of the imagination. But the victories of the imagination are not enough.[7]

The writer who engages with a genealogy of fiction – a genealogy to which she is added, and which she adds to in a process both intransitive and transitive – becomes enmeshed in a complex negotiation with forebears and with as-yet-unknown literary descendants. Whereas earlier models of feminist criticism proffered interpretative strategies of resistance, the genealogical model is predicated on resistance and affiliation, indebtedness and inauguration. Genealogy offers a map of interconnection where the writer is seen as involved in a complex inflection of earlier literary discourses; to interpret genealogically is to recognise writing as a *negotiation*.[8]

My discussion takes its cue from the historicised feminist scholarship of critics such as Annette Kolodny and Elaine Showalter (rather than the psychoanalytical school represented by, say, Judith Butler). The emphasis is upon the interpretation of texts within their historical context, and I read these stories or novels as products of a specific matrix of cultural forces, at a specific point in history. Placing texts within a particularised cultural 'moment', I go on to explore the narrative and rhetorical strategies forged by the individual writer. America's women writers have themselves acted as agents of change in an ongoing process of cultural transformation, often by unsettling old fictional patterns and creating new ones. Culture, as Sontag once remarked, is a way of thinking: through revision and inauguration within their literary culture American women have established new ways of thinking about themselves and their society. Sarah Orne Jewett's *The Country of the Pointed Firs* fashioned a folkloric, anthropological discourse about domesticity; Nella Larsen's two novels created a fabular, hallucinatory framework for stories of black selfhood; Sylvia Plath created a surreal discourse to represent the medicalisation of the female body. All these fictional languages anticipated shifts in the wider culture, adumbrating new structures of feeling.

No single, monolithic key is offered in this book to the totality of fiction by American women. I have presented a capacious survey and emphasised the quiddity of the specific novel or the individual career. Nonetheless, within each chapter I do advance more embracing arguments which encompass groups of writers from a specific literary–historical phase. Thus, my third chapter looks at modernists such as Djuna Barnes and Gertrude Stein, examining how their fiction configures space (and re-orders the familiar territory of the Victorian novel). Moreover, within the overall female genealogy several thematic and formalistic features do recur across a swathe of texts, and these provide leitmotifs throughout my study: folkloric modernism (manifested in an anthropological interest in folk culture and quotidian ritual); a fascination with the construction of national identities or what Gertrude Stein termed the 'making of Americans'; political engagement (women's narratives are more urgently bound up with cultural and political dispute than many commentators recognise); and a generic or formalistic latitude.

Folkloric Modernism

In works such as Cather's *My Ántonia* or Hurston's *Their Eyes Were Watching God* folkloric modernism became a means to construct radical fictional shapes which were informed by an anthropologist's sense that trivial or superficial features of everyday life (gossip, cookery, family anecdotes) contained the deep structures of a culture. Folkloric modernism has been one of the most significant well-springs for the woman writer; it has watered, in the past two decades, the heightened awareness to oral culture underpinning African–American and Asian–American fiction (notably, Toni Morrison's *Beloved* and Maxine Hong Kingston's *The Woman Warrior*).

Construction of National Identities

The question of what an American woman *is* has inspired a great array of novels and short stories. One of the quirkiest works I deal with, Alice James's *Diary*, is important for just this reason: the record of an invalid life in England, it is also an expatriate testimony, an account of being an American abroad. Expatriate writings are a key constituency in this literary culture, since they enfold explorations of both gendered and national identity (a womanly representation of sexuality and nation in Djuna Barnes's *Nightwood*, or throughout Gertrude Stein's career). Alongside expatriate narratives are two other major forms: the immigrant narrative, describing the arrival and assimilation of the European woman into American society (Mary Antin's *The Promised Land*, Willa Cather's early fiction); and what might be called the crisis narrative of ethnic identity. The latter constitutes a massive body of work in its own right, almost a distinct genre. For instance, in fabular fictions of the isolated self, a writer such as Nella Larsen explored the existential crisis of the mulatto heroine. Larsen's 1929 work *Passing* looks back to earlier studies of miscegenation, notably Frances Harper's 1892 text *Iola Leroy*; but the writer's construction of the miscegenation narrative is very different in each case. Whereas Larsen's text is a declensionist narrative of tragic conflict within the ethnically split self, Harper posits a progressive story of black 'uplift', as ethnic self-awareness and solidarity transcend division.

Political Engagement

Texts by American women debate, though sometimes indirectly or covertly, salient political questions of American life; they are, in the broadest sense, *engagée*. I argued in an earlier book, *Willa Cather in Context*, that the apparently escapist writer could be seen as profoundly involved in the war of political ideas, if we only looked to the right series of contexts for her fiction: progressivism, multiculturalism, 'Americanisation' in Cather's case. In this book, with its larger sweep of writers, it is harder to maintain that a central clutch of topics recurs across many works. Nevertheless, it remains the case that contextualised readings reveal the extent to which social history and cultural politics frame women's narratives. Women have often embodied in their fictions oblique, latent or allusive commentaries on what H. L. Mencken called the 'public psychology' of the day; political engagement is not necessarily synonymous with didacticism. Southern writers such as Flannery O'Connor or Eudora Welty have deployed symbolism and elliptical narratology to fashion stories which reveal themselves, on close reading, to be 'inside narratives' about their culture's political history. Other writers have addressed subjects which only reveal themselves as 'political' by reference to the contexts in which they were produced. Thus, I read Susan Sontag's *Death Kit* (1967) as a satire on the corporate male (a figure who had featured in a plethora of pop sociological accounts of suburban America); the novel also ironically meditates on the idealisation of romance and marriage which featured so widely in the domestic ideology of the 1950s and early 1960s. Indeed, several important 1960s texts can be read as a fictional counterpoint to the polemics then being published by feminists such as Betty Friedan: Sontag, Sylvia Plath and Joyce Carol Oates married formalistic experimentation to wry and often horrified meditations on what Friedan had famously termed 'the feminine mystique' in 1963.

Generic or Formalistic Latitude

Gillian Beer notes of Virginia Woolf's *The Waves*: 'Each of the books Woolf wrote around the time strained across genre, attempted to break through – or disturb – the limits of the essay, the novel, the biography, to touch realities denied by accepted forms. In all her work there was an astute awareness that apparently literary questions – of genre, language, plot – are questions that touch the pith of how society constitutes and contains itself.'[9]

I discuss works which show a similar willingness to disturb generic conventions and the constraints of 'accepted forms'; the revisionist canon is a new formation, not least for its acceptance of diverse and hybrid forms. Charlotte Perkins Gilman's 'The Yellow Wallpaper' is ostensibly a fictional narrative; but it contains well-documented biographical reference, and is often read as a quasi-political polemic. Women's fiction has often trespassed across the boundary between 'life' and 'art', taking on the shapes of writing close to biography: the memoir, the journal. For this reason I have included works of outright biographical origin (Alice James's *Diary*, Mary Antin's *The Promised Land*), and included accounts of fictions which are heavily autobiographical (Sylvia Plath's *The Bell Jar* or Elizabeth Hardwick's *Sleepless Nights*). For this reason, too, I like to use the word 'narrative' in place of 'novel': it frees us from prescriptive and proscriptive notions of form.

'Narrative' also has a pedigree as a term used by women to defend their work against accusations of formalistic incoherence. Willa Cather was attacked because *Death Comes for the Archbishop* seemed to possess little conventional coherence. She replied:

> I am amused that so many of the reviews of this book begin with the statement: 'This book is hard to classify'. Then why bother? Many more assert vehemently that it is not a novel. Myself, I prefer to call it a narrative. In this case I think that term more appropriate.[10]

Cather's nonchalance ('Then why bother?') is an index of the ease with which many women have transgressed the boundaries of genre. Cather had opened up her novel to include anecdotes and characters drawn directly from the history of the Spanish Southwest; her fiction appeared to many critics too close to history or biography. But this response predicates an ideal of fiction as flexible, narratologically relaxed, open to mixture, impatient with rigid classifications. Many of the key works of the past century are hybrid texts of indeterminate genre; the female writer has often worked as an amalgamator of disparate registers and forms. Cather blended history with fictional reconstruction; Flannery O'Connor wedded dense theological symbolism with the twists-and-turns of the magazine short story; Susan Sontag and Joyce Carol Oates have repeatedly fused genres to create a new fictional typology.

Even Cather would have to accept one form of classification: the marking of temporal boundaries, of beginnings and endings. This study encompasses a period from the 1890s to the 1990s; it charts a genealogy from the breaking-up of Victorian fictional models in the *fin-de-siècle* through to the formulation of a radical communitarian fiction by Toni Morrison at the next century's end. The image of the writerly genealogy or tree is an organic one, and implies an ongoing process of growth and succession (and, therefore, of growing interconnections). Books may themselves be made of trees, but cannot mimic this exfoliation. My study thus draws to a conclusion with writers born just before the Second World War (Oates, Sontag, Ozick, Morrison).

1

'Sickbed Deathbed Birthbed'[1]

Therapy and Writing in the 1890s

For a range of historical commentators (Christopher Lasch, Philip Reiff and T. J. Jackson Lears) much that is distinctive, and distinctively regrettable, about American life can be summed up by the word 'therapy'. These historians argued that the waning of Victorianism saw a shift from a culture of morality towards a world where feeling good and feeling better became the signals of worth. Newspapers and journals at the end of the nineteenth century were filled with articles regretting the collapse of American self-confidence and warning of a 'psychic crisis'. Prominent *fin-de-siècle* intellectuals – William James, Charles Eliot Norton, Henry Adams, Edith Wharton – suffered from the recently identified mental crisis 'neurasthenia'. For T. J. Jackson Lears this crisis in the American personality grew out of fundamental social and cultural shifts. The advent of consumer society meant that consumption and leisure began to constitute a way of life; Americans moved away from a 'bourgeois ethos' that 'enjoined perpetual work, compulsive saving, civic responsibility, and a rigid morality of self-denial'. The development of psychology, the advent of advertising and a consumer economy, the establishment of the guru of health (mental and physical), a general and pervasive emphasis on the need to feel vibrant and well: these symptoms indicated the shift from a Victorian world of individual moral choice towards a more therapeutic world. Jackson Lears argues that 'the crucial moral change was the beginning of a shift from a Protestant ethos of salvation through self-denial toward a therapeutic ethos stressing self-realization in this world – an ethos characterized by an almost obsessive concern with psychic and physical health defined in sweeping terms'.[2]

11

American literary women addressed this culture of therapy as it first appeared. They positioned a series of striking, hallucinatory and grimly ironic works within the sickrooms, bedchambers and living-rooms of the neurasthenic bourgeoisie. Charlotte Perkins Gilman's 'The Yellow Wallpaper' (1892), Alice James's *Diary* (1894) and Kate Chopin's *The Awakening* (1899) are all neurasthenic texts, taking sickness and the bourgeois body as their main subjects. Even Sarah Orne Jewett's *The Country of the Pointed Firs* (1896), superficially a less sickly text, contains more than a hint of neurasthenia in the narrator's writerly angst (she fretfully mentions the compositions she has to complete). These writers found a rich drama within the American psychic crisis; they embraced the doctors, sickbeds and medical jargon of the therapeutic culture. But for women, in particular, the therapeutic culture was more dangerous than it appeared; the writers of the 1890s were trenchantly sceptical about the value of therapy – evasion, madness or death might be preferable to the superficial attractions of the 'cure'.

Alice James: the Nomadic Invalid

At the end of the nineteenth century a short, privately printed book, issued in a minuscule run of four copies, presciently revealed many of the preoccupations that have marked subsequent prose by American women. The *Diary* of Alice James (1894) was distributed amongst her prodigiously gifted family; it finally made book form in 1934 as *Alice James: Her Brothers – Her Journal*. This diary, written by the invalid sister of Henry James (novelist) and William James (philosopher and psychologist) was composed in the confinement of the sickroom, and recorded Alice's observations in England, where she lived during the 1880s and 1890s. It records and dissects the salon culture fictionalised by her brother Henry; but its author was too sick to attend parties and literary gatherings, and so the *Diary* becomes a second-hand testimony to a life hardly entered into. It is a record, too, of reading and literary taste, written by an apprentice author who made it to the margin of the fictional page, but no further.

James's long disease, her life, places her alongside other marginalised and (at first) overlooked writers, notably Emily Dickinson. The position from which James wrote, with its combination of illness and powerful patriarchal presences (her father was also an eminent intellectual and writer), is suggestively analogous to that of many women writers: she wrote from the margins of life, and had to forge a voice independent of the clamour of the powerful males around her. Furthermore, the *Diary* takes us into a central debate about the relationship between women's art and lived experience. Alice James incarnated in her circumscribed world an extreme version of a dilemma sometimes said to handicap the female writer: how could she have earned the experiential right to create art when her knowledge of the world was so grievously limited? What Alice James *knew* was mediated through others: her brothers, or the French novels she read every day. James turned this poverty of experience into black comedy (she was so immobilised that the couch, rather than the larger confines of the house, became the limits of her world), while demonstrating that 'knowledge' is as much a matter of acuity and learning as direct 'experience' (thus trumping her brothers in demonstrating the primacy of the imagination). She also claimed a significance for her own experience, even in spite of its curtailment and poverty; such a claim might have to rest on solipsistic self-importance, but a self-importance made necessary because the wider culture refused to recognise the importance of a housebound female invalid. Note this enforced and poignant self-vaunting when Alice writes to her brother, William, that, 'Notwithstanding the poverty of my outside experience, I have always had a significance for myself.'[3]

In four areas Alice James's *Diary* adumbrates thematic motifs which recur across a century of American women's prose: authority; voice; borders; national identity. For women writers the questioning of authority and legitimacy means that the act of composition has been, even in its very inaugural moments, a fraught one. The simple right to write has been queried; or the right to address a particular subject is questioned by the (usually male) critic. We find echoes of Alice James's dilemma (the need to requisition authority or to assert legitimacy) again and again in the careers of women writers. When Willa Cather published her novel about the First World War, *One of Ours* (1922), her right to deal with the subject-matter of war was questioned by Ernest Hemingway:

> Then look at *One of Ours*. Prize, big sale, people taking it seriously. You were in the war weren't you? Wasn't that last scene

in the lines wonderful? Do you know where it came from? The battle scene in *Birth of a Nation*. I identified episode after episode, Catherized. Poor woman she had to get her war experience somewhere.[4]

Even at the end of the century, Toni Morrison's interviews reveal that a Nobel prizewinner is still concerned with the legitimacy of her subject-matter. Morrison has claimed to write a 'village literature' 'which is necessary and legitimate'. (One doubts whether a male Nobel prizewinner would be as concerned with legitimation.)[5]

For Alice James the authority of the writer cannot be taken for granted but has to be achieved. She establishes that authority by forging a distinctive literary voice. To talk of the 'voicing' of the *Diary* might appear rather redundant: how can a diary be anything other than the most personally voiced of first-person accounts? Alice James certainly begins her journal with an immediate claim for personal authorship; she looks forward to 'a written monologue by that most interesting being, *myself*' (p. 25). But the ironic, mordant wit of this statement already alerts us to the complexities of Alice's voice (a voice laced with jokiness, ironic understatement and mischief). And Alice was the sister and daughter of men already established as prominent voices in their own right; the relationship between the private female voice and the competing, public voices of men is one of the great tussles in the book. Alice James had a most distinctive literary voice: sarcastic, and 'witty' in the dual sense of comedy and conspicuous sharp intelligence. Yet she also places in her *Diary* the words of many other writers – sometimes in quite extended quotation, sometimes in reported speech:

> While I think of it I must note, lest unborn generations should think me a plagiarist, that a small joke I made about the cuckoo and the clocks, Kath. told me is in Dr. Holmes's *Hundred Days in Europe*. I never saw the book and never read a notice of it. As great minds jump (together) this proves conclusively what I have always maintained against strenuous opposition, that my mind *is Great*! Henry says that Wendell Holmes has had a most brilliant success in London and that he was as pleasant as possible, young-looking and handsomer than ever. Flirting as desperately too. – I suppose that his idea

of 'Heaven is still flirting with pretty girls,' as he used to say. (p. 61)

This typical passage encapsulates the sudden swoops and comic exclamations that make the *Diary* such an exhilarating text. James plays with the woman writer's indebtedness to her male masters; intertextuality here becomes a delightful game of quotation, reiteration, correction and annotation. Very little happens: Alice reads books, hears of her brother's engagements. But out of this second-handedness she creates a great performative voice, coining jokes out of vicarious experience. The voice, with its exclamatory enthusiasms, is that of the eager little sister, but a sister ironically and self-consciously aware of her own postition, and able to play with this role. Note, too, the fine tonal ambivalence of her assertions. 'My mind *is Great!*' is absolutely caught between the family's boastfulness (that they are great, that the Jamesian 'mind', above all, is an object of wonder), and self-mockery. There is both genuine pride and a manic self-parody here. The pitching and tilting from one tone to the other makes the *Diary* a vertiginous read. This textual mobility creates a sense of Alice James as what Rosi Braidotti has called a 'nomadic subject': nomadic not only in a literal sense (an American abroad), but also in a textual sense as Alice moves swiftly between registers or tones.[6]

Alice James's literary voice is both individuated expression and negotiated settlement with the voices of men. She allows into her reflections the words of her brothers (the *Diary* is a tissue of quotations), all the while shaping them and creating female literary spaces within which the male voice is allowed its room. As we shall see in later chapters, strategies of accommodation, modification and re-writing have energised much writing by American women: Toni Morrison's appropriation of William Faulkner's modernist narratives of the South; Sylvia Plath's rewriting of Salinger's *The Catcher in the Rye* in *The Bell Jar*; Susan Sontag's reworking of the male novel of middle-class angst in *Death Kit*.

All writing has a shifting and layered relationship with 'real life', but in the case of the diary the border between life and writing is particularly permeable. For the invalid Alice James her writing became the most significant part of lived experience, seeming to supplant the actualities of existence. Her life was hardly a life until she shaped and structured it through literature: 'If I can get on to my sofa and occupy myself for four hours, at intervals, thro' the day, scribbling my notes and able to read the books that belong to me, in that they clarify the density and shape the form-less mass within, Life seems inconceivably rich' (p. 113). The shift-ing discourse of the *Diary* is signalled not least in its ambivalent relationship with the facts of lived experience. Diaries transmute the stuff of life into inevitably subjective records; but a diary which keeps events at second-hand (Alice's report of what Henry told her about last night's party) further stretches the limits of authentic experience. The reader of the *Diary* becomes used to moving across the border from the grim authenticity of illness to a kind of shadow-world, where Alice James reads, writes, listens to gossip, fantasises. The paradoxical reality of the imaginary realm is one of the *Diary*'s motifs. As Susan Sontag's play, *Alice in Bed*, demonstrated, the privileging of a world of the imaginary creates affinities between this Alice and Lewis Carroll's child fantasist. But it also enables Alice James to outdo her brothers in privileging imaginative experience above the physical and the actual. In many ways the *Diary* is *the* major text produced by the James family, since it pushes their collective fascination with the workings of consciousness to its logical conclusion: bed-bound, Alice becomes the great Jamesian speculator, living out a life of pure mind. Neither dead nor alive, Alice James became a kind of imaginatively nomadic invalid whose consciousness provided mobility. And the creation of this private imaginative space also enabled James to resist well-wishers and their patronising acts of sympathy; she had her own resistant world of writing, a place where she could 'maintain selfhood in the face of forces seeking to strip her of that selfhood'.[7]

Generically, too, the *Diary* crosses borders and confounds our expectations. Alice James creates an amalgam of literary–critical record, family journal, political reportage, travel book, social satire and confessional testimony. There is a fictional edge, too, in the strange, half-hidden dramatic presences of figures who drift on the fringes of the book like minor comic characters in a Dickens novel (Bowles, Somers and 'Nurse': the bizarre trinity of helpers who assist James). Above all, the *Diary* is a topical account of British politics, dissected with verve and sarcasm. Alice felt her Irish ancestry keenly as she followed the Irish Home Rule debate in the British papers. She attacks British imperialism repeatedly, recording the celebratory smugness of the London newspapers as they record hollow victories: '*We* have just, with "great valour and skill" ', annihilated 1,500 more Dervishes, a 'brilliant victory'. 'After seven hours of fighting the starved naked wretches were cut to pieces' (p. 53). The *Diary* folds together an account of Anglo-Saxon manners with a savage debunking of imperial aggrandisement, as when she says of the English that 'taken en masse their bullying brutality made them simply odious' (p. 77). She crosses a border from domestic record of infirmity (a diary of comic discomfort) into a journal of politics and current affairs. The *Diary* can thus be read as a record of expatriate life and, by implication, an exploration of what it means to be an American. This is Alice James's answer to the accusation that the female invalid has no experience out of which to write; denuded as it is, her life possesses the irreducible fascination of expatriation, and this becomes her great topic.

The *Diary* therefore points forward to the literary nationalism that has underwritten many works by American women: nationalism in the broad sense – a quizzical reflection on national identity and 'American-ness'. Works as divergent as Mary Antin's *The Promised Land* (1912), Willa Cather's *My Ántonia* (1918), Maxine Hong Kingston's *Tripmaster Monkey* (1989) are records, to adopt Gertrude Stein's phrase, of the 'making of Americans'. Two genres have figured prominently in a century of women's national narratives: the narrative of expatriation (Gertrude Stein, Alice James); and the narrative of immigration (Willa Cather, Mary Antin, Maxine Hong Kingston). All these writers explore a territory of feminised literary nationalism. Their narratives trace apparently humble lives and are solidly embedded in a domestic world traditionally associated with women's fiction (the home, kitchen, family life); but, through their engagement with the quotidian or trivial experiences of either being or becoming an American, these women create powerfully understated stories of nationhood and identity. In fact, by positioning the momentous topic of national identity within the putatively trivial female sphere, the writer also transformed those fictional settings, finding a resonant politics in ordinariness.

Charlotte Perkins Gilman and Sarah Orne Jewett: Deconstructing Realism

Two writers command our attention at the century's turn: Sarah Orne Jewett (1849–1909) and Charlotte Perkins Gilman

(1860–1935). Each produced works which marked points of transition between the established women's cultures of the nineteenth century and the bracing, often disorienting, disestablishment of those cultures at the start of the twentieth. Each worked within a cultural matrix firmly grounded in Victorianism; but in their work we also catch a foretaste of modernism and the twentieth century. Gilman and Jewett established two literary discourses which have recurred, while being repeatedly transformed and revised, throughout the twentieth century. First, the heightened, expressionistic, first-person voice of 'The Yellow Wallpaper' has been enormously influential, leading to a whole genealogy of narratives. Although it is sometimes argued that Gilman herself was indebted to Edgar Allen Poe's sensational stories, her own tale has become a kind of alternative female point-of-origin for many later writers and critics. Her positioning of a first-person voice within a situation of female crisis reverberates in later writers (Plath, Oates); and her re-deployment of Gothic machinery (a bizarre and often enclosed environment, sensational effects, extreme pathologies) serves as a model for the female revision of an extant genre. Second, the regionally based realism – 'local color' – of Sarah Orne Jewett helped to create another discourse which later writers have found endlessly fertile. Jewett's combination in *The Country of the Pointed Firs* (1896) of regional focus, episodic narrative technique and domestic anthropology (folklore, ritual, crafts) served, for writers such as Willa Cather, as a model of what a womanly aesthetic might look like.

Charlotte Perkins Gilman's extraordinary career attracts modern scholars for its polymathic energy and political engagement. She was active in reform politics and nascent feminism. Married in the 1880s, she underwent, after the birth of a child in 1885, the notorious 'rest cure', as pioneered by the very Dr S. Weir Mitchell who is mentioned in 'The Yellow Wallpaper'. She was advised to give up intellectual work, but instead developed her ideas about the position of women in society, the domestic economy and the organisation of work. After her divorce she married George Houghton Gilman in 1900 and produced a series of works adumbrating in impressive diversity many of the concerns of twentieth-century feminism. Her writings cover a remarkable canvas, from progressive programmes for communal living to experimental fiction. *Women and Economics* (1898) posited one of the earliest arguments about the family's domestic economy; Gilman promulgated the professionalisation of domestic work (allowing wives to pursue careers outside the home). Later books such as *The Home* (1903) pursued this fascination with the financial nuts-and-bolts of family life. She was also a fiction writer, producing around 200 stories for *The Forerunner*, a radical magazine run by Gilman herself (1909–16). And she wrote one of the first Utopian fictions by a woman: *Herland* (1915), whose title is an early example of the naming and re-naming which has formed a tactic for feminist intervention in the politics of language.

But 'The Yellow Wallpaper' (1892) is the central Gilman text for literary scholars. Rejected by the *Atlantic Monthly*, it finally appeared in *New England Magazine*; forgotten for a period after Gilman's death, it is now one of the central texts in the re-formed American canon.[8] Gilman's brief, expressionistic monologue recounts the thoughts of a woman forced to take Dr Mitchell's 'rest cure'; confined to her room, she speculates with increasing frenzy on the yellow wallpaper of the title. By the end of the story she has become a hyperbolic, parodic vision of the female 'angel in the house' beloved of Victorian domestic ideologues – a woman solely and utterly defined in terms of her relations to home and family. In the final, critical sentences the speaker veers between a manic commitment to her own entrapment and a fierce desire to be freed. 'It is so pleasant to be out in this great room and creep around as I please!' But then she directs her rescuer to the key; is freed; and proclaims her freedom. " 'I've pulled off most of the paper, so you can't put me back!" '(pp. 18–19). Gilman expresses rebellion as a symbolic attack on home decoration.

The story has a powerful historical significance: 'The Yellow Wallpaper' is both summation of the nineteenth century's elaborately constructed domestic ideology, and the conflagration of that ideology. Gilman reduces the American woman's fate to its schematic, iconic essentials: woman, man, room. She then pursues the logic of that scenario to its conclusion: a woman committed by her husband and doctor to domestic containment; ensuing madness. The power of 'The Yellow Wallpaper' lies in its enmeshment of destructive and creative impulses. Gilman launches a fierce, corrosive attack on Victorian constructions of 'home' and 'wife'; but she also creates a new female discourse. As a tale of mental disturbance, domestic entrapment, and enforced (and supposedly regenerative) childishness, it foreshadows later attacks on the social conditioning of women (notably Plath's *The Bell Jar*). Gilman created a fractured, almost surreal first-person prose, establishing a discourse for the exploration of psychological distress and dis-integration. From Gilman creative continuities run down to the hallucinatory, crying voices of slavery which were 'freed' by Toni Morrison in *Beloved* or Susan Sontag's fractured speaker, Diddy, in *Death Kit*.

A stark, woeful and staccato voice tells its elliptical story:

> I don't know why I should write this.
> I don't want to.
> I don't feel able.
> And I know John would think it absurd. But I *must* say what I feel and think in some way – it is such a relief!
> But the effort is getting to be greater than the relief.
> Half the time now I am awfully lazy, and lie down ever so much.   (p. 10)

The tone and register of this voice indicate why the text has been important for later writers; the clipped sentences and staccato rhythms articulate a presciently modern idiom. With its series of isolated sentences, each formally separated from the next, this is a text whose composition reminds us more of poetry than prose. The reader is made to pause on the individual sentence or phrase; our engagement with this strange-looking text is encouraged to be as attentive as the speaker's fascinated gaze upon the wallpaper. The story would possess polemical but not literary force if it were simply a reiterated series of ideological statements; but the texture of 'The Yellow Wallpaper' encourages us to read it poetically, as a complex web of images and discourses. Gilman creates bitter, sarcastic comedy out of her speaker's fastidious obsession with home furnishings (a manic domesticity persisting in the midst of her disintegration); but this obsession also mimics the interpretative struggle which the reader has in making sense of the story. The speaker laments, 'One of those sprawling flamboyant patterns committing every artistic sin' (p. 5) – a comment, too, on the excessive stylistic sinfulness of 'The Yellow Wallpaper' itself. The narrator's search for a pattern encourages the reader to take a similarly active role in finding the embedded patterns and structures of Gilman's tale. References to the wallpaper's patterns suggest a degree of self-referentiality and promote the reader's own desire to discover patterns of meaning within the superficially random expostulations of the text. This is a wallpaper with a singular pattern, but a pattern that changes even as the light changes:

> You think you have mastered it, but just as you get well underway in following, it turns a back-somersault and there you are. It slaps you in the face, knocks you down, and tramples upon you. It is like a bad dream.   (p. 12)

This rhetorical self-awareness and self-reflexiveness help to make 'The Yellow Wallpaper' a quirkily modern, if not modernist, text. 'The Yellow Wallpaper' is also a radically minimalist text. The story inhabits the terrain of familiar domestic realism, but Gilman strips that form by pulling superfluous detail off the fictional skeleton. The latent framework of a fictional code is revealed. As minimalists, women writers such as Gilman and Sarah Orne Jewett pushed domestic realism towards this deconstructive turn. Drawn to what Willa Cather called 'The novel démeublé' (the 'unfurnished novel'), they produced stories whose revelatory spareness and slightness reveal realism's deep structures.

This makes a virtue out of what is often taken to be a weakness of women's writing. The slightness and miniaturised detail of women's writing has regularly attracted comment. The literary historian William Davitt Bell notes the faint praise granted by Henry James and William Dean Howells to Sarah Orne Jewett. James evoked in 1915 'her beautiful little quantum of achievement'; Howells emphasised the quietness of her work, compared to the noise of mainstream realism ('Your voice is like a thrush's in the din of all the literary noises that stun us so'). Scale, size and sweep are masculine virtues; women are left with miniaturised elegance. Bell summarises this argument as 'the bizarre but persistent critical interest in the *size* of Jewett's place in the canon'.[9] What is important in turn-of-the-century American writing is not the debate itself, familiar since Jane Austen felt the need to defend her miniaturised art; it is the uses to which women put the art of the small-scale. Increasingly, minimalism becomes an aesthetic in its own right; it becomes the space for some of the most experimental writing undertaken by women. Female minimalism, as practised by Gilman or Jewett in the 1890s, or the Cather of *My*

Mortal Enemy and the Stein of 'Tender Buttons', discovered a liberating plenitude within slightness.[10]

Sarah Orne Jewett's *Country of the Pointed Firs* owes much of its status to Willa Cather's championing of Jewett as a mentor. In 1925 Cather edited *The Best Stories of Sarah Orne Jewett*; her preface vouched for her status in the canon: 'If I were asked to name three American books which have the possibility of a long, long life, I would say at once, "The Scarlet Letter", "Huckleberry Finn", and "The Country of the Pointed Firs". I can think of no others that confront time and change so serenely.'[11] Cather's comment marked an inaugural moment for a woman's canon; it is an act of literary salvage and a demonstration of solidarity across the generations. Jewett's star had faded; Cather's own status was under attack by critics who felt that she was out of touch with modern life, a nostalgist or escapist. Cather's essay is thus coded: in recovering Jewett, and averring to the 'possibility of a long, long life' she fends off the local and, she hopes, temporary assaults of the critical establishment.

Jewett's bequest to later writers was an inverted one: she was as important for what she did not do, as for what she did. The literary generation before Jewett had written works marked by what Jane Tompkins has called 'Sensational Designs': sentimental, popular works with a didactic, polemic intent, structured around melodramatic plots. Harriet Beecher Stowe's *Uncle Tom's Cabin* (1852) is the classic example of the genre. Tompkins retrieves Stowe's novel from the imprecations of male critics who have disparaged its crudity and apoliticism. Tompkins 'holds that the popular domestic novel of the nineteenth century represents a monumental effort to reorganize culture from the woman's point of view'.[12] Tompkins demonstrates that polemicism, sensation and melodrama are all capable of artistic orchestration; and she maintains that such domestic, sentimental fiction performed great 'cultural work' (notably in the anti-slavery campaigns). *The Country of the Pointed Firs*, in contrast to *Uncle Tom's Cabin*, is marked by reticence, restraint and adumbration. Although it is still located in fictional settings that are domestic and sentimental, the tonal and formalistic arrangement of Jewett's narrative marks a break from the sensational tradition of female narrative. The narrating voice of *The Country of the Pointed Firs* implies significance, rather than stating explicitly. A loose, barely plotted structure supplants the strong, emphatic plotting of the sensational novel. Jewett's main bequest to Cather, and to twentieth-century women's writing in general, was an aesthetic of obliquity: a narrative voice of understatement, restraint and implication; a spare narrative; an eschewal of descriptive baggage and melodramatic dynamism.

Yet the novel deals, in its tentative and indirect way, with that most fundamental of subjects for the woman artist: the relationship between male and female cultures. The novel is mapped to embody the contrast between male and female spheres; a huddle of cosy small houses, Dunnet Landing looks out onto the sea where its men adventured and worked. The town is both villagey and all-encompassing, a world of its own (hence, the *country* of the pointed firs). The novel was published in the twilight of Victorianism, and seems to mark the fading of the dominant motifs of late-Victorian gender relations. On one hand, in the title of a classic article by Carroll Smith-Rosenberg, 'the female world of love and ritual', Smith-Rosenberg argues that this world of emotional freedom, tolerant of a wide spectrum of sentiment, including the homosocial, fragmented at the end of the nineteenth century.[13] On the other hand, a masculine sphere equally overshadowed by closure. The male seafarers described by Jewett are getting old and many have already died. Their adventuring days are over, as indeed America's own pioneering era had come to a close: the novel was published in 1896, three years after the official closing of the land frontier in the West. A wistful sense that heroic male endeavour is over, shadows Jewett's seafarers.

Jewett's episodic narrative finally comes to rest on the figure of Elijah Tilley; he is the first instance of a character who, we shall see, has achieved a curious permanence in American women's fiction: the male householder. When the narrator meets him he is even 'knitting a blue yarn stocking'. Not an unusual aptitude for a self-reliant seafarer, perhaps, but Jewett goes on to confirm the feminisation of this figure: 'There was something delightful in the grasp of his hand, warm and clean, as if it never touched anything but the comfortable woolen yarn, instead of cold sea water and slippery fish.'[14] Jewett repeatedly couches Tilley in terms of homemaking and domestic comfort, and this is also a sentimental portrait; the fisherman is a widower, and the dialogue shifts into an emotive account of how much he misses his lost wife. The characterisation moves between details of coded femininity (knitting, homemaking, sentiment) and references to Elijah's overtly manly pursuits as a fisherman. Jewett fastens the two spheres together in phrasing that conflates the masculine and the feminine: 'I saw that he had dropped a stitch again, and was snarling the blue yarn round his clumsy fingers. He handled it and threw it off at arm's length as if it were a cod line; and frowned impatiently, but I saw a tear shining on his cheek' (p. 97). The novel ends shortly after, as if with this improbable figure a sense of closure has been reached.

Elijah Tilley is a strangely foundational fictional creation who presages later masculine characters in women's fiction. He is a form of feminised 'American Adam' who recurs in varying guises throughout a century of fiction. Later writers, from Willa Cather to Anne Tyler and Toni Morrison, evince a fascination with the male householder. Cather fashioned such a protagonist in Professor St Peter, hero of *The Professor's House* (1925) – a novel whose title signals the obsessive domestic preoccupations of her academic. Anne Tyler's *Saint Maybe* (1991) pushed the idea further, finding transcendence and comedy in a hero who becomes a homemaker and mother-figure. Along the way, Toni Morrison has created characters like Paul D in *Beloved*, who are also grounded in the home and are made to feel the dependency traditionally associated with female characters.

The Country of the Pointed Firs was a pivotal text; it brought together, in one short work, the late-Victorian model of female community and a twentieth-century reading of that community. Jewett enmeshed the settings of the late nineteenth-century domestic–sentimental novel with an acutely anthropological sense of women's culture.[15] This is a highly *cultural* book, in the sense that Jewett is fascinated by the processes that form a culture. She understands community as an unfolding pattern of exchange, ritual and ceremony. Thus, Jewett's narrator is fascinated by herbalism, a topic imbued with folkloric significance. The narrator is herself initiated into the mystery of herbalism when she receives ink 'scented with bergamot' (p. 13) – a conflation of the herbalist's and writer's arts. A central figure in the book, Mrs Todd, is important for her role as cultural archivist, as a 'griot' who hands on to later generations the inherited stories and customs of the community. This fascination with folk culture now seems prescient; Jewett has been coupled with Toni Morrison as an explorer of 'folk roots'.[16] Oral culture, conversation, storytelling, domestic arts (quilt-making, herbalism, cookery): aspects of everyday life, these practices were given an added and inter-locked significance by their place in an inclusive and anthropo-logical reading of women's lives. After Jewett, this anthropological model becomes one of the major forms for later writers, informing in particular the work of Zora Neale Hurston.

Jewett's work is also valuable as a counterweight to arguments about 'relevance', since we soon realise that one era's relevance is another's thematic redundancy. In the 1970s, feminist critics were fond of contrasting the 'impoverishment' of local color writing with the larger-scale political engagement and aesthetic ambition of an earlier generation of sentimental novelists.[17] But Jewett's work has become topical. Her sensitivity to the labyrinthine affec-tive bonds that make up 'community' anticipates, strikingly, modern feminism's interest in the womanly community. Moreover, local color contained the seeds of a radical aesthetic: it provided a fictional framework for narratives about neglected, marginalised or unimportant lives. The local colorist finds a dignity and fascination in the quotidian and the provincial. From local color there is a short but usually overlooked step to early female modernism; local color foreshadowed modernism's fasci-nation with the poetic resonances of apparently ordinary life. Gertrude Stein's *Three Lives* (1904–5, published 1909) is not, in its basic narrative configuration, that far from *The Country of the Pointed Firs*: both are small-scale, tightly focused explorations of the female community; and both pledge an innate democratic commitment in their valorisation of forgotten lives. The writer, modernist or local colorist, creates a form of covenant between the author and 'ordinary' experience. The lives of the serving-women in *Three Lives*, like those of the elderly spinsters in Jewett's fiction, are apparently insignificant. Both Stein and Jewett pledge that, nonetheless, these are lives meriting the most concerted artistic consideration.

Kate Chopin's *The Awakening*

The Awakening's title irresistibly lends itself to critics seeking a novel to mark the end and beginning of centuries; that it was published in 1899 only helps this sense of occasion. It is often read as a novel on the cusp of change. For Elaine Showalter the work 'belongs to a historical moment in American women's writing'; it experiments with established traditions (local color, domestic realism), but inaugurates a freshly probing, sceptical examination of family life and marriage.[18] Certainly the book's first readers were alarmed by its pungent modernity; hostile reviewers attacked the novel's depiction of adultery and its apparent decadence. Even so, reviews like that in the *St. Louis Post-Dispatch* acknowledged Chopin's artistry: 'It is sad and mad and bad, but it is all consummate art.'[19] As with the career of Thomas Hardy, the accusations of impropriety seemed to have driven the writer into a chastened and resentful silence; Chopin produced little extra fiction before her death in 1904.

A tale on the 'Emma Bovary' theme of bourgeois boredom and extramarital passion, *The Awakening* follows Edna Pontellier, a Yankee Protestant who marries into the exotic Creole, Catholic world of New Orleans. Increasingly disenchanted, her impatience with husband and family leads to an 'awakening' to her circumstances. At the novel's end she is enticed towards the sea – deployed by Chopin as potent symbol of elemental seductiveness – in an ambiguous moment of suicidal destruction and self-assertion. *The Awakening* is set in the upper-middle-class demi-monde of New Orleans. Chopin places her heroine, Edna Pontellier, in the Creole culture created by the hybrid aristocracy of colonial French and Spanish America; it is an America within America. Chopin suggests a decadence or loucheness which Edna Pontellier, offspring of Presbyterian parents, is discomfited by. Part of Chopin's tactic is to draw on recognised cultural stereotypes about the decadence of this too-Europeanised, Catholic region of the United States. The Creole world is marked by linguistic pluralism, hybridity and a crude form of multiculturalism (not always, however, as welcome a concept for Chopin's heroine as it might be for modern liberals). There is a broad sense of cultural unease, of not being at home in this 'anti-puritan unAmerican mixture of races and nations'.[20] Edna 'was not thoroughly at home in the society of Creoles' (p. 20), even though she is married to a Creole and lives in New Orleans. Like other women writers of the 1890s, Chopin positions her heroine within an unsettling environment which eventually prompts breakdown and crisis.

A sense of unease and discomfort (even in the supposedly comfortable world of the home), is central to the domestic unsettling that takes place in the 1890s. The entry into the twentieth century witnessed a spate of fictions of the unhomely. In Alice James's *Diary* and *The Awakening* the protagonist finds herself confined to home, either through invalidity or the necessities of childcare, and then finds the home an unsettling blend of the comfortably known and the disconcertingly imprisoning. The settings of the *Diary* and *The Awakening* are both oddly familiar and strangely unknown for the American reader. New Orleans is markedly 'Other' in culture, religion and language. Alice James's England might be part of the Anglophone universe but, as she repeatedly discovers, a shared language reveals as many differences as similarities between America and Britain. Fictions of the 1890s *unmake* the home by a process of cultural dislocation, as the heroine, even within her domestic space, undergoes a defamiliarisation of the known and trusted.

The Awakening is striking for its frank, straightforward and trenchantly unblinkered account of the monotony and minor grumbles of married life; the 'affairs of the hearth', in Rod Edmond's phrase, are now 'affairs of the heat', as married life is now seen in rancorous terms.[21] In essence, *The Awakening* is a laconic account of marital tiffs, an account gradually rising in tempo and intensity. When Mr Pontellier ticks off his wife, 'He talked in a monotonous, insistent way' (p. 7). Mr Pontellier is symbolically referred to by surname; we never know his Christian name, as if such informalities were irrelevant within this tense marriage. The novel is anti-Victorian in its assault on an idealised domestic ideology, especially because its heroine is a woman who is categorically unsuited to be a mother: 'In short, Mrs. Pontellier was not a mother-woman' (p. 9). She steadily becomes less interested in her own children and 'would sometimes forget them' (p. 19). The rest of Edna's family fare little better. Of her father: 'Edna was glad to be rid of her father when he finally took himself off' (p. 68).

As with other *fin-de-siècle* authors, her work is as important for innovative tones, registers and voices as for subject-matter. Chopin, like James and Gilman, crafted a terse, abrupt style, devoid of flowery phrasing and prolixity:

> Despondency had come upon her there in the wakeful night, and had never lifted. There was no one thing in the world that she desired. There was no human being whom she wanted near her except Robert; and she even realized that the day would come when he, too, and the thought of him, would

melt out of her existence, leaving her alone. The children appeared before her like antagonists who had overcome her; who had overpowered and sought to drag her into the soul's slavery for the rest of her days. But she knew a way to elude them. She was not thinking of these things when she walked down to the beach.

The water of the Gulf stretched out before her, gleaming with the million lights of the sun. The voice of the sea is seductive, never ceasing, whispering, clamoring, murmuring, inviting the soul to wander in abysses of solitude. All along the white beach, up and down, there was no living thing in sight. A bird with a broken wing was beating the air above, reeling, fluttering, circling disabled down, down to the water.   (p. 108)

Crisply formulated, Chopin's sentences here modulate into a kind of icy, laconic impressionism. Compared to the excess or sentimental profligacy of the typical Victorian death-scene, this is a firmly understated tableau of despondency. Sentiment is expunged or allowed to infiltrate the passage obliquely, in the form of pathetic fallacy (the 'bird with a broken wing'). In its restraint and controlled repetitions ('down, down to the water'), Chopin's prose carries a foretaste of American modernism's fascination with a rhythmic spareness; we catch hints of the poetic understatement later deployed by Stein in *Three Lives* (and then adopted as the modernist manner by Hemingway).

The Awakening proffers its discontented heroine a classic avenue of escape: the seductive world of art. Edna's interest in painting antagonises her husband; she is also impatient with one of the few activities that seem to offer contentment. 'She liked the dabbling. She felt in it satisfaction of a kind which no other employment afforded her.' But then she looks at her work: 'After surveying her sketch critically she drew a broad smudge of paint across its surface and crumpled the paper between her hands' (pp. 12–13). This is a key moment in *The Awakening*; it signals, early in the text, the radical dissatisfaction which will eventually undo Edna. It embodies her frustration with the whole sphere of art and culture, a world which, as Chopin would have fully understood, was often used in nineteenth-century female texts as a place for the subject to find satisfaction and even a certain form of politicised independence from male structures of feeling. In Charlotte Brontë's fiction the female artist is a powerfully autonomous character (take the 'Vashti' figure of the actress in *Villete*). Chopin knew European models of the artistic heroine well; as a teenager she had read Mme de Staël's *Corinne* (a study of a feisty English poetess who flees to the romantic freedom proffered by Italy).[22] But in *The Awakening* she presents this route to female self-definition as in itself already decayed, degenerated and emptied-out of significance by weariness. Edna quite literally besmirches art, writing it out as a forum where a woman might become a heroine. A form of *fin-de-siècle* discontent afflicts Edna. She has no sense of the past or the future; she lives only for the moment. Her interest in painting is a manifestation of a languid, decadent aestheticism, ultimately devoid of great significance. Chopin's refusal to present the world of art in an optimistic manner is one area where *The Awakening* breaks with progressive Victorian women's fictions. Indeed, in its presentation of equally unattractive cultures, the book proffers no convincing, fulfilling space where Edna can create herself. The world of art is bleached of meaning; the Creole culture is too 'Other' to receive her; and her husband's job represents an utterly utilitarian culture. Edna's dilemma is as much to do with cultural entrapment – the lack of a viable and fulfilling women's culture – as it is to do with patterns of emotional disillusion. Edna thus becomes a form of 1960s feminist *in utero*; she has arrived at that state of pre-politicised anguish described by many of the women in Friedan's *The Feminine Mystique* (1963): radically (and in the eyes of her family, churlishly) dissatisfied, impatient with the cultural freedoms offered to her, but unable as yet to formulate a politics out of discontent.

If culture offers a bleak 'choice' between pointless gentility and vacuous commercialism, where might the self find fulfilment? *The Awakening* presents the sexualized world of nature, particularly the enchantments of the sea, as a domain where fulfilment might be found. The ocean is alluring for Edna: 'The voice of the sea is seductive; never ceasing, whispering, clamoring, murmuring, inviting the soul to wander for a spell in abysses of solitude; to lose itself in mazes of inward contemplation' (p. 14). The novel symbolically correlates sexual freedom, personal independence and erotic merging in water. The pattern of imagery here is somewhat insistently and mechanically handled; but it does mark out an increasing desire on the part of the female writer to explore the symbiotic interconnectedness of self and environment in a writing which can seem 'ecopoetic' (this complex interplay between female self and the natural world is discussed at length in Chapter 3).

The final causes of Edna's suicide – she is last seen walking into the water – are largely those of desperate resistance to the pathways before her. Chopin has cancelled out the more optimistic avenues: romance, art, children. All are found wanting, or compromise the self's integrity. 'She had resolved never again to belong to another than herself' (p. 76); 'she would never sacrifice herself for her children' (p. 108). This seems, at first sight, to be extraordinarily radical; Chopin goes beyond Flaubert, who diagnosed the threat to bourgeois marriage by the anarchic forces of sexual desire, to suggest that a woman's yearning for self-determination might militate against the family and children.

Structurally, *The Awakening* established a fictional shape whose pattern provides the skeleton of numerous, early twentieth-century works. This is the narrative of blunted or frustrated escape, whose plot-line concludes with frustrated liberty or compromised dissent. The protagonist encounters various ways of achieving freedom, integrity, fulfilment, only to find that each way forward is in fact an entrapment. For Edna Pontellier the freedoms offered by art and even romance are illusory; she is thrown back upon herself and her ineradicable status as mother and wife. This, too, is an entrapment, and the only way 'forward' is the almost-narcotised self-extinction as she wades into the water at the novel's conclusion. A later work, Nella Larsen's *Quicksand* (1928), traces a similar pattern of blocked release. There is, in these female novels of dissent, a very thin line between the celebration of the individual's antinomian energies and a recognition that these energies will be frustrated by societal containments. Unable to resolve this struggle between self and community, the writer achieves formalistic closure by means of melodramatic or even violent finales. Larsen's *Passing* (1929) and Ann Petry's *The Street* (1946) sit alongside *The Awakening* as novels whose endings possess the excess, melodrama and artifice of nineteenth-century serialised fiction. The roots of modern women's fiction in Victorian domestic realism show themselves in the recourse to melodrama as a means to 'solve' the heroine's dilemmas. As *The Awakening* demonstrates, melodrama proffers a narrative solution to apparently intractable dilemmas. Edna's proliferating crises – emotional, vocational, existential – are delineated with cool

precision, but Chopin's representation of psychological dissatisfaction does not extend to a wider societal solution to those
problems.

For the question begged by many women novelists, from
Chopin to Plath, is this: is the problem 'in' the heroine (and of her
making), or is it wider societal forces that have created these
dilemmas? Frequently, the novelist cannot resolve the dilemma; a
melodramatic ending (death, murder, escape) imposes some sort
of order on the messy incongruities of life for these protagonists.
Even in early twentieth-century works which do not opt for this
private apocalypse, disappointment, failure and domestic entrapment mark out an analogous narrative trajectory of decline and
disillusion. Many women's fictions trace 'declensionist' narrative
patterns, following protagonists downwards to frustration, failure, illness, loss and – surprisingly frequently – death. And yet
critics have often wanted to see, in the violently declensionist
fiction of a Chopin or Larsen, signs of rebellion, independence or
progress. The endings of these novels have attracted a great deal
of attention from critics concerned with the politics of closure.
Some readers see in Edna's suicide a non-conformist heroism;
others read Larsen's bleak fictions for signs that female desire has,
in some way, manifested itself. Discussing *Passing*, Jonathan Little
comments that, 'There seems to be a consensus among recent critics that Larsen should have rejected the ironic mode for something more explicitly affirmative.'[23] My own reading of *The
Awakening* (and, as we shall see, of Larsen's texts) suggests a
different interpretative model: readings which go with the grain
of these books, accepting the disillusion immanent in their pages,
but then see the declensionist narrative as a prelude to the female
stories of the later twentieth century, where a wider range of final-
ities added to the stock of available reality for the female author.[24]

African–American Women's Fictions: Pauline Hopkins and Frances Harper

Pauline Hopkins (1859–1930) worked as a playwright and sometime contributor to *Colored American Magazine*; she is known
primarily for her one published novel, *Contending Forces* (1900),
although her magazine fiction is now available as part of the
excellent Schlomburg project which has done so much to

recover these forgotten works by nineteenth-century black women.

Compared with the introverted chamber-pieces produced by white women in the 1890s, the African–American novel is notable for its outspoken political engagement. Pauline Hopkins, like Frances W. Harper, foregrounded a didactic narrating voice; the Preface pledges 'to raise the stigma of degradation from my race'.[25] Generically, this didacticism is embedded in a domestic, sentimental novel whose roots lie solidly in popular Victorian traditions; politically, Hopkins contributes to the ideology of 'uplift' advocated by black progressives. But it is the transformation and revision of literary conventions which make *Contending Forces* such an important text. *Contending Forces* is a family tale, a dynastic saga whose settings are hearthsides and salons; tonally, the overt didacticism and sentimental progressivism place the novel in kinship to *Uncle Tom's Cabin*. The family story, with its exfoliating great web of relationships, is bourgeois in origin; but Hopkins works both with and against the grain of the convention, especially because her families are racially hybrid and form miscegenated dynasties. Ultimately, the Victorian familial epic presents family as a site of comfort and reassurance; the coincidences and rediscoveries of relationship serve to embed the protagonist, say an orphan, in a web of relation which she or he had no inkling of. *Contending Forces* is driven by a plot-line equally indebted to coincidence; but here this dynamic encounters the complexities of race and miscegenation.

Whereas Chopin, Jewett and Gilman worked to strip down nineteenth-century literary forms, Hopkins preserved the capaciousness of Victorian popular fiction and its ability to absorb a plethora of themes. *Contending Forces* encompasses sub-plots about: miscegenation; the 'contending forces' of the North and South; female sexuality; the 'black Atlantic' linking America, Britain and Africa; the institution of marriage.[26] Hopkins's magazine fiction reveals a similar, sprawling breadth. *Of One Blood: Or, The Hidden Self* (1902–3) is a chaotically fascinating black appropriation of late-Victorian adventure narratives, centring on an archaeological trip to Ethiopa. Along the way, Hopkins articulates an early fictional version of the 'Black Athena' thesis (the argument that civilisation had its roots in Africa), and sweeps across a great range of late nineteenth-century scientific theories.[27]

But the multiplicity of topic contributes to an unevenness of

tone; and the formalistic dis-unity of Hopkins's fiction aggravates
critics who seek artistic cohesion. Richard Yarborough notes: 'As
one might expect, Hopkins's use of such diverse generic modes
causes marked inconsistencies in tone. Such discordances charac-
terize a great deal of early Afro-American fiction before World War
I, as black writers struggled to discover a vehicle that would
satisfy their urge toward realism without undermining their
adoption of popular literary forms.'[28] *Contending Forces* might, in
fact, be taken to refer to the range of discourses patterning this
novel; it is a distinctively patchwork narrative structure, informed
by a variety of registers and styles. The sentimental narrative, as it
evolved at the end of the century, here becomes a polyphonic
form, shifting between didactic homily, domestic sentimentalism
and lurid melodrama. Hopkins mixes further elements into this
amalgamated form: polemical social realism, anticipatory of the
protest fiction of Richard Wright; a homiletic voice which excori-
ates racism; and even historical essays which delve into the
African–American past.

The breaks and fissures of this text can be interpreted in two
ways. They testify to the latent polyphony of the sentimental
tradition, a generic form which, like the putatively artless vernacular architecture of its settings, is capable of endless extension,
renovation, modification and transformation. Also, Hopkins's
indifference to models of aesthetic cohesion anticipates the development, by an African–American modernist such as Zora Neale
Hurston, of the 'break'. Hurston articulated in *Jonah's Gourd Vine*
(1934) a narratology based not on smooth, organic evolution and
formalistic wholeness, but on abrupt fissures and breaks of
pattern (akin to the switch, in folk-musics, from instrument to
voice or from the single voice to the chorus). Hurston's notion of
the break can be seen as part of her African–American vernacular
aesthetic; but it is also continuous with the formal dis-integration
and discursive fissuring that had already begun to mark
African–American popular narratives in the late nineteenth
century.

Contending Forces presents a society which is essentially
(although it can hardly be said to possess a unitary essence)
miscegenated. At one point Mrs Willis voices her belief in the
ubiquity of miscegenation in America; the unfolding of the plot
underlines the centrality of this paragraph, which becomes a
governing model for the novel's representation of race. Mrs Willis

notes that 'the black race on this continent has developed into a race of mulattoes':

> Just bear in mind that we cannot tell by a person's complexion whether he be dark or light in blood, for by the working of the natural laws the white father and black mother produce the mulatto offspring; the black father and white mother the mulatto offspring also, while the *black father* and *quadroon* mother produce the black child, which to the eye alone is a child of unmixed black blood. I will venture to say that out of a hundred apparently pure black men not one will be able to trace an unmixed flow of African blood since landing upon these shores!   (p. 151)

As we shall see in later discussions of Zora Neale Hurston and Nella Larsen, the figure of the mulatto has often been associated in American writing with a 'mulatto tragedy': divided between the races, the half-caste has no real cultural home, and is fated to suffer. But Hopkins's novel posits a form of progressive miscegenation, where the 'natural' condition of American and British societies is hybridised. The very obscurity of racial origin ('we cannot tell by a person's complexion whether he be dark or light in blood') creates a world where anybody or everybody might have black blood. As the plot unfolds, Hopkins works out the logic of this proposition by showing that miscegenation is also reversible; it is the supposedly 'white' characters in the novel who are shown to have distant African origins. And the illustrations to the first edition confirm this sense of a mulatto text: the colour of the characters illustrated is difficult to discern, as they occupy a half-way house between black and white.[29] At the start of the novel Charles Montfort, an English plantation owner in Bermuda, is nonchalant about his own mixed heritage: 'there might even have been a strain of African blood polluting the fair stream of Montfort's vitality, or even his wife's, which fact would not have caused him one instant's uneasiness' (p. 23). Hopkins's mulatto world is a vertiginous realm, where sardonic comedy, sudden violence and latent tragedy swirl together. The mulatto can one minute be cynically accepted, the next moment feverishly desired for her exotic origins, and then lynched. Hopkins's formal structure, with its breaks between generic codes, serves to embody these tonal shifts, creating a heterogeneous narratological counterpart to the extraordinary 'contending forces' which assail the hybrid.

Perhaps the most fascinating aspect of *Contending Forces* lies in its configuration of the 'black Atlantic' – that Anglo-American–African, transatlantic world recently identified by Paul Gilroy. The novel, with its Victorian great web of social relations, binds black and white together in a complex hybrid matrix across the United States, the West Indies and Britain. The Montforts, an English family with (possible) black ancestry, move from Bermuda to North Carolina at the start of the novel. In conclusion, re-discovered relations with an English Member of Parliament draw the black American family back across the Atlantic. The North and South of the US; Bermuda; England – the space of *Contending Forces* is a wide one, presciently global in its sense of migration and cultural cross-fertilisation.

Frances E. W. Harper set her 1892 historical novel *Iola Leroy* during the Civil War and took for her subject a resonant topic for black women writers: the mulatto heroine's quest for fulfilment. As in Hopkins's *Contending Forces* or Hurston's *Their Eyes Were Watching God*, a complex interaction of gender, race and class is focused on a central character. Throughout all these novels a fundamental ambiguity characterises the mulatto. Light-skinned, such heroines might almost 'pass' for white (and in Nella Larsen's *Passing*, this is just what happens). Such fair heroines might almost be designed to appeal to a white readership – they are, after all, 'nearly' white. Yet at the same time, an inexorable racial determinism means that such characters, however superficially white they may be, are finally judged to be black by virtue of a remote but ineradicable African–American ancestry. This is the remorseless determinism which has unexpectedly benign results in *Contending Forces*, where a whole miscegenated dynasty is brought together by its origins in slavery. *Iola Leroy* voices at one point another, exclusivist vision of racial origin in a discussion between Alfred Lorraine and Eugene Leroy (Iola's father). Lorraine is appalled when his friend tells him, ' "The lady whom I am to marry has negro blood in her veins." '[30] Lorraine asks whether society does not have the right to ' "guard the purity of its blood by the rigid exclusion of an alien race?" ' because ' "One drop of negro blood in her veins curses all the rest" ' (pp. 41–2).

Nella Larsen's fiction, as we shall see in Chapter 4, has been read in terms of a 'mulatto tragedy' where this conflicted and

contradictory self is doomed to disappointment. But *Iola Leroy*
predicates an upbeat, progressive vision of the mulatto self; and it
also reverses the configuration of the 'passing' novel. Often, the
mulatto heroine has for male characters an elusive sexuality, a
seductive black eroticism which manifests itself through her
apparent whiteness. Eventually, this fantasy of hybridised sexuality will destroy the woman (thus Mrs Montfort is coveted and
then lynched at the start of *Contending Forces*). But in *Iola Leroy*
sexuality becomes a form of integrity rather than the cause of
destruction. ' "I was abused, but the men who trampled on me
were the degraded ones" ' (p. 75). Harper locates this resistance in
Iola's sense of racial belonging. Iola, in spite of her mixed origin,
remains defiantly part of the black race; the novel didactically
advances the need for racial solidarity. In place of division, Harper
advances solidarity; in place of tragedy, a story of moral uplift:

> 'To be', continued Iola, 'the leader of a race, to lead it to higher
> planes of thought and action, to teach men clearer views of life
> and duty and to inspire their souls with loftier aims is a far
> greater privilege than it is to open the gates of material pros-
> perity and fill every home with sensuous enjoyment.'   (p. 147)

Worthy sentiments like these can only be arrived at if one knows
what race one belongs to; and Iola never has doubts of her negri-
tude. The overall trajectory of the book can then be upwards:
towards emotional affirmation, confirmation of Iola's integrity,
and assertions of African–American progress. Iola's speeches in
the latter parts of the novel are suffused with the discourse of
'uplift': a heightened, religiose language which meshes together
personal commitment and identity politics. And Harper then
solves the problem of the mulatto heroine's sexual identity by
creating a marriage plot whose union is between Iola and the
equally miscegenated Dr Latimer (another potential 'passer' who
has remained loyal to the black race). Thoroughly Victorian in its
schematic resolution of political and social dilemmas by means of
a marriage, the novel presents a community of the miscegenated
who nonetheless remain defiantly African–American in their
racial ideology.[31]
Iola Leroy and *Contending Forces* are novels committed to the
power of the family; and both are thoroughly embedded in the
sentimental literary tradition. The figure of the mother in these

books is imbued with a rich, warmly luxuriant emotiveness. Thus *Iola Leroy*: 'Caressingly she bent over his couch, murmuring in her happiness the tenderest, sweetest words of motherly love' (p. 127). In these black fictions the sentimental power of family life, channelled through the figure of the mother, maintains its hold, and is then incorporated into a politics of resistance (familial solidarity as a means to resist the depredations of slavery, racism and war).[32] While, in white fictions of the 1890s, family bonds are starting to come apart, black writers continued and then deepened an earlier notion of the sentimental politics of the family (a process that continues through to the present, with Toni Morrison's *Beloved*). While white women were embarking on a long revolution against the established family, black women were renewing and revitalising family as the nexus for a politics of sentimentality. For white women such as Kate Chopin, 'mother' begins to be a term of dread; for black women such as Pauline Hopkins, the 'mammy' of nineteenth-century stereotype has increasingly suggested empowerment and resistance.[33] As we shall see in the next chapter, these shifts in the literary representation of the family had another corollary: a revolution in the significance of 'home'.

2

Re-making the Home, 1909–33

Gertrude Stein, Edith Wharton, Mary Antin

The authors gathered together in this chapter constitute a quirky grouping. Gertrude Stein (1874–1946) has long been recognised by scholars as a major modernist, a radical innovator (even if her difficult *oeuvre* still fends off a wider readership). Edith Wharton (1862–1937) has always maintained canonical virtue, though for reasons that are the reverse of Stein's case: as torchbearer of an older realist tradition – the Jamesian novel of manners and society. Mary Antin (1881–1949) is a newer arrival. *The Promised Land* (1912) is an early version of those migration and 'self-making' narratives later elaborated by Willa Cather and Zora Neale Hurston. The re-making of the canon over the past twenty years, and in particular the recovery of forgotten or neglected works of great worth, enable us to re-consitute literary groupings such as this one. But do these writers have anything in common beyond temporal coincidence? Are we not better off sticking with familiar and tested literary–historical periods and schools (local color, realism, regionalism)? A revisionist literary history sees continuities between writers and attempts to construct a nexus of cultural forces which shape literary production during a particular period; these early twentieth-century authors have more in common than first appears.

At the turn of the century American society was being re-shaped and transformed by two dramatic cultural shifts. First, this was now a mass immigrant culture. During the last decade of the nineteenth century and the first of the twentieth, vast numbers of migrants, mainly from eastern and southern Europe, arrived to transform America, particularly its cities. As over 1 million new citizens arrived at Ellis Island per year, society became more cosmopolitan, diverse and, in the eyes of some commentators, dangerously plural. For Henry James, returning to his homeland after a long absence, New York now seemed an alien place; but for progressives and radicals, the new society promised exhilarating multiplicity. Randolph Bourne in 1916 produced one of the first defences of what we would now call 'multiculturalism', praising 'trans-national' America: 'America is coming to be, not a nationality but a trans-nationality, a weaving back and forth, with the other lands, of many threads of all sizes and colors.'[1]

Second, old Victorian certainties (of class and marriage, of the role of women) were being dissolved by a rapidly changing economic order. Modern industrial capitalism gave birth to the Fordist workplace. Simultaneously, the twentieth century witnessed new technological consumerism – a consumerism associated with women who, it seemed, were the main beneficiaries of the industrial disciplining of masculine work. Advertising, the cinema, the department store, the car, magazines: a leisure society emerged, and it often appeared a *feminised* social order. In *The Great Gatsby* (1925) this feminised consumerism is familiar enough for F. Scott Fitzgerald to deploy a brief, sarcastic caricature of the female shopper, with her magazines and trivial purchases: 'At the news-stand she bought a copy of *Town Tattle* and a moving-picture magazine, and in the station drug-store some cold cream and a small flask of perfume.'[2]

Such typecasting entered American culture as early as 1899, when Thorstein Veblen drew attention to the psychological deformations wrought by consumerism. His *The Theory of the Leisure Class* presciently sketched the world fictionalised by many novelists in the early twentieth century, a world of consumption, technology and leisure. And, as with Fitzgerald's pen portrait of the female shopper, for Veblen the leisure society was inevitably feminised. Veblen's anthropological argument saw women as the occupants of a symbolic zone where men, themselves too busy making money to display it, vicariously expressed their worth. The world of leisure is a feminine one, an arena of 'conspicuous consumption': 'it has in the course of economic development become the office of the woman to consume vicariously for the head of the household; and her apparel is contrived with this object in view'. 'Propriety requires respectable women to abstain more consistently from useful effort and to make more of a show of leisure than the men of the same social classes.'[3]

The dual transformation of society in the early twentieth century can be seen as a re-making of the meaning of 'home'. First, home was radically re-shaped as a notion of national identity. On a macrocosmic level the metaphorical implications of the word 'home' had undergone a seismic shift, as new Americans entered the country, bringing with them different ideas of custom and culture, while long-established families (like the James dynasty) no longer recognised their 'own' cities. In the wake of the great immigration of the 1890s, the idea of a stable and readily identifiable homeland was disrupted: who 'we' are, and where 'we' come from were questions that would increasingly vex commentators. Simultaneously, consumerism and the development of a leisure class re-fashioned the home. In a very basic sense the home was transformed from a sanctified retreat from industrial capitalism into a crucible for the most significant changes in the economy. This development is most evident in the emergence of a political writing which addressed the material circumstances of home life, especially the economic structure of marriage. Charlotte Perkins Gilman's *Women and Economics* (1898) had, like Veblen's work on the leisure class, introduced a new materialism into discussions of the home and marriage: her critique of courtship is grounded in a brutally realistic economic analysis. Marriage is analysed, removed from the saccharine world of sentiment and placed solidly in the realm of financial need and dependency. It is worth quoting an extended passage from *Women and Economics* to see the formation of this analytical discourse, with its decoding of marriage as a form of consumerised choice:

> The girl who marries the rich old man or the titled profligate is condemned by the popular voice; and the girl who marries the poor young man, and helps him live his best, is still approved by the same great arbiter. And yet why should we blame the woman for pursuing her vocation? Since marriage is her only way to get money, why should she not try to get money in that way? Why cast the weight of all self-interest on the 'practical' plane so solidly against the sex-interest of the individual and of the race? The mercenary marriage is a perfectly natural consequence of the economic dependence of women.
>
> On the other hand, note the effect of this dependence upon men. As the excessive sex-distinction and economic dependence

of women increase, so do the risk and difficulty of marriage increase, so is marriage deferred and avoided, to the direct injury of both sexes and society at large. In simpler relations, in the country, wherever women have a personal value in economic relation as well as a feminine value in sex-relation, an early marriage is an advantage. The young farmer gets a profitable servant when he marries. The young business man gets nothing of the kind, – a pretty girl, a charming girl, ready for 'wifehood and motherhood' – so far as her health holds out, – but having no economic value whatever. She is merely a consumer, and he must wait till he can 'afford to marry.' These are instances frequent everywhere, and familiar to us all, of the palpable effects in common life of our sexuo-economic relation.[4]

The *mélange* of languages in this piece is what makes it important. A hard-headed stress on simple domestic economics ('marriage is her only way to get money') rests alongside a quasi-anthropological diction, with its roots in Darwin ('the sex-interest of the individual and of the race'). And then there are the references that place these passages specifically in the leisure society of modern America: the 'young business man', the wife as 'consumer'. Gilman's account is of what H. L. Mencken was to call 'public psychology'.[5] These arguments, often drawing on the nascent social sciences, turned a putatively scientific eye towards modern marriage. This blend of domestic economics, Darwinist anthropology and social observation recurs again and again in the first decades of our century. When Mencken himself wrote *In Defence of Women* (1918) he regarded many of the assumptions of Gilman and Veblen as representing inherited clichés to be taken for granted. The central passage in this book is Mencken's trenchant, cynical account of why women get married:

But of all things that a woman gains by marriage the most valuable is economic security. Such security, of course, is seldom absolute, but usually merely relative: the best provider among husbands may die without enough life insurance or run off with some preposterous light of love, or become an invalid or insane, or step over the intangible and wavering line which separates business success from a prison cell. . . . She seeks a husband, not sentimentally, but realistically; she always gives thought to the economic situation; she seldom takes a chance if it is possible to avoid it. It is common for men to marry women who bring nothing to the joint capital of marriage save good looks and an appearance of vivacity; it is almost unheard-of for women to neglect more prosaic inquiries.   (pp. 86–7)

Mencken turns the screw of Gilman's materialist analysis a little tighter; marriage is now a matter of 'joint capital', and courtship the subject of fiscal surveillance. Mencken, as ever, takes great delight in pushing his arguments to the limit, in a some-times tiresome display of intellectual bravado; but the underlying significance of *In Defence of Women* is clear – that money is the centre of the marital contract.

The three writers in this chapter might be thought of as authors responding to these economic and social transformations in the meaning of 'home'. For Stein, Wharton and Antin what home might signify, in both literal and metaphorical senses, becomes the animating dynamic of narratives which encompass diversity of homeland (Antin), the re-making of home by a Veblenesque commercialism (Wharton) or the radical re-configuration of domestic space by a modernist aesthetic (Stein).

Gertrude Stein's 'Simply Complicated' Aesthetic

No American writer of this century presents us with more of an interpretative and evaluative task than Gertrude Stein. Her vast *oeuvre* has been barely absorbed by the academy; and the works of canonical status ('Tender Buttons', *Three Lives*) are recondite, elusive, allusive and at times opaque. Stein was a high modernist, a consciously experimental author working at the edge of received nostrums about literature. Championed by Alfred Stieglitz in 1912 as an example of modernist aesthetics, Stein's early work followed avant-garde movements, like Cubism, in its deconstruction and reconstruction of representation itself. Jayne Walker notes that Stein moved with staggering rapidity from the 'colloquial realism' of *Three Lives* to the 'radical iconoclasm' of 'Tender Buttons', as part of a project to enage 'radically [with] what we have come to recognize as the most crucial issue of modernist art – the problem of representation'.[6] Increasingly, feminist and post-structuralist critics are drawn to Stein as re-maker of literary language; she is praised for her ability to invent a new writing, a literary language *ab initio*. This project of inauguration fits into critical frameworks which call for an *écriture féminine*, a womanly writing free from the entrapments of language created within a patriarchal order. Shari Benstock sees Stein's career evolving towards a 'lesbian modernism', as her friendship with Alice B. Toklas freed her into innovative ways of thinking, feeling and writing: 'In accepting Alice's love, Stein learned a new language (or rather rediscovered a language she had known in childhood) and exchanged monologue for dialogue, preaching for joking. Her writing suddenly ceased imitating the patriarchy.'[7] Such arguments deploy Stein's lesbianism alongside her experimentalism to make a formidable case about sexuality and writing: Stein's sexuality, with its explicit rejection of conventional polarities, called forth a writing equally impatient with the settled discourses of conventional fiction. Instead, it is argued, Stein destabilises accepted categories; her restless prose reformulates an idea of what writing might be, and therefore what our selves might be or become.

Even in the early work *Three Lives* (1909), Stein's 'realism' stetched the limits of this genre to create a new form and an experimental voice. She stripped out the encumbrances and baggage of Victorian fiction to fashion a distinctly modern idiom: spare, unfurnished, plain. Stein gave to American modernism an artistry based on exclusion and excision; Hemingway was her keenest disciple, but we might trace her influence, too, in the careful excisions of *The Great Gatsby*. The Stein sentence is a superficially simple artefact, constructed around coordinated clauses, repetitive use of conjunctions and a calculatedly circumscribed lexicon; but repetition and echoes within paragraphs create a densely poetic texture. The architecture of paragraphs is central to Stein's compositional technique. She cuts and edits her paragraphs to lend emphasis to particular phrases or sentences; she was a great user of the single-sentence paragraph, allowing an individual statement to stand forth from the page with sudden clarity. In the opening pages of 'The Good Anna' Stein deploys the sentence, 'Anna led an arduous and troubled life', in a stark, repetitive pattern as a choric statement which occurs between longer paragraphs of exposition. A kind of chorus, the statement tolls through these opening paragraphs.[8]

But Stein sited her exploratory technique within a terrain that was now familiarly female: the world of domesticity, sentiment and a form of miniaturised realism. *Three Lives* is a novel about housekeeping. Two of its protagonists are servants. The action of the book consists of the quotidian lives of these women, their routines, friendships, partnerships; the writing is defiantly unmelodramatic, and the conventional features of plot (choice, chance, event) are eschewed. The very ordinariness of the topic strikes the reader: this is a topic celebrated by late-Victorian American culture, but rarely admitted into fiction in such deliberately prosaic detail. Stein, along with Gilman, Chopin and Alice James, marked the end of the Victorian ideology of domesticity simply by acknowledging its underside, by bringing the home, housework, and the routines of married life into the purview of fiction.

Thus, *Three Lives* stakes a claim to the importance of the ordinary and the everyday. Its title suggests that these will be significant or important lives by hinting at the exemplary biography beloved of nineteenth-century *littérateurs*; but these are the lives of the unseen, if not the marginal. The title of the book might equally be 'forgotten lives'; it is a compendium of characters usually excluded from the bourgeois novel (migrants, the serving class, lower-class women). The radicalism of *Three Lives* lies in its re-writing of what we might call the 'representational ratio' of nineteenth-century fiction. Whereas the loose baggy monster mocked by Henry James had, in spite of its size, frequently maintained a social exclusivity (where are the urban working classes in a supposedly compendious work like *Middlemarch*?), Stein's compressed and stripped-down work is, paradoxically, more encompassing in its outreach to the overlooked classes and castes beyond the literate bourgeoisie.

The first life, 'The Good Anna', opens with the daily routines of a domestic help: 'she had every day her busy time. She cooked and saved and sewed and scrubbed and scolded' (p. 46). Stein makes from such banality a rich, quasi-poetic, rhythmic narrative. The plainness of the prose is redeemed from dullness by idiosyncratic locutions and rhythms, which often catch the immigrant roots of her protagonists (here, the Germanic inversion of 'she had every day her busy time'), and by the rhythmic structuring of sentences by repetition and cadenced variation. Like Lawrence and Hemingway, Stein fashioned out of the ordinary stuff of everyday language a supple, musical and fluid net to catch shifting emotional patterns. 'Melanctha' is a prose poem centring on the tonal shifts of intimacy between Jeff Campbell and Melanctha. These domestic scenes have an acuity about them, representing as they do a detailed and supple geography of the inner life. Stein deploys a third-person narrative voice, but places it close to the thoughts and feelings of her characters; an idiomatic free indirect discourse is inflected with distinctive speech patterns:

> And so it was Melanctha Herbert found new ways to be in trouble. But it was not very bad this trouble, for these white men Rose never wanted she should be with, never meant very much to Melanctha. It was only that she liked it to be with them, and they knew all about fine horses, and it was just good to Melanctha, now a little, to feel real reckless with them. But mostly it was Rose and other better kind of coloured girls and coloured men with whom Melanctha Herbert now always wandered. (pp. 190–1)

As a postgraduate student at the School of Medicine at Johns Hopkins University, Stein had developed experiments to demonstrate that consciousness was often not what it seemed. Her work on 'Motor Automatism' (1896) ranks alongside William James's commentary on the 'stream of consciousness' as a moment when radical theories of the mind's workings begin to emerge and intersect with fledgeling modernist aesthetics. Stein argued that experiments with 'spontaneous automatic writing' demonstrated that her subjects displayed a 'marked tendency to repetition'.[9] The belief that repetition was part of the basic structure of the mind, informed Stein's own experimental prose, with its choric recurrences and echoing syntax. (Repetition has since become part of the aesthetic of the twentieth-century American avant-garde in a range of media, leading to Andy Warhol's series of Elvis Presley icons and to Philip Glass's endlessly circling symphonic scores.)

To write of the ordinary or the banal, and to regard repetition as a central dynamic of consciousness, is to risk becoming banal oneself. In the absence of melodrama, or a strong narrative line, the reader can become disengaged. Stein's work helped to bring into being a new kind of reader, a reader whose conscious attentiveness would pick up subtle echoes and tonal modulations across a page. Moreover, Stein's narratives often move towards moments of great poignancy and pathos dependent, for their effect, on our having carefully worked through a mass of accumulated, everyday detail. Stein is trying to chart the rhythms of ordinary life, with the contrast between swathes of triviality and sudden moments of great pain and tragedy. 'The Good Anna' ends with simple words, but they have immense power as they conclude a story that encompassed the fine grain of her life: 'In a few days they had Anna ready. Then they did the operation, and then the good Anna with her strong, strained, worn-out body died' (pp. 75–6). Each of the three lives ends with death (the narrative has the spare, clean shape of a triptych); Stein presents these fates in a flattened style, but the very lack of overt sentiment moves us through understatement:

> Melanctha went back to the hospital, and there the Doctor told her she had the consumption, and before long she would surely die. They sent her where she would be taken care of, a home for poor consumptives, and there Melanctha stayed until she died.   (p. 215)

In her lectures, *Narration* (1935), Stein was very keen to distinguish American from British English. For Stein, language incarnated national identity. For the British, an island people, this was done by a strict bifurcation between what was 'inside' and what was 'outside': 'because otherwise the outside might come to be inside and the inside might come to be outside and then their way of telling about the way they lived their daily living every day would have gone away'.[10] But for the new nation, a more mobile and unsettled form of English was culturally necessary; Stein saw American English as disturbing the rigid forms of British English so as to express movement: 'the Americans move with them move always move and in every and in any direction' (p. 14). American literature would free itself from the idea of succession (succession implied tradition – a hallmark of the genealogy of European literatures from which American writing would escape): 'American writing has been an escaping not an escaping but an existing without the necessary feeling of one thing succeeding another thing of anything having a beginning and a middle and an ending' (p. 25). This sentence tries to make concrete these ideals of fluidity and movement by miming the restlessness of thought itself. Stein's expository prose often contains a self-contradictoriness, as she brings forward qualifications and paradoxes into her syntax, rather than excluding them (thereby leaving a finished, static syntax which occludes the *processes* of thought): 'an escaping not an escaping but an existing'.

Stein's work recurrently focuses on questions of race, nationalism and cultural identity. As an expatriate American, born to German–Jewish parents in Pennsylvania, she had biographical affinities to the exiles and emigrés of international modernism (Stein as sister to James Joyce or Joseph Conrad). But her modernism developed readings of culture which stresssed particular and peculiar national features, not overarching international or transnational cultural motifs. Stein was in many ways an expatriate *provincial* writer. She was a close friend of Sherwood Anderson, and much of her work about local French life is strongly redolent of Anderson's fondly ironic portrayals of the provincial small town. Even though she was a German–Jewish American who spent much of her life abroad, Stein was surprisingly uninterested in notions of the hybrid. National cultures are always monolithic in her work. In fact, after her death she was mobilised into the service of American nationalism by one of her readers. Gilbert Harrison collated her comments on Americans and foreigners in order to demonstrate that, in spite of long exile, she remained a defiantly American writer. *Gertrude Stein's America* (surely one of the curios of modernism) testifies to her breathless, nervy pleasure in her own innate American identity. When she meets some soldiers from Colorado: 'I do not know Colorado but that is the way I felt about it lovely Colorado and everybody was tired out and they gave us nice American specialities and my were we happy. . . .'[11]

Stein's defiant Americanism and her fascination with the provincial or local are manifestations of her interest in the home and 'ordinary' life. Similarly, *The Autobiography of Alice B. Toklas* (1933) re-writes the artist's life into a biography of epic normality. Generically framed by a tried-and-tested formula (the account of an artist by her friend – one thinks of Elizabeth Gaskell's *The Life of Charlotte Brontë*), the *Autobiography* quirkily plays with convention: Stein adopts the position of her friend, Toklas, to write an account of herself in the third person. This perspectival trick, reversing positions to create a memoir from the outside, allows Stein to write with intimacy and distance about her own life. The assumption of the third person also allows Stein to gain a certain authority for her deliberately outrageous comments, as when 'Alice' claims she has known three geniuses in her lifetime: Picasso, Alfred Whitehead . . . and Gertrude Stein. At such points the technical conceit of the book, with its immediate defamiliaris-ing of the writer's life, collapses into pretentious solipsism. Elsewhere, the reversing of perspective takes on a more exploratory and investigative rigour. As in the Cubist paintings she so admired, a radical shift in the position of the viewer opens up disconcertingly new perspectives on familiar material. Stein explicitly mentions Cubist art as the font of her early inspiration: 'She had begun not long before as an exercise in literature to translate Flaubert's *Trois Contes* and then she had this Cezanne and she looked at it and under its stimulus she wrote Three Lives.'[12] The disconcerting mundanity of Cubism continued throughout Stein's work; she admired Cubism's conjunction of the familiar and the disorientating. Stein favoured remarkably humdrum settings and subjects, but brought to this quotidian subject-matter a bracingly avant-garde technique.

Given Stein's reputation for difficulty and abstruseness, it is surprising to come across her forthright defence of the 'ordinary' in art:

> She always says she dislikes the abnormal, it is so obvious. She says the normal is so much more simply complicated and inter-esting.   (pp. 91–2)

The idea of a 'simply complicated' aesthetic might stand as an epigraph to Stein's work; she also cited the 'normal' as one of the reasons why she could not get on in her medical studies of *abnor-mal* psychology. And the fiction cleaves, with great rigour, to the textures of everyday life. In *Three Lives* she formulated a democ-ratic modernism, sensitive to the neglected interstices of quotid-ian existence; in the *Autobiography* this led to a highly original rendering of artists' lives. Here, Stein revealed the backing of the life of art: domestic arrangements, parties, friendships. When 'Alice' tells us, 'In this way my new full life began' (p. 9), we might expect a fullness that will deal with the high politics and aesthet-ics of modernism. After all, this is a book cluttered with references to some of the great modernist theorists (Picasso, Cezanne, Wyndham Lewis). But their declarative manifestos are a world away from Stein's representation of the artistic *demi-monde*. For

Stein, art is a ceaseless round of parties, visits, chance encounters. The discovery of painters, buying and selling artworks, the rituals of writing, the doings of a literary salon: this is the stuff of the *Autobiography*.

Yet the work does have a lot to say, by implication, about the role of art in society, and the importance of artistic passions for the individual self. Life in the *Autobiography* is more or less entirely defined in terms of artistic interest, interests largely confined to visual art. Politics hardly figures, and there is relatively little self-analysis. The calculated triviality of the *Autobiography* reinforces this emphasis on the primacy of aesthetic experience. Look, Stein seems to be saying, these parties and visits are sanctified because they take place within the hallowed world of art. The relentlessly quotidian terrain of the *Autobiography* also has implications for Stein's womanly aesthetic. Stein invokes the clichéd assumption that it is in the trivialised world of everyday social encounter that women have their place; the 'visit' is the very stuff of this book. The wit of the *Autobiography* is to invoke a hackneyed coupling of women and genteel conviviality, but to renew it by association with the avant-garde and modernistic. Having dinner with friends becomes tremendously significant if one's companions are Picasso and Gris.

Stein's modernism, a modernism of the normal, became part of a larger paradigmatic shift: the development of an aesthetic which yoked together innovation and ordinariness, thereby grounding experimentalism within the everyday. Stein's work is here comparable to that of James Joyce; but one can identify a specifically womanly strain of this quotidian experimentalism. Female modernists fostered a modernism attuned to the underside of existence, the customary and anti-melodramatic. In 1925 Willa Cather made analogous claims for a compositional method based on the 'other side of the rug':

> *My Ántonia*, for instance, is just the other side of the rug, the pattern that is supposed not to count in a story. In it there is no love affair, no courtship, no marriage, no broken heart, no struggle for success. I knew I'd ruin my material if I put it in the usual fictional pattern. I just used it the way I thought absolutely true.[13]

This is one of the earliest statements by a woman to link novel-writing to folk arts such as weaving. What intrigues me here is the extension of this analogy to encompass ideas about banality or the ordinary; the notion of a folksy 'pattern' expresses Cather's commitment to those subjects which are supposed 'not to count in a story'. We can see that folk arts might be important as a source of aesthetic principle for women, not only because such activities are grounded within the female sphere, but also because they are redolent of trivial experience (an ordinariness which American women writers have found inexhaustibly and paradoxically rich).

Analogies between writing and quilt-making have become a feature of modern feminist criticism, pushing the link between folk crafts and women towards the constitution of a 'female aesthetic'. Rachel Blau DuPlessis, in her classic essay 'For the Etruscans' (1979/84), argued that 'the "female aesthetic" will produce artworks that incorporate contradiction and nonlinear movement into the heart of the text'. DuPlessis read Monique Wittig's *Les Guérillères* as a 'verbal quilt':

> Monique Wittig's *Les Guérillères*, a form of verbal quilt. We heard her lists, her unstressed series, no punctuation even, no pauses, no setting apart, and so everything joined with no subordination, no ranking. It is radical parataxis. Something droning. Nothing epitomizes another.[14]

A corollary of faith in the ordinary or everyday (the 'other side' of the rug, the quilt of the quotidian) is that women have projected aesthetic models free of large-scale mythographic, political or religious schemas. Stein's avant-garde aesthetic is almost improvisational and *ad hoc*: she folded together fascination with Cubism, commitment to American English, and a democratic belief in ordinary experience; she allowed these ideas to rest informally together. Perhaps one of the reasons why female modernism is hard to identify as a discrete body of work is that its theoretical pronouncements lacked the stamp of the grandiloquent or visionary. 'Vision', if anything, is a masculine preserve in Anglo-American modernism. Pound, Eliot, Yeats, Lewis: all forged polemical theories of art, framed by totalising structures which combined political, mythic, religious and aesthetic imperatives (Eliot's Anglo-Catholic modernism of reaction or Yeats's gyres). Thus, the manifesto is a major discourse for male modernists, but rarely encountered in the work of female modernists. Women modernists (Stein, Cather, Hurston) instead fashioned critical statements that were informal, improvisational, off-the-cuff. Cather's commentary on the narratological experiments of *Death Comes for the Archbishop*, an incisive plea for formalistic latitude, was framed in nothing grander than a letter to a magazine. And in place of the prescriptive, vatic utterances of male modernism, a writer such as Zora Neale Hurston operated on a more *deductive* level. Her essays on black folklore and culture are pragmatic and observational; they derive a model of culture from careful observation, relying on the individual author's willingness to learn from what is already out there. One might call this approach 'low-tech' to distinguish it from the 'high-tech' critical articulations of the male modernists; but the distinction is not meant to carry pejorative connotations. If anything, the improvisational and deductive aesthetic theorising of women is likely to become more attractive due to its very eschewal of grand pronouncements. An improvisational aesthetic suits our increasing suspicion of the prophetic utterance.

Edith Wharton and the Crisis of Masculinity: 'To Slave for Women is Part of the Old American Tradition'

Edith Wharton's fiction often derives its dynamic from the pressurised masculinity diagnosed in the treatises of Mencken, Veblen and Gilman. Her stories mark out a fairly familiar territory of courtship and romantic intrigue; but the question of money is now becoming, at the start of the century, an overriding concern for the hero. Whereas nineteenth-century fictions of courtship typically witnessed a compromise between money and sentiment (the heroine needs to find a man she can love, but financial security is also part of the equation), in Wharton money is achieving its own power – a form of disembodied agency as if it were a character in its own right. Now, the suitor understands that his love has, almost as soon as it is recognised, to be confirmed with financial guarantees.

A novella, *The Touchstone* (1900), embodies this dilemma in crisp format. In eighty pages Wharton tells the tale of Glennard, a young man whose romantic friendship with a famous novelist left him with a clutch of her love letters. After her death, his romance with a Miss Trent leaves him desperately in need of money, to confirm and embody his desire. He publishes the letters, and they become a huge hit; he has sold one confidence to gain another. His new wife cries out at the end of the novel:

> His wife's cry caught him up. 'It isn't that she's given *me* to you – it is that she's given you to yourself.' She leaned to him as though swept forward on a wave of pity. 'Don't you see,' she went on, as his eyes hung on her, 'that that's the gift you can't escape from, the debt you're pledged to acquit? Don't you see that you've never before been what she thought you, and that now, so wonderfully, she's made you into the man she loved? *That's* worth suffering for, worth dying for, to a woman – that's the gift she would have wished to give!'
>
> 'Ah,' he cried, 'but woe to him by whom it cometh. What did I ever give her?'
>
> 'The happiness of giving,' she said.[15]

Read in isolation from the text, a passage like this one might seem to be saturated in a familiar romantic language of gifts, giving and pledges. But as a culmination to a story whose dynamic was a very literal process of pecuniary giving (and buying, too), the language takes on a harsher and more material edge. 'Gift', 'debt', 'pledged', 'giving': all such words are now freighted with connotations of base materialism, even when they are uttered in such a passionate vignette. The emotional realm has become utterly penetrated by fiduciary values.

Money is everywhere in Wharton's fiction. One might respond that there is nothing new in this, and that the novel, the quintessential bourgeois art-form, has always been fascinated by the intersections of sex and money. What is new in Wharton's work is a highly particularised fiscal crisis: a male crisis, produced by financial inadequacy or emotional debility or vocational indecision. Hence the sheer range of male discomfort in Wharton's *oeuvre*: the betrayal of Ralph Marvell in *The Custom of the Country*; the domestic entrapment in *Ethan Frome*; the unrequited romance, verging on a paralysis, that afflicts Newland Archer in *The Age of Innocence*. Two of Wharton's lesser works display even more bizarre masculine predicaments: the strange midlife crisis that afflicts Martin Boyne in her late novel, *The Children* (1928); and the alcoholism and suggestions of incestuous desire scarring Charity Royall's guardian in *Summer* (1917).

A tactic of recent criticism has been to rehabilitate Wharton, previously seen as a snob or a nostalgic novelist of manners, as an avatar of modernity. Wharton is increasingly seen as a transitional writer, an author who catches the moment when Victorian domestic ideology gives way to a twentieth-century sexual politics. Elaine Showalter reads *The House of Mirth* as marking 'the death of the lady novelist' and sounding the knell for Victorian domestic ideology. In this novel Wharton creates 'one of our American precursors of a literary history of female mastery and growth'.[16] Showalter's Wharton secretes proleptically radical narratives within the Trojan horse of her bourgeois fiction. The emphasis here is on re-reading Wharton as creator of a new woman's narrative; but what catches the male reader's eye is how often this transitional Wharton is a novelist of *masculine* crisis.

The Custom of the Country (1913) is a major representation of the bifurcated, gendered social and economic order laceratingly attacked by H. L. Mencken: a world where women shop and men make money. Undine Spragg is a new kind of heroine. Unlike the Victorian heroines who featured so heavily in Wharton's own reading (her indebtedness to 'the good George Eliot' was remarked on by Henry James), this is not a complex self.[17] There is none of the self-division of Jane Eyre or the maturation of a Dorothea Brooke; indeed the novel flouts the assumption that characters should, in some way, 'develop'. Undine Spragg is basically the same character on the final page as on the first, with similar desires and motives. Her ambition and materialism are established at the start ('she was going to know the right people at last – she was going to get what she wanted!') and continue through to her wistful, final reflection that marriage to an ambassador would have guaranteed the money and social position she desired. Undine Spragg's is a female self without subtlety, a self constructed by simplistic social and material yearnings. The very lack of moral substance or characterological texture is the point of Undine Spragg. As if drawn up by Thorstein Veblen himself, in his account of the 'leisure society', Spragg is a consummate consumer: of people, of men, of society. Thus, she bases her behaviour on 'the manner described in the articles on "A Society Woman's Day" which were appearing in *Boudoir Chat*'.[18] And rather like the 'Other-directed' individuals diagnosed by social scientists later in the century, Undine is wholly constructed by how she appears in the eyes of others. In one fine phrase, 'ripples of self-consciousness played up and down her watchful back'

(p. 31). Undine is also furious when she becomes pregnant. Wharton imagines desire and eroticism as themselves created by social ambition and consumerism. The heroine is not attracted to men for sexual reasons, but for their significance as emblems of taste or social standing. Wharton describes a materialist romance (the submission of the erotic to pecuniary and social imperatives):

> She wanted, passionately and persistently, two things which she believed should subsist together in any well-ordered life: amusement and respectability; and despite her surface-sophistication her notion of amusement was hardly less innocent than when she had hung on the plumber's fence with Indiana Frusk.   (p. 211)

Complexity, ambivalence and representational depth are channelled by Wharton into her portrayal of the male protagonist, Ralph Marvell. He is an aesthete, a languid connoisseur deeply unfitted for the rough-and-tumble of business America. Whilst Undine is rapacious and single-minded, Ralph exhibits the self-doubt and self-consciousness more readily associated with the *ingénues* of Henry James. Intriguingly, Ralph reads his own future by means of a Veblen-esque, quasi-anthropological terminology. His family, he thinks, are 'Aborigines': he 'likened them to those vanishing denizens of the American continent doomed to rapid extinction with the advance of the invading race'. Such a language, drawing perhaps crudely on a kind of popular social Darwinism, is found throughout Wharton's work. Newland Archer, for example, has undertaken 'his readings in anthropology': 'He knew that the southern races communicated with each other in the language of pantomime'.[19] Indeed, Wharton is much more of an overt anthropologist than her mentor, Henry James; her commentaries on national character are repeatedly framed by appeals to notions of racial and cultural identity. A year before *The Age of Innocence* Wharton had published *French Ways and Their Meaning* (1919), a work which approached her adopted homeland with a curiously mixed diction of belle-lettristic enthusiasm and pseudo-anthropological scholarship; the title itself conveys this mixture, with its rather laboured advertisement of the 'meaning' of France.

Wharton provides, then, a sociological and anthropological framework for the masculine crisis at the centre of *The Custom of the Country:* the inability of Ralph Marvell to reconcile his artistic dreams with the brutal necessity of earning enough to keep Undine in the privilege she demands. 'What can he do, then?', asks one of the novel's major passages:

> 'What *can* he do, then?' the future father-in-law inquired.
> 'He can write poetry – at least he tells me he can.' Mr. Dagonet hesitated, as if aware of the inadequacy of the alternative, and then added: 'And he can count on three thousand a year from me.'
> Mr. Spragg tilted himself farther back without disturbing his subtly calculated relation to the scrap basket.
> 'Does it cost anything like that to print his poetry?'
> Mr. Dagonet smiled again: he was clearly enjoying his visit. 'Dear, no – he doesn't go in for "luxe" editions. And now and then he gets ten dollars from a magazine.'
> Mr. Spragg mused. 'Wasn't he ever *taught* to work?'
> 'No; I really couldn't have afforded that.'   (p. 73)

Ralph is a useless male, economically; his father-in-law has to provide a pension for the couple to cover the son's fiscal disability. For Ralph lacks the one thing that will define him in American society: ruthless financial efficacy. He is listless and dreamy in a society that demands utilitarian discipline. Ralph exists in an inverted marriage, where business-like pragmatism has become, perversely, a female and not a male quality. 'What hurt him most was the curious fact that, for all her light irresponsibility, it was always she who made the practical suggestion, hit the nail of expediency on the head. No sentimental scruple made the blow waver or deflected her resolute aim' (p. 100). Ralph's agony is that society demands forthright pragmatism and acquisitiveness from men: 'To slave for women is part of the old American tradition' (p. 124).

Wharton put her finger on a dilemma that obsessed many male American writers of the early twentieth century: the place of the male artist in a culture with definite ideas about the cultural roles of men and women. For male writers and *littérateurs* in the 1910s and 1920s, masculinity itself seemed jeopardised by interest in the arts. According to Harold E. Stearns, one of the most prominent of the 'lost generation' literary critics, intellectual life itself had become the victim of 'feminization': 'Hardly any intelligent foreigner has failed to observe and comment upon the extraordinary feminization of American social life, and oftenest he has coupled this observation with a few biting remarks concerning the intellectual anaemia or torpor that seems to accompany it.'[20] It might be that the creation of an overtly masculine aesthetic by so many American modernists was a self-defensive act, a means to construct a cultural resistance to feminization.[21] Placed in this context, *The Custom of the Country* emerges as a curiously prescient and sympathetic work, written by a female novelist with a keen eye on the dilemmas of the American male. Wharton heavily slants the book to elicit the reader's sympathy for the increasingly wretched Ralph while portraying Undine as a character with, as it were, a bottomless reservoir of superficiality. Although recent criticism has claimed Wharton as a proto-feminist writer (the creator of women's stories, of narratives of domestic space and female conscience), the creator of *The Custom of the Country* occupies another position: analyst of masculine crisis and satirist of feminised materialism.[22] The 'feminism' of a novel like this does not rest in the creation of female icons (for that we might look at Willa Cather's pioneer novels of the 1910s), but in re-orientations of stereotyped gender characteristics. And one might even argue that there is a form of 'post-feminist' awareness in Wharton's creation of a hollow, greedy, superficial heroine: she adumbrates a women's writing which accommodates negative as well as positive representations.

Wharton's career had begun with a work of anodyne upper-class consumerism. *The Decoration of Houses* (1897), co-written with the deliciously named Ogden Codman, initiated the reader into interior design and home-furnishing; it might stand as a totemic text of Veblen's 'conspicuous consumption'. But her mature work often contorts or distorts this cosy image of domestic comfort, finding strangeness by the hearthside. Two novellas, *Ethan Frome* (1911) and *Summer* (1917) focus on houses which invert, parody and mock the bourgeois comforts celebrated in 1897. The home in these later works becomes the site of emotional turmoil and familial fracture; both works centre on stark houses, symbolically denuded of comfort. 'Family' in both works stands for a broken and non-conventional structure. In *Ethan Frome* Wharton created a strange *ménage à trois* of adulterous husband, wife and mistress, living in a harsh household – a kind of New England counterpart to the Flaubertian novel of adultery, where romance has turned to ice and ash. The heroine of *Summer* is utterly deracinated. Charity

Royall, the offspring of an alcoholic father and a 'loose' mother, is brought up by a guardian in a desolated and isolated village; her very name ironically incarnates the pathetic hope that through adoption (Charity) she can be elevated to a better position (Royall). Charity Royall is Wharton's representation of a self stripped of roots, of family and of the cultural apparatus which for the author gives meaning to life. She works in a library, but has little understanding of books; her romantic fascination with the cultured visitor to North Dormer, Lucius Harney, is pitifully fostered by a desperate yearning to better herself.

The Decoration of Houses was underwritten by a classic Victorian piety: that the home was a site for cultural production, the fostering of manners and taste. But *Summer* envisages a hollowed-out and desiccated environment, where the bare houses of North Dormer signal a kind of spartan anti-culture: 'There it lay, a weather-beaten sunburnt village of the hills, abandoned of men, left apart by railway, trolley, telegraph, and all the forces that link life to life in modern communities. It had no shops, no theatres, no lectures, no "business block." '[23] North Dormer is Sarah Orne Jewett's fictional community, Dunnet's Landing, advanced further into decline; Jewett's picturesque, local color version of rural simplicity has devolved into a nightmare of deserted houses and philistinism. Both *Summer* and *Ethan Frome* reveal Wharton's cynicism about the idealised beloved communities projected by the local colorists. She claimed in her 1934 autobiography, *A Backward Glance*, that she was drawing New England realistically rather than looking 'through the rose-colored spectacle of my predecessors'.[24] At the start of the century a spate of best-sellers had turned local color's vision of the country good life into populist pastoralism. John Fox's 1908 smash *The Trail of the Lonesome Pine*, Kate Douglas Wiggin's *Rebecca of Sunnybrook Farm* (1903 – a novel set, like Wharton's works, in rural New England), Gene Stratton-Porter's *A Girl of the Limberlost* (1909): all these hugely popular works fostered an image of bucolic idyll, a simple life satisfyingly conducted in America's vast green spaces. Such fiction fed the appetite of the homesteaders then vainly pursuing their dreams in landscapes, like that in eastern Montana, of unremitting harshness.[25] *Ethan Frome* and *Summer* read like dystopian fictions, bitter deconstructions of the pastoral naivety fostered by popular fiction.

Towards the end of *Summer*, Charity Royall establishes her tryst with Lucius Harney, a touching but doomed romantic idyll

(Charity finally submits to her guardian's offer of marriage, a conclusion underwritten by a brutally ironic sense of the determining triumph of societal circumstance over individual desire).[26] In these scenes the representation of domestic space is again important. Charity and Harney meet outside the bounds of the village, in an echo of those earlier American adulterers, Hester Prynne and the Reverend Dimmesdale. In an empty house they fashion an austere simulacrum of the marital home, imbued with a spare sensuality. Charity experiences 'the wondrous unfolding of her new self' in a room 'furnished in primitive camping fashion'. The marital bed: 'in one corner was a mattress with a Mexican blanket over it' (p. 115).

A thesis could be written on the ruined, emptied and haunted houses that recur so often in American women's writing this century. It is as if the plenitude of the Victorian home has become too linked with a constricting domestic ideology; the modern writer prefers domestic spaces of unconventional decoration which symbolically incarnate alternative spaces outside the realm of established morality. Willa Cather's Mesa houses in *The Professor's House* (1925) and *The Song of the Lark* (1915) fulfil this function. Anne Tyler, in *Ladder of Years* (1995), depicts Cordelia Grinstead's self-renewal in a stark rented room, an antidote to the busy, cramped home she has fled. And in *Beloved* Morrison uses the haunted house, 142, as a trope to stand for the domestic disturbance and familiar hauntings wreaked by slavery upon the black household. More recently, Morrison has placed the female community of *Paradise* (1997) in a ruined convent, a shell of a building that invokes and inverts the ideal of home (and disturbs the local men to the extent that they wreak terrible vengeance on the women). All of these twentieth-century fictional households are spartan and unconventional homes. In place of the nineteenth-century home, over-furnished in both literal and ideological senses, these twentieth-century writers have created domestic configurations based on a kind of radical simplicity or even emptiness: the home as a stripped box or a shell or ghostly space.

Mary Antin's *The Promised Land*: 'I Have Been Made Over'

The Promised Land, published in 1912, was a great success; it told of the Americanisation of its author, a Russian Jew, but managed to achieve a wider popularity outside Antin's own community. The title of Mary Antin's autobiographical account of immigration into the United States suggests a familiar biographical pattern: a neo-theological journey of upbringing, formalistically derived from saints' lives and allegories such as *The Pilgrim's Progress*. But Antin's relationship with Christian culture was distant, ironic or quizzical; she hints at a Christian narrative but then subverts it. This is at the outset a Jewish autobiography, and the 'promised land' of the title – the United States – is as likely to be a new home for the Israelites as a Christian paradise.

Mild subversion or ironic displacement is typical of *The Promised Land*. The immigrant autobiography was to become one of the major popular genres of early twentieth-century America, serving up a heartening stew of self-improvement and nationalist sentiment. The fervour with which the migrant looked forward to her new home confirmed American exceptionalism; and the migrant's success provided a narrative of model citizenship. The immigrant autobiography, a narrative of Americanisation, is thus a form of national epic. It suggests that the individual life will have a wider significance as a symbol for the national culture. But Antin's exploration of these motifs is more searching, more meditative than the overtly populist manifestations of the genre (although her book also sold widely). Compared with a work like *The Americanization of Edward Bok* (1920) this is a highly self-scrutinising and poetically meditative work. For one thing, she turns the Americanisation narrative towards an essay on selfhood, memory, identity itself:

> I was born, I have lived, and I have been made over. Is it not time to write my life's story? I am just as much out of the way as if I were dead, for I am absolutely other than the person whose story I have to tell. Physical continuity with my earlier self is no disadvantage. I could speak in the third person and not feel that I was masquerading. I can analyze my subject, I can reveal everything; for *she*, and not *I*, is my real heroine. My life I have still to live; her life ended when mine began.[27]

This is a fascinating passage; Antin deconstructs stable pronouns ('*she*, and not *I*') to project a sense of a lifetime as fissured rather than a steadily organic evolution. Antin advances a theory of the self that seems modern, if not post-modern (breaks, transformations, the production of selfhood through the act of writing); but the power of the passage lies in its simple vernacular testimony to selfhood. 'I am just as much out of the way as if I were dead', 'I have been made over': this is a radically transformed self expressed in a common idiom – the vigour of the American demotic itself a sign of the wondrous transformation.

One of the recurrent tropes in *The Promised Land* is that of the boundary or the division – a physical manifestation of the borders in her own inner life. As a child she lives within the 'Pale', a Jewish enclave in Russia. A later chapter, 'The Boundaries Stretch', witnesses the breaking of those earlier geographical and cultural rigidities. That early life is marked by ritual, custom, the inherited ways of Judaism. It is an ordinary life, as Antin ceaselessly reminds us, a life shared by many thousands of East European Jews. Antin then alerts us to the boundary between the collective, historical circumstances of her life, and the stirrings of the individualism which flowers in the United States:

> I have now told who I am, what my people were, how I began life, and why I was brought to a new home. Up to this point I have borrowed the recollections of my parents, to piece out my own fragmentary reminiscences. But from now on I propose to be my own pilot across the seas of memory.   (p. 64)

The ship setting sail is a hackneyed image; but elsewhere, Antin develops a highly idiosyncratic language of individualism and self-transformation. Her prose is striated with a range of vocabularies: transcendental meditative prose (there are obvious echoes of Emerson, whose work she knew well); social history; family memoir. Antin finds few continuities, correspondences or bridges between her childhood as a Russian Jew and her Americanised adolescence. The self is fissured and divided; the new life in America is just that, new, creating a radical discontinuity. This conception of the self creates intriguing epistemological problems for the writer. If I have changed utterly from how I was then, is it at all possible to conceive of the earlier self? Antin's solution is to present us with separate discourses of the self. The earlier sections are historical, sociological, anthropological; they are the testament of a collective or familial memory. The latter part of the book – more earnestly individualistic – is written by the new American Antin. Here the writing becomes anecdotal and personal.

The Promised Land shows its turn-of-the-century context most clearly in the use of a quasi-Darwinist language. Darwinist evolutionary theory provides one way for Antin to maintain a vision of the collective; she stresses the adaptability and communality of the Jewish people as if they constitute a species developing through time. But, with that characteristic crossing of boundaries and 'making over' of an earlier mode of life, this quasi-Darwinist argument (the Jewish people as a species) is succeeded by transcendental individualism:

> If I had died after my first breath, my history would still be worth recording. For before I could lie on my mother's breast, the earth had to be prepared, and the stars had to take their places; a million races had to die, testing the laws of life; and a boy and girl had to be bound for life to watch together for my coming. I was millions of years on the way, and I came through the seas of chance, over the fiery mountain of law, by the zigzag path of human possibility. Multitudes were pushed back into the abyss of non-existence, that I should have way to creep into being.   (p. 48)

'Social Darwinism' sanctioned the triumph of a specific race, nation or culture as a result of the 'survival of the fittest'. Antin, however, pursued her own idiosyncratic model of transcendental, *individualist* Darwinism: the vast operations of evolution have taken place 'that I should have way to creep into being'. This is the central passage in *The Promised Land* since it enlists a scientific discourse to support individualism and to sweep away inheritance: 'Such creatures of accident are we, liable to a thousand deaths before we are born. But once we are here, we may create our own world, if we choose' (p. 49).

The change from Europe to America, from the religious certainties of Judaism to atheism, is a transformation from the collective to individualism. Now, collective identity is formed through nationalism and the myths of the American state. Antin's schooling is partly a matter of individual assertion and enterprise; it is equally a process of acculturation, as the myths and symbols of national identity are imbibed by the hungry new American. She writes of the great numbers of immigrants 'who next February will be declaiming patriotic verses in honor of George Washington and Abraham Lincoln' (p. 163). Antin's exuberant reponse to the

United States is largely formed by her delight in the educational opportunities it offers the individual young woman. Immigrant testimonies were, of course, often largely about education; *The Americanization of Edward Bok*, a best-seller and Pulitzer Prizewinner, is typical of the genre in its emphasis on learning and language acquisition. Antin's book, adopting this educational emphasis and then feminising it, relentlessly stresses the exceptional opportunities America offers its young women. The young Jewish woman is denied in her homeland an extended education; the Hebraic education of a traditional Jewish community is reserved for its bright young men. Mary Antin is lucky enough to arrive in the United States while young enough to take advantage of these opportunities (her elder sister is brought up in the old ways, and is abruptly married in her teens). *The Promised Land* can thus be read as a quasi-feminist national epic, since it celebrates the unique virtues of a country with a public education system of rare egalitarianism.

As *The Promised Land* advances, and its heroine becomes assimilated into American society, the narrative becomes less interesting; the latter stages are celebratory and banal in equal measure. However, our reading of the book is framed by Antin's pitiable life story. Marital break-up and political alienation seem to have played their part in a life of gathering obscurity; she only published two pieces in the last twenty-three years of her life.[28] As with other women writers (one thinks of Nella Larsen, Zora Neale Hurston or Tillie Olsen), early creativity and recognition were succeeded by marginality and silence. Therefore, one reads the optimistic testimony of *The Promised Land* ironically. Its triumphs were temporary and its motto might be the Virgilian epigram quoted at the start of Willa Cather's *My Ántonia*, 'Optima dies ... prima fugit' ('the best of days are the first to fly'). *The Promised Land* thus marks another stage in the ongoing struggle in American women's writing between progressive, optimistic narratives and declensionist plots. I noted earlier that *The Awakening* has become a major site for this debate, as critics spar over whether the heroine succumbs to her fate or rebels against it. *The Promised Land* introduces a further biographical twist to this argument: the optimism of the text is shadowed by another narrative, the story of the writer's life, which cannot help but inflect our reading. As with so many of our writers (Chopin, James, Hurston, Larsen) the biographical details press down on the texts left behind after a brief spell of truncated creativity.

Narratologically, works such as *The Promised Land* or *The Custom of the Country* inhabit a familiar formalistic lexicon; their structures would have been recognisable to a reader of the late nineteenth century. The social, economic and cultural forces of modernity are registered in these works as topics or themes, but the writer's template for the construction of her story remains an inherited one. Modernism has not impacted on form. Even the apparent radicalism of Stein's *Three Lives* can be seen as indebted to the established discursive codes of local color realism. It was with the next stage of modernism, overlapping with the works in this chapter and extending into the 1920s and 1930s, that a more thoroughgoing structural change to the shape of women's narrative took place. At the level of the individual sentence, and also within the broader grids of structure (plot, chapter, paragraph), Djuna Barnes's *Nightwood*, Stein's 'Tender Buttons' and Willa Cather's *My Ántonia* effected a more fundamental revolution in storytelling. It is to what I will call their 'modernist geographies' that I now turn.

3

Modernist Geographies

Space in the Fiction of Willa Cather, Djuna Barnes and Gertrude Stein

If an anthropologist were to consider late nineteenth-century American society, she would note the central role played by the organisation of space in that culture. The Victorian 'female world of love and ritual' praised by many feminists might well have had a radical edge, and it certainly allowed for a greater range of emotional expressiveness than stereotypes of nineteenth-century stuffiness would suggest; yet it was also a confined world of the interior, of sitting-rooms and parlours. It is a cliché, but also a truth, that nineteenth-century American literary culture associated the open spaces of a new country (frontier, sea, wilderness) with freedom, while female culture was locked within the home (often constructed, as in *Huckleberry Finn*, in terms of a tyrannical space ruled by womanly culture's petty rules). Women themselves, of course, often explored the home as a site of emotional plenitude and a sentimental politics of renewal (as in Harriet Beecher Stowe's *Uncle Tom's Cabin*). And historians such as Ann Douglas have pointed to the 'feminisation' of American society as these values gradually took on a wider resonance and importance. But a time was bound to come when women would want to break out, in their writings and their lives, from this relentless association between themselves and the home. Women's literary modernism of the early twentieth century saw, above all, a re-configuration of these familiar domestic spaces and an opening-up of new environments. The Victorian interior world was radically deconstructed and re-imagined; new, outdoor spaces became the settings for female fictions. In Willa Cather's work the spatial matrix of America was amplified, both geographically and historically: various American pasts (aboriginal, Hispanic, French) exfoliate in her work, even as she sweeps across heterogeneous environments (Mesa land and prairie; Québec and New Mexico; modern cities and ancient dwellings). In Gertrude Stein's experimental texts a familiar domestic setting (parlour, kitchen) is deconstructed and then re-assembled by her kaleidoscopic literary Cubism. And in Djuna Barnes's *Nightwood* (1936) a female cityscape becomes the carnivalesque site for models of shifting identity and sexuality.

And if there is a womanly 'signature' in American modernism, it is surely here: in spatial re-configuration, especially of the familiar Victorian settings of female fiction. Stylistically, Stein, Cather and Barnes have little in common. Stein's avant-garde nursery rhymes are a world away from Cather's careful splicing of the lapidary and the idiomatic; Barnes's lyrical and ludic modernism is different again. But all three writers do share a common project, which is both thematic and formalistic: to re-imagine the places where women's writing might be set, and in so doing to re-make the female narrative aesthetic. All three arrive at a modernist tectonic – a revised sense of the shape that narratives might take. Intriguingly, all three of these writers were lesbians (although the public presentation of sexuality, and the importance of sexuality in their creative lives, is once again very different for each writer). Might there be some connection between sexual 'otherness' and the willingness to see familiar fictional environments in a new way? Might the spaces of American female modernism be 'queer spaces'?

Willa Cather's America(s)

Willa Cather (1873–1947) is the exemplary instance of a female author castigated for disengagement from the contemporary world. Her novels of the 1920s and 1930s (*Death Comes for the Archbishop*, *The Professor's House*, *Shadows on the Rock*) occupied a geographical and temporal space that seemed far from American modernism's great subject, the accelerating futurity of the city. Cather instead wrote of the nineteenth-century Catholic missions in Mexico, of seventeenth-century French Canada, of the ancient civilisations on Mesa tablelands. Public statements such as her remark that the world 'broke in two in 1922 or thereabouts' hardly helped foster an image of an author welcoming modernity. For a critic such as Granville Hicks, Cather seemed damagingly divorced from contemporary realities.[1]

Cather's *oeuvre* seemed, to her critics, part and parcel of a tepid female historicism which dominated the best-seller lists but resisted the aesthetic crusade of modernism. Furthermore, Cather won the Pulitzer Prize for *One of Ours* (1922), a novel about the Great War which aroused Ernest Hemingway's wrath as it trespassed on all-too-masculine subject-matter (the war has been 'Catherised', he complained to Edmund Wilson). We need to see attacks on Cather by men such as Hicks and Hemingway in the context of the era's literary politics. Two years later, after the success of *One of Ours*, Edna Ferber won the Pulitzer for *So Big* (1924). Ferber's heroine, Selina De Jong, settles in the Illinois prairies as a pioneer and a school-teacher; the novel thus echoes Cather's early fiction in its deployment of a 'strong' female protagonist who carves out a space in a typically masculine world. Few would now claim much merit for Ferber's utilitarian language; but her novel is interesting on sociological grounds, as it reveals a great appetite amongst readers for pastoral and historical works imbued with a mildly progressive ideology. In reading Cather, and the adversions cast by Hemingway on her work, we need to be aware of the 'culture war' in which Cather became caught up: a *Kulturkampf* where Hemingway's aesthetic of self-conscious experiment, strident modernity and iconic masculinity became pitted against a female writing often rooted in the pastoral and the past – the world of Ferber and, apparently, Cather. Hemingway probably read Cather as just one of a host of populists who had turned history into a middlebrow, money-spinning genre.[2]

Yet Cather grew up in environments which revealed to her, on a daily basis, the whirling and exhilarating cultural forces that shaped the modern United States. Although Cather's family were of long-established stock, her work showed relatively little interest in the Anglo-American heritage mined by predecessors such as Hawthorne and James. Cather was interested in newer, rawer varieties of national identity. After her family moved to the barely settled state of Nebraska in the 1880s, Cather grew up amongst the new immigrants who populated the Midwest: Scandinavians, Germans, Bohemians and Slavs. Cather knew this area as a land of cultural, linguistic pluralism. Admittedly, this was predominantly a European cosmopolitanism; but it was, nonetheless, a context of greater variety than that of many literary contemporaries. The daily experience of life in Nebraska exposed the burgeoning forces of what the radical critic and harbinger of multiculturalism, Randolph Bourne, would call in 1916 'Trans-National America'.[3] This was a culture which worshipped Italian opera and Shakespeare, even as it mutated into a society *sui generis*: a cosmopolitan immigrant community established on landscapes littered with the archaeological traces of earlier indigenous peoples.

Another way to frame these biographical observations about Cather is to say that her situation was that of many postcolonial writers: she voluntarily surrounded herself with the accoutrements of European civilisation, even as she recognised the manifold ways in which modern America pulled away to create a new civilisation. Cather grew up as a disciple of the high European arts; she reviewed opera and drama as a young woman, and idolised British poets and French novelists. Her early reviews are indebted to European cultural heritages, but they equally point to the need for an autonomous literature. During Cather's student days it was still customary to regard American literature as simply a minor offshoot of the 'mother tongue', British English. But like that other female experimentalist, Gertrude Stein, Cather's early work was partly driven by a form of literary nationalism. In Stein's case she often envisages American identity in terms of linguistic difference: the divergences between American and British English. In Cather's case nationalism is expressed more obliquely, and largely in terms of genre and geographical setting.[4]

Cather's postcolonial literary nationalism operated in two ways. First, she adopted and revised the fundamental classical genres underwriting the Western canon. Second, she explored the geographical variety of America, creating fictions reponsive to the spatial heterogeneity of the United States; and in mapping the unexplored New World she fashioned an innovative tectonic for the American novel – a literary architecture able to accommodate vast shifts of space and time. Cather *Americanised* genres rooted in the oldest of Old World traditions. She deconstructed the European traditions to find the fundamental genres (tragedy, epic, pastoral) which she then embedded in her American narratives. The early pioneer novels (*O Pioneers!* and *My Ántonia*) draw heavily on pastoral, epic and elegy; they signal their indebtedness to Latin and Greek models. *My Ántonia* carries an epigraph from Virgil ('Optima dies . . . prima fugit': 'The best of days are the first to fly'); Virgilian themes of migration, cultural transmission and elegy echo throughout the novel. Cather's lapidary style, with its chiselled concision and marbled elegance, has also been seen as a 'classic voice' indebted to the Latin masters.[5]

Cather's classicism shaped her literary nationalism; and her adoption and re-formulation of ancient genres strikingly anticipate the strategies of recent postcolonial writers. Her setting of Virgilian pastoral on the Nebraskan prairies is analogous to Derek Walcott's revisionist Caribbean setting of Homeric epic in *Omeros* (1990). Walcott's work has provoked critics to ask whether generic indebtedness constitutes cultural submission. For some readers, adoption of classical models marks fealty to the European heritage and a betrayal of his African–Caribbean and Creole roots. As Joseph Farrell has argued, this is to misread the heterogeneity implicit in many classical genres. Although writers have sought, by using classical genres, to gain the imprimatur of authenticity and tradition, Farrell suggests that classical scholarship increasingly sees these forms as themselves marked by difference, hybridity and transformational potential. Farrell regards Walcott's classicism as polyphonic: capable of accommodating a variety of voices. The postcolonial writer of classical forms creates an indeterminate space, an intertextual arena where ancient and modern, classical and postcolonial can coexist without necessarily signalling cultural obeisance to the European order of things. The postcolonial classicist places ancient and modern, European and Creole, in open-ended conversation with one another.[6]

Similarly, Cather's classically enriched fictions create indeterminate, intertextual spaces, where cultures and eras can overlap in fruitful complexity. On her Nebraskan prairies, where Czech-speaking pioneers move in an Anglophone culture, their lives echoing Greek pastoral, Cather adumbrates an indeterminate classicism: indebted to ancient models, undoubtedly, but capable of renewal – stamped with the cultural authority of the ancients but never in sway to them.

Cather's fictional project also embraced the heterogeneity of America: the various and often-unfictionalised spaces of a country which in her work is coming into being. More than any other American writer, Cather's career is marked by promiscuous restlessness within the continental boundaries, as she moves from one zone of the United States to another: each phase of her career can be read as a configuration of a new space or the exploration of a fresh environment. Her early work, with its epic celebrations of the gains and losses of pioneering, grasps the prairies as the site for heroic endeavours with a classical resonance. *My Ántonia* (1918) and *O Pioneers!* (1913) also staked a claim for the Midwest on account of the area's extraordinary mixture of cultures. Indeed, Cather claimed that 'it is in that great cosmopolitan country known as the Middle West that we may hope to see the hard molds of American provincialism broken up'.[7] Cather went on to represent the diverse spaces of America; she fictionalised a mosaic of peoples, places, cultures. Even in the early novel, *The Song of the Lark* (1915), the heroine's psychological renewal takes place against the background of the Southwestern tablelands, with their ancient 'Cliff-Dweller' Indian settlements. *Death Comes for the Archbishop* (1927) is set in the hinterlands of Spanish America, and takes place in the mid-nineteenth century; it focuses on a Latin, Catholic America, alongside the aboriginal world of indigenous peoples. *The Professor's House* (1925), above all, imagined a nation of juxtapositions: modernity and technology (the novel is partly set in a university, and its protagonist invents a jet engine); antediluvian landscapes and ancient dwellings. *Shadows on the Rock* (1931) furthered this geographical sweep, as she turned towards French Canada in the seventeenth century by setting her work in colonial Québec. At the end of her life she was still exploring diverse terrains; she set her final novel *Sapphira and the Slave Girl* (1940) in plantation-era Virginia. And when she died, Cather was planning a novel about medieval Avignon.

If Cather's work was simply an extended exercise in fictional mobility, then it would not be as interesting as it is. However, this peripatetic energy had fascinating consequences for Cather's fiction in other ways, too. First, the locking of the multiple spaces of America within a fictional form impacted on the shape and construction of her novels: how was the novelist to internalise vast heterogeneity within a cohesive fictional format? Second, Cather's mobility was not merely geographical but also historical: drawn to the new spaces of her country, she also imagined the temporal extension of the United States; Cather's fictions have a historical reach way beyond the modern America in which they often unobtrusively begin. In particular, she was fascinated by the ancient Pueblo communities of the Southwest. One biographer credits a trip to Arizona and New Mexico in 1912 for Cather's decisive transformation from journalist and short-story writer into fully fledged novelist.[8] *The Song of the Lark*, *The Professor's House* and *Death Comes for the Archbishop* all feature ancient, indigenous communities; but to account for these cultures, temporally so distant from modern America, created further problems of narrative organisation.

Cather saw narrative in terms of architectural analogies. Asked about the discontinuous and broken-backed format of *The Professor's House* (1925), she replied that the inset narrative, 'Tom Outland's Story', was like a view within a Golden Age Dutch painting:

> In many of them the scene presented was a living-room warmly furnished, or a kitchen full of food and coppers. But in most of the interiors, whether drawing-room or kitchen, there was a square window, open, through which one saw the masts of ships, or a stretch of grey sea. The feeling of the sea that one got through those square windows was remarkable, and gave me a sense of the fleets of Dutch ships that ply quietly in all the waters of the globe.[9]

Here Cather invokes a recognisably feminine world of interiors, warm kitchens and so on; but this womanly space is, above all, now a representation rather than a cultural given. Through the analogy with Dutch painting Cather can both invoke and then distance herself from a familiar interiority. Moreover, the passage then mimes, quite literally, a movement out of enclosure into open space, the sea, as the viewer's eye tracks outwards through the square window. The sea, as in Jewett's work, is coded with masculine features; it is an imperial domain, although also an empire that has been subtly feminised (the ships 'ply quietly' their business – the violence of empire is absent). What occurs here, in one of Cather's most famous commentaries on her work, is a 'doubled' argument, as the woman writer both returns to expected territory and revitalises that terrain to carry a new aesthetic importance.

These analogies served Cather as a means to deconstruct and re-shape traditional realist narrative. Early in her career she pursued an accretive, monolithic realism where the mimetic power of fiction depends on the novelist's stacking-up of representative detail. She later revised *The Song of the Lark* by cutting superfluous material, and her essay 'The Novel Démeublé'

(1922) called for a stripping-out of extraneous detail. The space of Cather's work then seemed to narrow, as she produced leaner and sparer works such as *My Mortal Enemy* (1926). But at the same time she was expanding the interior space of her work, throwing the net around the terrains of the Southwest or French Canada. Novels like *The Professor's House* or *Death Comes for the Archbishop* have a *trompe l'oeil* effect: superficially these elegantly chiselled narratives are unfurnished; but in terms of historical and geographical space they open up a vast interiority. 'The Novel Démeublé' opposed the relentlessly accretive realism of the early twentieth-century novel (Theodore Dreiser, although not named, exemplifies the kind of writing she complains of). Cather here claimed for her *selective* realism the imprimatur of modernity:

> There are hopeful signs that some of the younger writers are trying to break away from mere verisimilitude, and, following the development of modern painting, to interpret imaginatively the material and social investiture of their characters; to present their scene by suggestion rather than by enumeration. The higher processes of art are all processes of simplification. The novelist must learn to write, and then he must unlearn it; just as the modern painter learns to draw, and then learns when utterly to disregard his accomplishment, when to subordinate it to a higher and truer effect. In this direction only, it seems to me, can the novel develop into anything more varied and perfect than all the many novels that have gone before.[10]

Cather is often seen as a conservative or a nostalgist; but this passage commits itself to the 'modern' and to a progressive theory of art. Furthermore, in its use of examples from visual art, Cather's essay learns from that most avant-garde of art forms in the early twentieth century. Modern painting is in the vanguard; the novelist must follow. This essay also makes numerous references to French art and culture – further indices of a progressive modernity.

At the end of the piece (itself slight, as if embodying the virtues of economy and concision), Cather explicitly imagined a minimalist aesthetic:

> How wonderful it would be if we could throw all the furniture out of the window and, along with it, all the meaningless

reiterations concerning physical sensations, all the tiresome old patterns, and leave the room as bare as the stage of a Greek theatre, or as that house into which the glory of Pentecost descended; leave the scene bare for the play of emotions, great and little – for the nursery tale, no less than the tragedy, is killed by tasteless amplitude. The elder Dumas enunciated a great principle when he said that to make a drama a man needed one passion, and four walls.   (pp. 55–6)

Cather articulates a modernist aesthetic of spare simplicity which tantalisingly looks forward to contemporary avant-garde theory (the 'scene bare for the play of emotions' is curiously similar to statements made by the British theatre director Peter Brook about the empty space of radical dramaturgy).[11] And this 'bare' scene, in a further intriguing twist, is given a theological implication. Cather compares the new *mise-en-scène* of the stripped-out novel to the empty room where the Pentecost (the gift of tongues) took place. It is a surprising analogy, and one which fuses modernism and theology within a minimalist aesthetic: all three elements are pitted against overburdened realism. These artistic ideals are extrapolations away from the local color aesthetic of Sarah Orne Jewett; 'The Novel Démeublé' thus re-fashions Jewett's spare realism, using local color to create a progressive, minimalist formalism.

Writing about the geographical and cultural multiplicity of the United States, Cather was inevitably drawn to a series of questions which anticipate the concerns of contemporary cultural theory: how do civilisations inter-relate? What is the meaning of cultural exchange? Are cultures discrete, or can they be hybrid? Recent critics of Cather have used her sporadic anti-Semitism as a touchstone for reading her work's representations of race, culture and nationalism; but Cather did attempt to make amends for early lapses in judgement.[12] And her later work elevated exchange, hybridity and cultural interconnection over racial or cultural insularity. The most successful individuals and cultures in her work tend to manifest polymorphic, multifaceted diversity. Fictional representations of the composite and the diverse recur in her work. Conversely, exclusivist and insular cultures in her work will always collapse. When Tom Outland, in *The Professor's House*, discovers the spectacular remains of a Pueblo settlement, he at first idealises its insulated incorruptibility; here is an ancient, indigenous version of the 'City on the Hill', a *polis* constructed by the vanishing American. Cather, however, undercuts this dream of an insular, indigenous American Utopia. The horrifying remains of a martyred woman reveal the cruelty of the community; proudly autonomous, this was nonetheless a culture divided against itself.

In contrast, Professor St Peter illustrates the virtues of cultural diversity by incarnating a mixed-European heritage from both the South and the North of the Continent; he brings together the Latin and Anglo-American heritages of the United States:

> Though he was born on Lake Michigan, of mixed stock (Canadian French on one side, and American farmers on the other), St. Peter was commonly said to look like a Spaniard. That was possibly because he had been in Spain a good deal, and was an authority on certain phases of Spanish history.[13]

St Peter is a composite, hybrid European settler of America. Derived from French and Anglo stock, in terms of looks and interest he embodies too the Hispanic world. Such conflations are not unusual in Cather. García María de Allande, in *Death Comes for the Archbishop*, combines a 'long Spanish face' with a complexion derived from his English mother.[14] These patterns of amalgamation and hybridity are typical of Cather's fiction from the 1920s; she found cultural strength in a mélange of cultures. Usually, of course, this is a mixture of predominantly Western civilisations. At the end of *Death Comes for the Archbishop* Father Latour supervises the construction of a cathedral which brings together the architecture of the French Midi and the Mexican landscape of its settings; the clear implication is that a powerful New World culture will be an amalgam of the American and the European. But elsewhere in that book Cather describes a pluralism open to other, non-Western ways of being. For example, when Latour hears the Angelus rung, he imagines the Islamic roots of this Christian celebration. Father Latour reflects that 'the silver of the Spaniards was really Moorish, was it not?':

> A learned Scotch Jesuit in Montreal told me that our first bells, and the introduction of the bell in the service all over Europe, originally came from the East. He said the Templars brought

the Angelus back from the Crusades, and it is really an adaptation of a Moslem custom.   (pp. 44–5)

This is one of the most benign references to Islamic culture in non-black American writing. Cather traces the cultural roots of the Angelus, in Latour's rapid flitting across the eras, to the Moorish mosques. It is a quite audacious moment of historical reasoning since it predicates an American origin not in the chuches of Iberian Christianity, but further back: in the Arabic Islamic world. As important as the claim for Islamic origin is the way Latour reasons here: he considers culture as a process of exchange and transference across eras, cultures and countries. His is an analysis of cultural transmission. Intriguingly, in a letter to Dorothy Canfield Fisher about the First World War, Cather followed a similar line of historical reasoning. She used the analogy of the Crusades, which she claimed saw the conflict between the 'advanced' culture of Islam and the more backward civilisation of European Christianity.[15]

Cultural transmission is one of Cather's great subjects. The early works traced the transplanting of central Europeans to the Midwestern prairies; their fascination with cultural transmission and linguistic translation grew from Cather's analysis of what happened to the European migrants as they entered America. Her readings in archaeology and anthropology confirmed this model of culture as a process of exchange and transference. She was familiar, for instance, with early work in American anthropology and archaeology by scholars such as Adolph Bandelier and Charles Lummis.[16]

A genealogical strand runs down from these American anthropologists through the women who appropriated their work, and then into the work of later novelists (for example, Maxine Hong Kingston and Toni Morrison). Willa Cather and Zora Neale Hurston engaged with an academic discipline which was then in its early stages, and used anthropology as the animating dynamic of new fictional shapes. Their discoveries – of a folkloric America saturated with oral narratives and littered with shards of overlooked history – have provided a powerful precedent for later writers. All of these writers had or have a fascination with folk culture, storytelling and oral tradition; all have explored a dynamic of exchange and transference between cultures (Kingston: California and China), between eras (Morrison: the enduring relevance of the black past), and between nations (Cather: the transmission from Europe to America). Scholars have long recognised the importance of anthropology for male authors (noting, for instance, the influence of J. G. Frazer's study of myth, *The Golden Bough*, upon T. S. Eliot); but female 'anthropologised' fiction deserves attention as a literary discourse in its own right.

Alongside these themes of literary nationalism and cultural transmission, Cather's other great topic is what might be called 'ecopoetic': the relationship between (female) self and landscape.[17] Most readers will know Cather as the pioneer novelist; her early famous works, *O Pioneers!* and *My Ántonia*, are representations of the settlers who populated the Midwest at the end of the nineteenth century. Each novel positions a heroine at the centre of a narrative of settlement; each follows the territorial expansion of the United States into the 'empty' Great Plains, appearing to celebrate the heroic virtues of endeavour, steadfastness, and sheer brute determination. Cather is credited with grafting these stereotypical masculine pioneer virtues onto narratives of the female life. Hermione Lee reads Cather as a feminist revisionist who re-cast male narratives in female terms, 'intervening in a masculine language of epic pastoral'.[18] But Cather's exploration of the relationship between the land and the female subject is more complex than simple insertion of a heroine into male plots. Her early fiction, in particular, insistently maps the interdependence of humankind and landscape, adumbrating ways of thinking about nature and civilisation that go beyond a merely instrumental notion of pioneering. Early American women, as Annette Kolodny has shown, had fostered in their diaries and journals a rich heritage of 'green' writing which imagined the myriad encounters between womanly self and American landscape.[19] But Cather was perhaps the first woman to establish a fictional, and therefore public, language of womanly American landscape.

Cather's ecopoetic writing emerged with great force early in her career as a novelist. In *The Song of the Lark* Thea Kronborg, an opera singer, undertakes a restorative spiritual trip to the desert places of the Southwest. Cather's writing in this section, 'The Ancient People', entwines anthropological reference to the Pueblo civilisation, lyrical landscape description and an extended meditation on the creative consciousness:

In the afternoon, when she had the shade of two hundred feet of rock wall, the ruins on the other side of the gulf stood out in the blazing sunlight. Before her door ran the narrow, winding path that had been the street of the Ancient People. The yucca and niggerhead cactus grew everywhere. From her doorstep she looked out on the ochre-coloured slope that ran down several hundred feet to the stream, and this hot rock was sparsely grown with dwarf trees. Their colours were so pale that the shadows of the little trees on the rock stood out sharper than the trees themselves. When Thea first came, the chokecherry bushes were in blossom, and the scent of them was sickeningly sweet after a shower. At the very bottom of the cañon, along the stream, there was a thread of bright, flickering, golden-green – cottonwood seedlings. They made a living, chattering screen behind which she took her bath every morning.[20]

Rebecca West acclaimed Cather as 'The Classic Artist': 'The most sensuous of writers, Willa Cather builds her imagined world almost as solidly as our five senses build the universe around us.' And Ellen Moers, in one of the first critiques of Cather and landscape, read these canyons and gullies in symbolic terms, as an overtly feminine landscape of grooves and recesses and swellings, a 'female self-assertion in terms of landcape'.[21] Perspicacious as these comments are, Cather seems to me to produce effects beyond the 'sensory' or 'symbolic' in this writing. For she carefully weaves attentively observed detail into a seamless web of natural history, impressionism and a sensory, almost luxurious, observation. The shadows 'sharper than the trees themselves' demonstrate a beautiful precision; but in a passage whose ostensible purpose is to set the scene Cather's prose is in surplus, exceeding the requirements of a simple representation of landscape as impassive backdrop or picture to be consumed. In heightened passages of landscape writing, Cather adumbrated ways of thinking about nature, gender and creativity. The canyon acts upon Thea, fostering a renewal of the self:

Here she could lie for half a day undistracted, holding pleasant and incomplete conceptions in her mind – almost in her hands. They were scarcely clear enough to be called ideas. They had something to do with fragrance and colour and sound, but almost nothing to do with words. She was singing very little now, but a song would go through her head all morning, as a spring keeps welling up, and it was like a pleasant sensation indefinitely prolonged. It was much more like a sensation than like an idea, or an act of remembering.   (p. 373)

The passage downplays the overt, instrumental, active dimensions of Thea's consciousness, exploring instead her intuitive and semi-conscious imaginings as she is artistically renewed by the antediluvian landscape. Creativity is described via analogies with nature. There is nothing new in this, of course, but Cather is careful to find an apt and fit image for Thea's creativity. The 'welling' spring feels absolutely right; it is an image of natural abundance in a terrain of great aridity. Cather weaves contemporary accounts of consciousness into her essentially Romantic conception of a 'fit' or reciprocity between the creative self and the responsive landscape. Behind the passage lie William James's ideas about the processes of the mind, particularly the notion that thought is a 'stream of consciousness' rather than a more regular or linear phenomenon. As Daniel Joseph Singal has argued, William James was one of the two philosophical architects of American modernism (the other was John Dewey). 'The Jamesian stream' of modernism 'centres its interest on the individual consciousness, celebrates spontaneity, authenticity, and the probing of new realms of personal experience'.[22] An interweaving of modernist psychology with an American vision of the Romantic sublime, which is then framed by concentration on female and not male consciousness, makes up Cather's account of Thea's meditations.

Later in *The Song of the Lark* Thea Kronborg feels a kinship with the women who created the hallowed space of Panther Cañon, and who had spent 'so great a part of their lives going up and down it'. In a moment of imaginative transference, Thea thinks of herself as quite literally stepping into the shoes of these Indian women: 'She could feel the weight of an Indian baby hanging to her back as she climbed' (p. 376). Here, the ecological landscaping of Cather's writing takes on a further, layered significance. Having enmeshed the landscape and Thea's artistic creativity, Cather goes on to construct further linkages between terrain and history, and in particular to read the landscape in terms of its feminised historical significance. Panther Cañon thus becomes the site for an audacious extension of the methods of local color

realism. Like her mentor, Sarah Orne Jewett, Cather was fascinated by the specific geography of a narrow locale; and she
shared Jewett's interest in quasi-anthropological female folk arts.
What is new in Cather's anthropological local color writing is a
dramatic opening-up of the chronological scale (we are suddenly
back in an ancient America), even as local color's fascination with
place and community is maintained.

Cather's landscapes are markedly different from those imagined by earlier, usually male, creators of the written American
landscape. Annette Kolodny has described an archetypal relationship between an acquisitve male pioneer and a feminised landscape, a pairing which recurs in the writing of the Frontier.
'America' is figured as virgin, awaiting the ravishment of the
pioneer, or as mother, proffering a sensual abundance and an
almost regressive fantasy of fulfilment. (Cooper's Leatherstocking
tales exemplify the former, while the famous raft scene in
Huckleberry Finn contains echoes of the latter).[23] Landscape in
Cather's fiction, though, reverses this figurative pattern by acting
upon the self. Even in the pioneer novels we find alongside a celebration of the transitive actions of the settlers an exploration of the
symbiosis of female settler and landscape. In one of Cather's most
renowned sentences, the last line of *O Pioneers!*, the protagonist
achieves an ecological fusing with the earth itself: 'Fortunate country, that is one day to receive hearts like Alexandra's into its bosom,
to give them out again, in the yellow wheat, in the rustling corn,
in the shining eyes of youth!'[24] The recycling action of the earth,
taking in the dead body to provide further nourishment for future
generations, here provides the template for a near-mystical vision
of the interpenetration of humankind and nature. Such moments
of ecstatic intermingling or fusion occur throughout Cather; she
imagined transcendence as a dissolution of boundaries, especially
between self and natural environment. Demarcations fall away.
Another instance of this is the strange masculine household
created by Tom Outland and his companions in *The Professor's
House*: a cabin in the wilderness that seems to merge with the landscape surrounding it. Later in this book, Tom encounters a
dystopian image of a culture which is nothing *but* boundaries, the
Washington where he takes his archaeological finds. Outland
'used to walk for hours around the fence that shuts in the White
House grounds' (p. 233). At such moments Cather constructs
profoundly *spatialised* representations of America – vignettes and

vistas where geography itself expresses the paradisal or dystopian qualities of a place.

For Willa Cather, to read her culture was to read its many spaces. Cather's historical imagination was profoundly geographical. She understood America's past times in terms of the different spaces inhabited and constructed by civilisations such as the Pueblo Indians or the French colonists of Québec. The shaping of her narratives was also governed by dramatic geographical paradigms: contrasts between city and wilderness, tablelands and university campuses, the raw wilderness that greets her pioneers and the settled farmland they bequeath to their children. Cather re-drew and re-mapped her nation, creating odd conjunctions and parallels, new pathways across the disparate space of America. For Djuna Barnes and Gertrude Stein, two other geographical modernists, such re-mappings were also central, although in their work innovative cartography tended to focus on two specific sites: the city in Barnes's fiction; the home for Gertrude Stein.

Djuna Barnes: the Carnival of Urban Modernism

American modernism sited itself in the city. Male writers produced a series of works in the 1920s and 1930s which took the city as geographical setting and subject-matter: Hart Crane's *The Bridge*, John Dos Passos's *Manhattan Transfer*, and of course, F. Scott Fitzgerald's *The Great Gatsby* and T. S. Eliot's *The Waste Land*. All share the quintessential modernist belief that the city is the locale for new ways of thinking and feeling; and all use the city in a symbolic way, as icon of progress or more disturbingly as index of cultural disintegration. The American city novel, in the hands of a Dreiser or Dos Passos, also valued urban experience because a new, technological, machine aesthetic could be seen at its most developed in that environment. For Lewis Mumford, a great theorist of American urbanism, it was natural to argue that the city always embodied the *Zeitgeist*. His essay, 'The City' (1922) began: 'Around us, in the city, each epoch in America has been concentrated and crystallised.' In particular, the nation's industrial development was written into the fabric of the city: 'It is possible to telescope the story of America's colonial expansion and industrial exploitation by following the material growth and the cultural impoverishment of the American city during its transformations.'[25]

Acounts of urban modernism, even those written by women, tend to reflect the male domination of this cultural space. Blanche Gelfant, in *The American City Novel*, hardly mentions female writers. For Cecelia Tichi, in *Shifting Gears: Technology, Literature, Culture in Modernist America*, Willa Cather's creation of an engineer in *Alexander's Bridge* (1912) was a rare instance when women addressed the technological motifs of the age.[26] Women *were* writing about the city, but their chosen city space happened not to be mechanical, industrial or technological or, indeed, American. Paris was the modernist urban cynosure for American women such as Gertrude Stein, Anaïs Nin and Djuna Barnes (as well as a whole supporting cast of critics and *littérateuses*). Whereas the male city aesthetic often looked to the machine as analogue and inspiration, the female city space, in a work such as Djuna Barnes's *Nightwood*, is often said to be carnivalesque. Moreover, while male fictions by Dreiser or Dos Passos deal with a traditional politics of class, the politics of female urban modernism is focused on identity, especially the construction of sexual and national selves.

Nightwood (1936) is steadily moving towards the centre of the canon, supported by admirers of its lesbian erotic writing. Carolyn Allen has identified a 'Barnesian' tradition of female modernism, marked by 'lyrical prose, nonlinear form, and fascination with the psyche' (she adds Jeanette Winterson and Rebecca Brown to this tradition).[27] *Nightwood* is a book of changing identities, chance encounters; its setting is the polymorphous, decadent modernist European city, with its kaleidoscope of cultures and languages. The novel represents the city as shifting, carnivalesque, phantasmagoric space; it prefigures the extravagant, chimerical fictions of later women writers such as Angela Carter. Critics have celebrated Barnes for the multiplicity and heterogeneity of her fiction, a polyphony which reminds them of Bakhtin's 'carnival' or 'what Gilles Deleuze and Felix Guattari might call a "nomadic assemblage" ': 'The novel traverses, combines, and juxtaposes American puritanism and French pornography, French surrealism and American realism.' Barnes 'articulates the distance between "flaneur realism" and "lesbian realism," between the city of surrealist revolution and the state of lesbian exile: a queer space', continues Dianne Chisholm.[28]

Whether Djuna Barnes's literary politics are as progressive as

many of her supporters believe is a key question. It is worth looking at *Nightwood* in some detail to explore how female urban
modernism worked: the politics of female modernism, like the
politics of male modernism, could encompass a disturbing fusion
of formalist experiment and crude cultural stereotyping. While a
'carnivalesque' fictional discourse is wholeheartedly endorsed by
many critics, one notes that carnivals can also be grotesque,
frightening, dangerous and illiberal places. Critics often enlist
Bakhtin's idea of the carnival in the cause of their own progressive readings of an author, but it seems less clear how the anarchic
pleasure of carnival translates into progressive ideology, if at all.
For carnival in many countries serves as a release-valve for the
dominant culture, as a social convention rather than an oppositional force. Revolutionary societies (France, for instance)
commemorate their foundation with carnivals, but the revolution
itself certainly did not *begin* with a carnival.

Furthermore, the notion of a 'nomadic' text, while often a valuable insight (see my earlier discussion of Alice James), jars when it
is applied to Djuna Barnes. *Nightwood* has a central character who
is a nomad – the Jew Guido Volkbein – but the text is unsparing in
its satire of him due to the very fact that he is a nomadic
wanderer:

> The child's father had gone six months previously, a victim
> of fever. Guido Volkbein, a Jew of Italian descent, had been
> both a gourmet and a dandy, never appearing in public with-
> out the ribbon of some quite unknown distinction tinging his
> buttonhole with a faint thread. He had been small, rotund, and
> haughtily timid, his stomach protruding slightly in an upward
> jutting slope that brought into prominence the buttons of his
> waistcoat and trousers, marking the exact centre of his body
> with the obstetric line seen on fruits, – the inevitable arc
> produced by heavy rounds of burgundy, schlagsahne, and
> beer.[29]

The Jew symbolically embodies a shifting, rootless, de-histori-
cised identity which is the epitome of inauthenticity. Pretentious,
self-indulgent, absurd: Volkbein is a model of deracinated greed.
The problem with *Nightwood* is that these malicious caricatures,
which could possibly be ascribed to the weight of the general
culture on a writer (as with Fitzgerald's anti-Semitic parody of

Wolfshiem's accent in *The Great Gatsby*), are part of rampant theorising about Jews and Judaism. For example, Hedvig Volkbein has
a child at the start of the novel, 'in spite of a well-founded suspicion as to the advisability of perpetuating that race which has the
sanction of the Lord and the disapproval of the people' (p. 1). Her
husband, Guido Volkbein, is the outcast Jew, trying to root himself
in Christian society. When he expires on his wife's breast, we are
told: 'When a Jew dies on a Christian bosom he dies impaled.
Hedvig, in spite of her agony, wept upon an outcast' (p. 2).
Caricature is just one manifestation of a larger pattern of speculation and theory about race, culture and nation; the speculation
hinges on the figure of the Jew.

Barnes lampoons Guido as a tragicomic figure and something
of a buffoon because he attempts to imitate Christian ways. The
charge, then, is not of being Jewish, as such, but of pretending to
be that which one is not. The Jew is represented as an inauthentic
figure, an incompetent confidence man whose attempts at
disguise are doomed to failure because his racial essence is ineradicable (Guido, in a moment with unfortunate historical overtones,
imitates his wife's 'goose-step of a stride' which becomes 'dislo-
cated and comic'). The novel's comedy of identity is thus
profoundly bound up with its readings of Jewishness. Guido is a
fake: even the portraits of his family were discovered by happenstance 'in some forgotten and dusty corner' (p. 6). This detail is a
telling one. For the problem of the Jew is a problem of *origins*. The
Jew, writes Barnes, 'seems to be everywhere from nowhere' (p. 7).
The Jew is a profoundly paradoxical figure, a character who
confounds geographical categorisation: he is a figure we find
everywhere but he has no absolute origin. He is a supremely
deconstructive figure, a con man who drastically upsets place and
genealogy. He produces identity when he has none; he finds a
family – Christian – when he has none.

Nightwood presents the reader with a phantasmagoric, shifting
gallery of eccentric and bizarre characters; but a recurrent contrast
runs through this cast. On one hand, inauthentic characters, of
whom the paragon is the Jew. Other examples of these inauthentic and dangerously mutable figures include the Irish–American
doctor Matthew O'Connor, who is also a wanderer and something of a con man: he even steals from his own patients. On the
other, there are the lesbian lovers, Robin and Nora. The lesbian
lovers possess a solidity and a confirmed sense of their own

integrity; only the passion between Robin and Nora is portrayed as having sincerity and authenticity. Theirs is an *amour fou*, a wild and intense romance that might well end in death. Their passion is predicated on a model of possession. The world outside their cocooned intimacy is seen as dangerous, as Other; it is the enclosed world of their love which Nora, particularly, wants to hold tight in its integrity:

> Yet sometimes, going about the house, in passing each other, they would fall into an agonized embrace, looking into each other's face, their two heads in their four hands, so strained together that the space that divided them seemed to be thrusting them apart. Sometimes in these moments of insurmountable grief, Robin would make some movement, use a peculiar turn of phrase not habitual to her, innocent of the betrayal, by which Nora was informed that Robin had come from a world to which she would return. To keep her (in Robin there was this tragic longing to be kept, knowing herself astray) Nora knew now that there was no way but death. In death Robin would belong to her. Death went with them, together and alone; and with the torment and catastrophe, thoughts of resurrection, the second duel.   (p. 52)

The voice of the passage is the free indirect discourse common to many modernist texts and extensively deployed in *Nightwood*; it is a third-person narrative position which can also mime or represent the internal musing of a character. When Barnes writes, 'In death Robin would belong to her' she is ambivalently writing from an authorial position and from Nora's own position; there is a simultaneity of perspective. Free indirect discourse can enable the writer to explore a lucratively hazy tonal range where irony and sympathy mingle; the reader is both empathically on the side of the character and subtly distanced from her. While Barnes exploits these commingled tones elsewhere in the novel – we are led to see Guido Volkbein as both comic and tragic hero – the portrayal of lesbian love is resolutely unironic. Most commentators on *Nightwood* see the central romance between Nora and Robin as a complex, meditated representation of lesbian eroticism; and the unironic timbre of this passage seems to suggest that this, indeed, is where the novel discovers integrity and authenticity.

Barnes portrays lesbian desire as a form of narcissism. The two women, holding one another, are like one creature ('their two heads in their four hands'). Nora asks Dr O'Connor, ' "have you ever loved someone and it became yourself?" ' (p. 126). It is writing like this which has encouraged scholars to construct intriguing arguments about *Nightwood* and psychoanalytical readings of narcissisim and desire. But the enshrining of lesbianism, and specifically an erotics of narcissism, at the text's discursive centre, is not without its problematic aspects. For lesbian narcissism becomes the obverse of the Jew's endlessly displaced and 'unhomely' identity: while the Jew is continually displaced from imaginary homelands, the lesbian finds herself reflected in the eyes of her lover. The novel's reading of same-sex female desire is thus predicated on a cultural map which positions the Jew as its other pole. *Nightwood*, due to this contorted representational logic, adumbrates a form of lesbian anti-Semitism. Whereas the Jew is a figure without origin and a proper home (a figure whose desires will never be satisfied), the lesbian is for Barnes a figure who finds everything, who discovers absolute fulfilment, in the arms of her lover: 'Everything we can't bear in this world, some day we find in one person, and love it all at once' (p. 135). Such plenitude, however, is understood in *Nightwood* as part of a polarity; and at the other pole, embodying emotional vacuity and a dangerous rootlessness, is the Jew.

Gertrude Stein's Cubist Domesticity

Gertrude Stein's 'Tender Buttons' (1911) is another experimental revision of the spaces inhabited by American fiction. Whereas Cather had opened up, cartographically and historically, the areas where American women could write, Stein's early work adapts a familiar interior to create innovative perspectives on a known world. 'Tender Buttons' is a prose poem whose strange, riddling paragraphs suggest in glimpsed or snatched echoes of quotidian domesticity an interior space being dissolved and re-configured; Stein creates a modernist dream where the details of the nineteenth-century home are seen in unexpected configurations. As in a Cubist still-life, the ordinary world is present in terms of crude subject-matter (Stein's subtitles: 'Objects', Food', 'Rooms'); but a radical aesthetic fractures, re-shapes and renews known scenarios. Stein here creates a syntax to jolt us into strangeness:

SINGLE FISH

Single fish single fish single fish egg-plant single fish sight.

A sweet win and not less noisy than saddle and more ploughing and nearly well painted by little things so.

Please shade it a play. It is necessary and beside the large sort is puff.

Every way oakly, please prune it near. It is so found.

It is not the same.[30]

The overall shape of 'Tender Buttons', its narrative geometry, is based on a thematic core of homelife and on a series of oppositions between textural and spatial polarities: cleanliness–dirt; curvature–linearity; top–bottom. But the experience of reading closely is more bewildering than these simple categories would suggest. Stein entitles sections of 'Tender Buttons' with captions, evoking the titles accompanying a painting. But this stasis, the stasis of a still-life or a name, chafes against the restless movement engendered by Stein's syntax. She was fond of repetitive phrases embedded in barely punctuated sentences, thereby creating a mimetic impression of speeded-up or blurred movement.

Stein's sentences are both familiar and strange; in their allusions they suggest a homely familiarity, even as Stein uncouples language from referentiality to create unhomely estrangement. The reader catches echoes of and references to the languages of kitchen, nursery and parlour. Verbal shards and rhythmic echoes from these intensively feminised realms can be found throughout 'Tender Buttons'. Many of her sentences echo the generalising shape of domestic proverbs, but these are not quite proverbs. They present a slanted and surreal domestic wisdom. Thus: 'A little called anything shows shudders.' Or: 'A little lace makes boils. This is not true' (p. 173). 'Tender Buttons' is also full of sentences with the syntax and interrogative diction of questions; but there is not a single question mark in the entire text. Words such as 'what' or 'why' inaugurate sentences that seem to curve towards questions, but never quite become questions (they hang instead in a grammatical space of Stein's making). Is this (not) a question(?):

Why should that which is uneven, that which is resumed, that which is tolerable why should all this resemble a smell, a thing

is there, it whistles, it is not narrower, why is there no obliga-
tion to stay away and yet courage, courage is everywhere and
the best remains to stay.   (pp. 178–9)

Such sentences have a teasing and radical indeterminacy; Stein
creates a trembling and nervy grammar which hovers on the edge
of the explicit but ultimately refuses to commit itself to an outright
question. To bring such a syntax into the home (specifically, into
the kitchen) is to present epistemological uncertainty in a context
where easy platitudes are normally the order of the day (hence,
Stein's invocation and then transformation of household
proverbs).

'Tender Buttons' occupies a feminised terrain of home and
hearth. Male characters emerge only at one or two points, and
then in a surreal mode which seems to transform male characteristics into strange jokiness. 'Suppose a man a realistic expression
of resolute reliability suggests pleasing itself white all white and
no head does that mean soap' (p. 175) – where masculine 'reliability' is equated with the utility of a bar of soap. The deliberately
coded femininity of 'Tender Buttons' is also confirmed by its use
of the language of children. In its repetitiveness, absurdity and
jokiness, 'Tender Buttons' reminds the reader of nursery rhymes.
Stein's prose, with its simple diction and sometimes unintelligible
syntax, mimes out a baby language. As Wayne Koestenbaum
remarks, 'Stein's paradigm of the writer was the baby: the author
as infant.'[31] By becoming a child in her writing, Stein could invoke
one of the central Victorian paradigms of womanhood: woman as
child, as infant. In fact, a form of empowered infantilism has energised several of America's most avant-garde female writers. Emily
Dickinson, Alice James, Gertrude Stein: all three writers become,
at points in their writing, big babies who exploit the association
between women and the nursery to create a radically experimental literary discourse that is playfully and liberatingly nonsensical.

I began this chapter by speculating that the covert or overt
homosexuality of these three women writers might have something to do with their creation of strangely alternative fictional
worlds. Attempts to decode literature in terms of its creator's
sexuality are notoriously prone to either an overly mechanistic
causality or a vague imprecision. Whether or not the alterity of a
text such as 'Tender Buttons' was 'produced' by Stein's lesbianism
will remain a vexed question. What we can say is that Stein,

Cather and Barnes shared a readiness to re-shape established narrative patterns. In their work a radical re-configuration takes place: of general narrative trajectory (Cather's shifting locales), of the syntax of individual sentences (Stein) and of generic codes (Barnes's yoking together of realism and surrealism). Looked at this way, lesbian modernism defined itself primarily in terms of *form*: a shared desire to re-shape narrative, which in turn led to a new poetics of space or a radical fictional geography. And one can almost hear Gertrude Stein calling this aesthetic into being at the start of her incantatory prose-poem from 1923, 'Geography':

As geography return to geography, return geography. Geography. Comes next. Geography. Comes. Comes geography.

As geography returns to geography comes next geography. Comes. Comes geography.

Geography as nice. Comes next geography. Geography as nice comes next geography comes geography.

Geographically, geographical. Geographically to place, geographically in case in case of it.[32]

4

The Interwar Social Problem Novel

Zora Neale Hurston, Nella Larsen, Jessie Fauset, Agnes Smedley

In 1932 fifty-two writers, including Sherwood Anderson and Edmund Wilson, publicly backed the Communist Presidential ticket. This was the 'The Red Decade', a period when writers became enmeshed in politics, usually of the liberal and leftist variety. In general, the radical creative works of the era were marked by a code of social realism and social protest, often coupled to representations of 'proletarian' life and a fascination with vernacular speech (the climactic work in this protest tradition was, of course, John Steinbeck's *The Grapes of Wrath* in 1939). However, I want in this chapter to suggest a more capacious and fluid reading of the political fictions of the late 1920s and 1930s. Two female literary histories of this time are now familiar to us: the upsurge of polemical, committed writing (Meridel Le Sueur, Agnes Smedley and Tillie Olsen); and the emergence of black female modernism in the work of Zora Neale Hurston, Jessie Fauset and Nella Larsen. This chapter suggests that these two bodies of work might be thought of in conjunction. The white leftists and the black modernists shared a commitment to a form of social problem novel. They identified a nexus of social or political problems, and then created around those issues (often identified explicitly *as* issues) new fictional shapes, or gave voice to the problem in an innovative, experimental register. Thus, Agnes Smedley's *Daughter of Earth* (1929) moves across an almost-programmatic range of topics (women and the workplace, female education, radical internationalism) but it also creates a distinctive discourse: an angry, rough-hewn yet poetic and highly personalised narrative voice. Meanwhile, Nella Larsen's two novels, *Quicksand* and

Passing (1928 and 1929) lock other 'problems' (the sexual desire of black women; the 'passing' of African–Americans as whites) into haunting, fabular tales of identity.

The 'social problem' novel is primarily associated with so-called English industrial fiction of the 1840s and 1850s. Charles Dickens, Elizabeth Gaskell, Benjamin Disraeli and Charlotte Brontë staged debates about the social and economic conse-quences of industrialism, and addressed other pressing problems encountered in 'the way we live now' (the fate of the 'fallen woman'; class conflict; the role of religious dissent). Besides their overt topicality and positioning of the novelist as chronicler of contemporary society, these works were notable for creating a distinctive fictional discourse: a form of bourgeois realism, heav-ily dependent on melodrama, where separate characters embody or articulate differing sociopolitical viewpoints, and where a final resolution attempts to reconcile clashes between ideologies, classes or between men and women. Relying on what Catherine Gallagher calls the 'providential plot', a novelist such as Elizabeth Gaskell attempted to discover a formalistic response to the politi-cal, social and religious debates of her age. Gallagher's arguments are specific to British culture in the mid-nineteenth century, but they do resonate when we consider American women's writing in the interwar period: these writers moved towards an *engagé* fiction where narrative structure (the shape of a story) embodies an attempt to grapple with, and thereby 're-form' (in Gallagher's phrase), social problems.[1]

Not all political subjects were as obvious as the totemic crises of the 1920s and 1930s (Crash, Dust Bowl, Depression): another form of social problem fiction deals with cultural issues, with questions about identity and ethnicity. For African–American writers the identification and articulation of their specific cultural identity became a central project. Zora Neale Hurston, Nella Larsen and Jessie Fauset created a fiction whose discourse is closer to cultural anthropology than to the political pamphlet; the tracking of local rituals and customs forms a fictionalised investigation of ethnic identity. Whereas the work of an Agnes Smedley or Meridel Le Sueur addressed socioeconomic problems (and is underwritten by a Marxist sense that capitalism itself degrades human rela-tions), Hurston and Larsen placed cultural and existential dilem-mas at the centre of their novels. Smedley's barely veiled autobiographical account of her early life in *Daughter of Earth* presents a series of economic crises (how can I subsist?); but for the heroines of Larsen's work the dilemma is one of identity, both personally and collectively: who am I and to what culture do I belong? For the African–American novelists, identity and recognition become central. The light-skinned heroine of *Passing* moves in white society, fearful that her blackness will finally be exposed; meanwhile Hurston wrote extensively about the folkloric practices of the black community, constructing maps of African–American culture.

This modern form of the social problem novel evolved into a great variety of aesthetic models; and even within individual novels there is a multiplicity of discourses and generic registers. For example, Hurston's sensitivity to the oral folklore of the African–American community led to an accommodating fiction; her work is fissured and aerated by a freewheeling digresssiveness into the pathways of oral culture and popular domestic arts. Discursive consistency tends to be sacrificed in favour of a patchwork, piecemeal writing, with the forgotten voices of black culture now admitted into increasingly porous fictions. A similar point can be made about Nella Larsen's work: composed in what seems at first to be an evenly toned social realism, *Passing* and *Quicksand* mutate generically. As their explorations of identity deepen, these novels shift towards a hallucinatory and almost anti-realistic mode; Larsen's fictions about identity crisis prefigured the African–American existentialist novel which is often thought of as coming-into-being with Ralph Ellison's *Invisible Man* (1952).

Zora Neale Hurston: Voicing African–American Culture

In the early years of this century commentators increasingly recognised American English as a distinctive language in its own right rather than a bastard offspring of the British mother tongue. In 1919 H. L. Mencken published his first edition of *The American Language*; and in 1925 *American Speech*, an academic journal of linguistics and folklore, was founded.[2] Not surprisingly, many writers were equally fascinated by the newness of their tongue, and began to stress the inspirational and unique qualities of American English; the cosmopolitan lexicon fostered by mass immigration added to this process of forging a language. For women writers the process of forging their own womanly language intersected with the broader national project of fostering American English. The woman writer of the early twentieth century was therefore in a unique position of inaugural creativity: her American, female English was doubly innovative, since it marked out a terrain new both for her gender and for her nation. Meanwhile, ethnic or minority writers brought into being their own community's voices (another language with little written grounding until this point). A sense of inauguration is everywhere in women's literature of the early twentieth century; but these various newnesses could create conflict, division and instability within a text. It is one thing to be granted a language stamped with freshness, but another thing altogether to be granted two or even three new idioms. For one of the central writers of this period, Zora Neale Hurston, the double- or triple-voicedness of her writing creates ceaseless tension; cross-hatched languages jostle and wrestle with one another, as she writes out of and towards overlapping communities (black America, female America, the white establishment where she was educated).

Born in Alabama and educated at Barnard College in New York, Hurston (1891–60) was schooled in a thoroughly interdisciplinary manner across a number of academic subjects; she was always to straddle disparate cultures. Trained as an anthropologist by a pioneer in that field, Franz Boas, she wrote fictions informed by social science and folklore. In fact, Boas wrote a Preface to her *Mules and Men* (1935), applauding its collation of African–American folklore in classic anthropological terms: 'It is the great merit of Miss Hurston's work that she entered into the homely life of the Southern Negro as one of them and was fully accepted as such by the companions of her childhood.' Boas's praise for Hurston as a fieldworker now seems more problematic than his professorial commendation allows. The plain implication is that because Hurston was black, she would inevitably have advantages over the white folklorist: 'she has been able to penetrate through that affected demeanor by which the Negro excludes the White observer effectively from participating in his true inner life'.[3] But Hurston's work reveals a more complex and ambivalent relationship between the writer and her fieldwork. On one hand she sometimes pursues an almost impassive observation of the folkloric object (the writer as dispassionate recorder, as camera-eye). On the other hand, this putatively 'objective' anthropology is enmeshed in works which demonstrate the creative writer's desire to animate this material, to turn it towards fiction.

A typical movement in Hurston's critical essays is to move from observation towards theory; she used anthropological fieldwork to construct paradigms of what an African–American language might look like. In 'Characteristics of Negro Expression' (1934) Hurston adumbrated a reading of black oral culture informed by anthropology, African–Americanism, and by a modernistic concern to 'make it new'. She emphasised the activity and mobility of African–American speech: 'His very words are action words. His interpretation of the English language is in terms of pictures. One act described in terms of another. Hence the rich metaphor and simile.'[4] Hurston's essay is an exercise in sociolinguistics and a celebration of her people's verbal dexterity; but it also appropriates earlier (white) polemics about American creativity. Note the tang of Emerson in the following claim, with its sense of endless cultural renewal: 'Negro folklore is not a thing of the past. It is still in the making.' In this quest for originality the black speaker emerges as a paradigmatic modernist because he converts extant culture to fresh usage: 'So if we look at it squarely, the Negro is a very original being. While he lives and moves in the midst of a white civilization, everything that he touches is re-interpreted for his own use.' And Hurston then goes further, to the exchange of ideas between culture; she comes close to notions of exchange and hybridity which anticipate postcolonial theory: 'Thus has arisen a new art in the civilized world, and thus has our so-called civilization come. The exchange and re-exchange of ideas between groups.'[5]

Hurston's narratology, her construction and shaping of stories, was influenced by her discoveries in African–American popular culture. At one point in *Jonah's Gourd Vine* (1934) she introduces the idea of the 'break', and places black American music directly in an African genealogy:

> Furious music of the little drum whose body was still in Africa, but whose soul sung around a fire in Alabama. Flourish. Break.
> Ole cow died in Tennessee
> Send her jawbone back to me
> Jawbone walk, Jawbone talk

Jawbone eat wid uh knofe and fork.
Ain't Ah right?

CHORUS: Yeah!
Ain't I right? Yeah!

Hollow-hand clapping for the bass notes. Heel and toe stomping for the little one. Ibo tune corrupted with Nango. Congo gods talking in Alabama.[6]

The 'break' is an overt shift or break in tone, rhythm, voice; it is now familiar to us from its adoption and development within African–American musics. Hurston's deployment of the 'break' as a formalistic device endorsed a vernacular aesthetic; but it also 'broke' with a familiar interpretative matrix (a matrix created by the white mainstream). The break signals a break with notions of the novel as organically composed and as steadily evolving. Hurston's narratives are marked by fissures, shifts, sudden switches of tone or tempo. In place of cohesion or organic integration, the novel now follows patterns closer to the improvisatory techniques of folklore, oral performance and live music – an exhilarating dis-integration.

Hurston's folkloric methods are not always easily understood, especially for readers outside the 'village', in Toni Morrison's phrase, of the African–American community. She presented the reader with unmediated passages of black patois, and on first reading makes few concessions to those unfamiliar with the rhythms and idiolects she charts with such meticulousness. In *Jonah's Gourd Vine* she does not adopt the familiar technique, often found in fictions rooted in a specific idiolect, of placing explanatory footnotes within the text. Instead, a glossary at the end of the text sheds retrospective light on unfamiliar words and phrases. Hurston's explanatory addendum is certainly a help; but it is markedly distant from the main body of the text, and embodies Hurston's anthropological approach (the author as fieldworker and etymologist). In its formal structure and narratological shape, *Jonah's Gourd Vine* embodies two rather paradoxical relationships between writer and folkloric subject. First, a writing from within the culture: the African–American vernacular is presented on the page in unframed immediacy. Second, the framing of folklore by etymology and glossary, the intrepretative apparatus of anthropology:

BITTER BONE, the all-power black-cat bone. Some hoodoo doctors select it by boiling the cat alive with appropriate ceremonies. (See 'Hoodoo in America', *Journal of American Folk-Lore*, vol. 44, no. 174, p. 387) and passing the bones thru the mouth until one arrives at the bitter bone.   (p. 171)

At such points Hurston writes from within the discourse of the academy, framing her commentary with a studiously objective diction, and adding the full apparatus of footnotes. *Jonah's Gourd Vine* reads, then, as both 'inside' and 'outside' text, a dualistic fiction with two imagined communities of readers: the African–American community for whom explication is not necessary; and the white readership with a need for mediating analysis.

Hurston's fiction represents society as a carnival of voices. Her fictions are polyphonic in the most elemental sense: they free the multiple voices of black America. In particular, argues Houston Baker, a character such as Janie in *Their Eyes Were Watching God* can be seen as the inheritor of a 'blues' tradition which gives voice to black pain: Janie 'can, indeed, be interpreted as a singer who . . . recapitulates the blues experience of all black women treated as "mules of the world".'[7] Yet we are often aware in her work not of the immediacy and unselfconsciousness of the vernacular, but of the academic orthodoxies and scholarly distancing implied by 'anthropology'. To state this sounds like a writing-off of her achievement: a suggestion that it is tainted by pseudo-scholarship. But we might read the academic mimicry of *Jonah's Gourd Vine* as part of its meaning. Hurston adopts and adapts the discourse of the white anthropologist, enfolding his 'objective' language into her rendering of black speech. The novel, like much of Hurston's work, folklorically embodies the African–American vernacular, and at the same time appropriates the white, mediating apparatus brought by scholars to such raw 'data'.

Hurston wrote her anthropological essays in the discourse of academic orthodoxy; a black tyro, she took on the language of a white – and overwhelmingly male – community. There is a destabilising effect in this, since Hurston seems to talk of blackness using an authority imputed by white language: does the speaker, in using another's language, inflect or even ironise that discourse? And if there is irony here, what is it doing to the authority of the writer herself?

Their Eyes Were Watching God (1937) is written, so it seems, from within the black community. Very rarely is there mention of white folk; they are seen in glimpses or flashes, for instance on a bridge during the flood at the end of the novel: 'White people had preempted that point of elevation and there was no more room.'[8] Hurston dramatises racism in poignant vignettes which reveal the inequities of Southern society in glancing but lacerating detail. Tellingly, these details are themselves often grounded in the vernacular speech of the black and white characters. After the flood the rescuers have difficulty distinguishing black from white bodies. A guard says, 'don't lemme ketch none uh y'all dumpin' white folks, and don't be wastin' no boxes on colored' (p. 253). The dialect makes the spitefulness of the discrimination especially graphic, reducing the black community to the shorn adjectival bluntness of 'colored'.

Throughout *Their Eyes* Hurston's narrative voice has a rough-hewn, incantatory, earthily poetic quality. Extensive use of anaphora (repetition of the same grammatical pattern at the start of each sentence) suggests a culture rooted in the syntax of the Old Testament. Hurston's prose is studded by imagistic riffs, vigorous idioms combining the domestic and the surreal: 'Daylight was creeping around the cracks of the world when Janie heard a feeble rap on the door' (p. 189). (An image where we expect to hear 'cracks of the door', but where there is a sudden and strange magnification of effect into 'cracks of the world').

At such moments Hurston seems to write, in a vernacular poetry, from out of her community. But as I have suggested, this is just one of a number of rhetorical strategies in the novel. In fact, a fixed and authoritative narrative centre remains elusive in *Their Eyes Were Watching God*; a volatility (of tone, of point-of-view) results. Take the trial at the end of the novel. Janie is arraigned for the accidental killing of her husband. The courtroom scene (black public; white officials) is engineered to suggest that Janie will become the victim of an unsympathetic, racist system. But Janie is the happy recipient of the white jury's clemency, while the black public is depicted as brutally indifferent to the context of the killing: 'They were all against her, she could see. So many were there against her that a light slap from each one of them would have beat her to death' (p. 275). The cross-hatching and conflict of voices confounds our expectations: we expect Janie to be made a victim of the system, but the court saves her from the brutal instincts of the crowd, who are less concerned for her as a black than aggravated by the fact that a woman killed her husband. The prose shifts into free indirect discourse, creating a hybrid space between Janie and the author; free indirect discourse sanctions her inner thoughts with an authority derived from the third person but abjures the moral certitudes of omniscient narration. Such shifts of tone and point of view are, perhaps, partly a result of the divided audience addressed by the novel. As I noted earlier, Hurston had been trained within the white academic discipline of anthropology (a discipline which, some would argue, particularly incarnates the inherent patronage offered by whites to the 'Other'); she spoke from within a space partly defined by whites, and she had the authority derived from being a witness to her own race (an authority granted by white culture). But at the same time, Hurston could speak of and to her own people in a more immediate manner. Alice Walker recounts that when she read *Mules and Men* to her relatives, 'a kind of paradise was regained . . . Zora's book gave them back all the stories they had forgotten or of which they had grown ashamed'.[9] Thus, the imagined community of listeners or readers is a bifurcated one: formed partly by the white liberal establishment (the readership one predicates for Nancy Cunard's 1934 *Negro* anthology, to which Hurston contributed); and partly by the African–American community. When Janie suddenly expresses her fear of her fellows in the courtroom, and when the white court unexpectedly acquits, the reader senses, in a quite vertiginous way, Hurston moving backwards and forwards between these two audiences.

The sense of a variegated and heterogeneous text is further confirmed by the manuscript of *Their Eyes Were Watching God*. Emily Dalgarno has shown that the novel's structure was shaped by re-writings, and that this revisionary work on the manuscript was done to accommodate anthropological material. The 'folk material' was 'added after the manuscript was completed, in some subsequent draft'. Furthermore, this re-casting of folk material which had been printed earlier in specialist black journals, suggests that Hurston 'wished to appeal to another, more diverse reading public'. Structurally and tonally, then, *Their Eyes Were Watching God* is deeply moulded by Hurston's anthropological interests and by a desire to 'voice' that material to differing, if not conflicting, audiences.[10]

The famous account of *Their Eyes Were Watching God* in Henry

Louis Gates's seminal work, *The Signifying Monkey*, described Hurston as the author of a 'speakerly text' who mobilised and gave voice to a folkloric tradition. Hurston's legacy 'is a lyrical and disembodied yet individual voice, from which emerges a singular longing and utterance, a transcendent, ultimately racial self'. 'Hurston realized a resonant and authentic narrative voice that echoes and aspires to the status of the impersonality, anonymity and authority of the black vernacular tradition.'[11] Gates forcefully advocates Hurston as the avatar of a vernacular tradition, here equated with the 'authentic' and 'authority'. But *Their Eyes Were Watching God* seems to me too discontinuous and polyphonic to sustain the idea of a unitary and transcendent folkloric self at its centre. Hurston's revisions to the manuscript and her engagement with (and re-voicing) of white anthropology suggest instead a writing that is *intertextual*, a palimpsest of different discourses rather than a *singular* writing. Franz Boas, in his 'Preface' to *Mules and Men*, had assumed that Hurston, because of her colour, could become closer to her subject-matter than the white ethnographer. In effect, this is analogous to Gates's argument: that Hurston collapsed the distance between the black ethnographer–writer and her subject to produce a text where the vernacular tradition emerges in all its authenticity. But the various discourses infiltrated into Hurston's texts (folklore, glossary, anthropological survey) suggest instead that Hurston's encounter with black culture was 'framed' by mediating languages. The reader of *Their Eyes Were Watching God* or *Jonah's Gourd Vine* continually senses their 'madeness' as texts. Changes of register, discourse and tone indicate a complex negotiation between Hurston and the black vernacular. Her work is marked by dialectics: spoken and written; black folklore and white anthropology; the male academy and the female writer. The vernacular is in dialogue with other representations of African–American culture.[12]

Sometimes, Hurston replaces the buzz of folklore with a meditated silence. The violence shown by one African–American towards another – specifically, the violence of black men towards women – arises at numerous points in *Their Eyes*, and elicits just this muted voice. Of Tea Cake's aggression, Hurston writes, 'He just slapped her around a bit. . . . Everybody talked about it next day in the fields' (p. 218). So little is made of such comments that we might also pass over them; but there they are, and one is inclined to take this as ironic commentary on Janie's 'love' for Tea

Cake and on the community's acquiescence. Hurston allows such moments of violence to rest in the novel, unflagged by narrative commentary, as if they were an utterly expected feature of such communities. One senses a kind of ironic silence at such points, a restrained pointedness as the writer allows the action to speak for itself.

But elsewhere, Hurston does in fact adopt a much more explicit, polemic and forthright narrative voice. Take, for instance, the episode where Mrs Turner, a 'yellow' negro of mixed blood, harangues Janie about the hierarchy of colour within the community and complains that: 'We oughta lighten up de race' (p. 209). This is an intriguing set-piece that plays out, in a homely and comic setting, a debate about miscegenation and the racism amongst the black community itself. The point seems to be made obliquely but powerfully: Mrs Turner is a ridiculous figure, her views contemptible. But then Hurston makes the point absolutely explicit in a vitriolic, polemic passage where the narrating voice attacks this character in an explicitly satirical thrust: 'she was cruel to those more negroid than herself in direct ratio to their negroness' (p. 215). What happens here is that Hurston switches from a recognisably modernistic presentation (in Wayne Booth's well-tried formulation, she 'shows' rather than 'tells' the reader that Mrs Turner is absurd), into an older style, a preachy and didactic voice rooted in nineteenth-century writing. *Their Eyes Were Watching God* becomes at such junctures a volatile mixture of oblique modernism and forthright polemicism; the narrative voice shifts, uneasily at times, between showing and telling. Moreover, the tonal conflict is most evident here, in a discussion of the internalised racism of the black community, as if to reveal the problems of finding a fit fictional voice to address this dilemma.

At many points *Their Eyes Were Watching God* furthered the deconstruction of married life implicit in American women's fiction since *The Awakening*. Hurston's book is as transgressive as Chopin's; it depicts violent emotion (hatred, indifference) as part of the tapestry of domestic life, and it traces a desire that takes Janie into the arms of a much younger man, Tea Cake. Hurston helped to ground boredom, dislike and even hatred in the sentimental palette of women's writing, while eschewing the sometimes sugary celebration of family and children seen in the work of earlier black women such as Pauline Hopkins. Janie is a heroine with a remarkable lack of familial attachment: 'Digging around inside of herself like that she found that she had no interest in that seldom-seen mother at all. She hated her grandmother . . .' (p. 137). These are amazing sentences, locking as they do an acidic and biting hatred into the received emotional range of women's fiction; they complicate still further the politics of the novel, since the grandmother epitomises a radicalism and a nascent feminism which Janie seems distant from. The novel captures, too, a kind of self-justifying and self-blinding rhetoric which lures Janie into accepting Tea Cake's violence and gambling: 'It was part of him, so it was all right' (p. 188). And this is also a novel of widowhood, and the freedoms it brings. At her first husband's funeral, Janie 'sent her face to Joe's funeral, and herself went rollicking with the springtime across the world' (p. 137). Hurston significantly amplified the range of fiction in two ways: first, like Chopin, she created a new temporal space by following women's lives after the apparent finale, the moment of marriage when romance is fulfilled, into the mundanities of wedded life and even into a post-marital state (widowhood, adultery). Second, within this expanded narrative space, Hurston enriched fiction by drawing in hitherto unwritten structures of feeling.

Yet in the eyes of her contemporaries Hurston seemed to lack decisive political engagement. Two of the leading African–American intellectuals of the day, Richard Wright and Alain Locke, argued that her fiction lacked polemical force and radicalism. Writing for the leftist magazine, *New Masses*, Wright praised *Their Eyes Were Watching God* for its representation of the 'Negro folk-mind', but was disconcerted by the novel's lack of bitterness or anger:

> Miss Hurston can write; but her prose is cloaked in that facile sensuality that has dogged Negro expression since the days of Phillis Wheatley. Her dialogue manages to catch the psychological movements of the Negro folk-mind in their pure simplicity, but that's as far as it goes.
>
> Miss Hurston *voluntarily* continues in her novel the tradition which was *forced* upon the Negro in the theater, that is, the minstrel technique that makes the 'white folks' laugh. Her characters eat and laugh and cry and work and kill; they swing like a pendulum eternally in that safe and narrow orbit in which America likes to see the Negro live: between laughter and tears.[13]

Just as Willa Cather was lambasted in the 1930s for failing to react to the 'significant tendencies' of the age, so Hurston was also attacked for lack of political responsiveness and naivety. Both women faced a leftist critical coterie which decoded fiction in terms of a narrow set of signals. The 'masses', urban experience, social protest, documentary style: these were the motifs and stylistic registers of radicalism. Alain Locke, Hurston's former teacher and editor of the seminal anthology, *The New Negro* (1925), felt that, in contrast, Hurston had become too preoccupied with folklore. When, he asked in 1938, was she going to 'come to grips with motive fiction and social document fiction'? Hurston responded angrily, writing a vicious and probably libellous portrait of Locke which the editors of the magazine *Opportunity* refused to publish. Robert Hemenway, Hurston's biographer, summarises this spat as a dispute about the status of folklore:

> It shows the frustration of an author whose novelistic talents were deprecated because her fiction dealt with intraracial folkloric situations rather than with interracial confrontations – it was not 'social document fiction.' The difference in these perspectives is not between protest and accommodation, as Wright implied, but between different conceptions of the folk community.[14]

Hemenway summarises a critical manoeuvre already noted in this book: the attack on the female writer because she lacks overt political engagement. As I noted in my discussion of Willa Cather, these arguments often lose their force in time; we gradually realise the radicalism immanent within texts formerly castigated for ideological blandness or evasiveness. Similarly, a writer such as Sarah Orne Jewett, with her apparently genteel representations of the female community, is now read as a prescient analyst of womanly cultures. These authors obliquely, indirectly but nonetheless powerfully established radical aesthetics with political implications. Analogously, Hurston's folkloric modernism increasingly seems more imaginatively resourceful than straightforward 'social document fiction': in her responsiveness to the vernacular, and her willingness to write *across* stylistic registers, Hurston had moved beyond such a prescriptive model of what radical writing should be. And in her mobilisation of various discourses, including the discourse of white anthropology, she showed that the 'interracial' conflict identified by Hemenway was also a struggle between different idiolects and discourses. Political writing, as Hurston demonstrated, would now be marked by a writer's fleet-footed trespasses into the linguistic territory of another community.

Nella Larsen: the Female Jeremiad

Nella Larsen produced two books at the end of the 1920s, *Quicksand* (1928) and *Passing* (1929); she is one of the great re-discoveries of feminist scholarship after falling into obscurity for much of her lifetime. She has now become one of the central novelists within the African–American canon. *Quicksand* was recognised at the time as a major achievement; she was praised by W. Du Bois and awarded a Harmon Foundation medal for achievement amongst African–Americans. Then she infamously retreated from the literary stage after *Passing*; one of her short stories led to an accusation of plagiarism, and the ensuing scandal drove her into silence. It is hard, though, to imagine where she could have gone in her writing after these two novels. Each seems to represent a full-stop, an abrupt closure, as if Larsen had thought through an argument and presented her own unanswerable reply.

What, then, are the hallmarks of this tantalisingly short but highly influential *oeuvre*? Three motifs recur across these two books: racial identity (Larsen deals extensively with the hybrid figure of the mulatto); sexuality – Larsen brought black female sexuality explicitly into fiction for the first time; and a trenchant scepticism about the patterns of fulfilment offered to black women. The prevailing tone in both works is sardonic, caustic and mordantly disillusioned. Helga Crane, the protagonist of *Quicksand*, is a 'despised mulatto'.[15] Her father was 'a gambler who deserted my mother, a white immigrant. It is even uncertain that they were married' (p. 23). Helga begins an itinerant journey through black society. She encounters political activists and African–American polemicists; she travels to Harlem; and she even goes to Denmark to live with her mother's white relatives. In all contexts Helga is dissatisfied and restless; nowhere is home. For many critics *Quicksand* becomes a tragedy of hybridity centred on the mulatto's split existence and her conflicted origin.[16]

But the cause of Helga's crisis has as much to do with sexuality as with racial identity; the novel crosses and intertwines Helga's racial origin and her sexuality in a complex knit of causality. Miscegenation brings sexuality and race together in socially unacceptable ways. As one character, Mrs Hayes-Rone, says: 'For among black people, as among white people, it is tacitly understood that these things are not mentioned – and therefore they do not exist' (p. 39). Whether Helga's miscegenated origin causes her downfall is less clear. Larsen's novels evince a repeated impatience with a strictly arithmetical definition of racial origin, even as they acknowledge the fantasies often woven around the figure of the mulatto woman. It is this particular alchemy of miscegenation and gender which is so constricting for Helga. She suffers from an 'indefinite discontent' (p. 81), but this is unlikely to be resolved when others figure her in stereotypical terms. A white suitor notes: 'You have the warm impulsive nature of the women of Africa, but, my lovely, you have, I fear, the soul of a prostitute' (p. 87). Another character imagines 'the vagrant primitive groping toward something shocking and frightening' within Helga (p. 95).

Placed within a web of stereotypes, a clichéd fomulation of what the words 'black' and 'female' mean when put together, what is the African–American woman to do? Helga does have her own utterly legitimate desires, but she is torn by the disjunction between the self's wants and society's constructions of desire. Sometimes this disjunction is comic, as when Helga misconstrues Dr Anderson's drunken kiss as a serious commitment; but more generally, Larsen's heroine finds a grim, if not tragic, lack of fit between self and society. The problematic balancing of self and community is finally reconciled when Helga marries the Reverend Green, minister at the Church where she finally merges her troubled individuality into the collective fervour of evangelism: to marry a minister ties together the secular and profane, and seems to offer Helga the solace of a ready-made community. But the marriage leads only towards relentless procreation. *Quicksand* concludes grimly; the heroine hates her husband, dreams of other places and faces the grinding repetition of endless childbirths.

Quicksand's metallic asperity remains with the reader for a long time. Larsen was on the fringes of the Harlem Renaissance, that creative flowering in New York's black quarter, but there is little of the movement's utopian hopefulness in her work. Instead, Larsen takes the shape of classic Victorian narrative – the heroine's journey through a series of different environments and different spaces – but removes the benign conclusion usually embedded within these narratives. Whereas a novel such as *Jane Eyre* traces a symbolic map of the options available to the female subject in Victorian England (the heroine ineluctably finds fulfilment in marriage), *Quicksand*'s pilgrim faces a series of disappointments: each option is cancelled out with grim finality; each apparent new beginning is frustrated and disappointed. Throughout the journey Larsen's tone remains icily sarcastic – Helga, for instance, tries to ignore her husband's 'self-satisfaction which poured from him like gas from a leaking pipe' (p. 122).

Where did Larsen go after *Quicksand*? *Passing*, written immediately afterwards, pushed Larsen towards a more existential investigation into the nature of racial identity itself. The novel has the structure of a politico-philosophical thriller: a black woman, herself light-skinned, meets an old friend who has passed for white and married into that community. Strongly drawn towards Clare Kendry, Irene Redfield is also disconcerted by the racial conundrum she presents (the novel also intimates that the fascination might be homoerotic). Racial identity, it seems, is polymorphously subtle even as society codes such variegation in the crudest of ways; Clare's husband is utterly unaware of his wife's racial origin, and launches into a frenzy of racial insults in the company of other black women who have 'passed'. The novel prises open this dilemma: is one's identity structured absolutely by race, or is it possible to be 'oneself' in such a way that racial identity is kept at a distance?

> She was caught between the two allegiances, different, yet the same. Herself. Her race. Race! The thing that bound and suffocated her. Whatever steps she took, or if she took none at all, something would be crushed. A person or the race. Clare, herself, or the race. Or, it might be, all three. Nothing, she imagined, was ever more completely sardonic.   (p. 225)

The dilemma goes beyond the hybridity represented in *Quicksand*; it is a self-division which turns into agonising conflict within the self, between individualised determination and racialised identity. At the end of the novel, Clare is finally 'outed' as a black, bringing forward her husband's inevitable and immediate insults. Irene, meanwhile, is aware that her husband is having an affair with Clare, so this outing raises the spectre of Clare leaving the white community to flee towards her husband and the black community. This intractable dilemma – race, identity, sexuality, all bound together in a Gordian knot – shapes the end of *Passing*. Then Clare abruptly faints, and falls out of the window (there is a sugges-tion of suicide). Irene is left to live on, but the novel stops here, in shocked and intractable stasis. Both Larsen novels end abruptly and melodramatically. The problems her fiction raised permitted no adequate resolution beyond a stylised melodrama; they are simply too complex for 'realistic' resolutions. Larsen takes her reader into a fictional cul-de-sac; the only way out inevitably smacks of a degree of artificiality.

Larsen's work does not fit easily into recent readings of African–American literature because it offers little purchase for the rich theories of oral, vernacular traditions developed by critics such as Henry Louis Gates and Houston Baker. Baker's essay on the Harlem Renaissance traces black modernism to Booker T. Washington by noting 'a *mastery* of stories and their telling that leads to Afro-American advancement'.[17] Larsen, a heterodox writer even within an already oppositional culture, eschews the vernacular African–American tradition. Hers is an almost deliber-ately bland narrative voice, uninflected by the idiolect of a minor-ity culture (contrast Hurston's foregrounded, folkloric idiom). Even Larsen's dialogue is marked by careful excision of anything resembling dialect; her characters consistently talk in 'straight' middle-class American English. But the absence of a marked or conspicuous black folkloric culture, and the careful settings within the bleached comfort zones of bourgeois society (tea salon, drawing-room), articulate a devastating point: that the African–American might create an apparently comfortable, safe domestic space, but the issue of race will, nonetheless, inevitably erupt. The opening chapter of *Passing* makes this point with great economy: afternoon tea, the spotting of a stranger who seems strangely familiar, and suddenly the whole psychodrama of blacks who 'pass' as whites begins to unfurl.

W. Du Bois had argued in his 1903 essay 'The Talented Tenth' that an educated African–American elite would act as a vanguard for the race: 'The problem of education, then, among Negroes must first of all deal with the Talented Tenth; it is the problem of developing the Best of this race that they may guide the Mass away from the contamination and death of the worst, in their own and other races.'[18] Larsen's fiction is an antiphonal voice within the 'talented tenth', as she creates fictions out of the sexual and racial tensions splintering the progressive, African–American bourgeois harmony yearned for by Du Bois. Both of her novels create tragedy not only out of sexual and racial displacement (the 'mulatto' tragedy often remarked on by critics), but also out of a highly specific anxiety about *class*. Both Larsen heroines are, as some might now say, aspirational; in both novels the desire for social advancement, material comfort and the company of the 'Best of this race' motivates the heroine. But in each book the allure and political progressivism of this social uplift are shown to be chimerical. The particular horror of *Quicksand* rests in part on Helga's marriage being to a Church minister. She marries her better, achieving respectability in an archetypal manner; but the relentlessly ironic cast of Larsen's imagination turns this fulfilment to ashes. The heroine might marry into the talented tenth, she suggests, but do not imagine that this will solve the problems of the black female subject.[19]

Writing at the end of the nineteenth century, Pauline Hopkins and Frances E. W. Harper looked to the sudden violence of Southern society as a cruelty about to be succeeded. Harper and Hopkins represented deeply miscegenated societies, as did Larsen. But both *Iola Leroy* and *Contending Forces* end on what might seem unduly upbeat notes; both implicitly contrast the past (where miscegenation is a fact of life, but remains a crime liable to sudden and arbitrary punishment) with a present or future America more accepting of racial intermixing. In the hands of Larsen the miscegenation genealogy turns, first, inwards. Whereas Hopkins and Harper painted on a broad societal canvas, Larsen focuses on isolated heroines. And the tenor of Larsen's work is, second, profoundly pessimistic: contrast the recognitions of racial difference and admixture which are sentimentally represented at the end of *Contending Forces* with the abrupt death that brings *Passing* to a sudden climax.

Quicksand and *Passing* form a jeremiad; Larsen's work is one of several such woeful laments or complaints produced by American women over the past century. From 'The Yellow Wallpaper' and *The Awakening* to *Quicksand*, and then on to Ann Petry's *The Street*, Plath's *The Bell Jar* and Susan Sontag's *Death Kit*: all these texts are harshly, fiercely contemptuous of bourgeois conventionality. All attack 'the way things are'; all are lamentations, often couched in a sarcastic tone. Gilman, Chopin, Larsen, Petry, Plath and Sontag: a genealogy runs down through these writers, a genealogy linked by cantankerous dissatisfaction with American realities. This female jeremiad represents an inflection of a nineteenth-century masculine tradition, the ironic and often pessimistic register of Melville's 'Bartleby', Poe's fiction and the Twain of 'The Mysterious Stranger'. Their 'power of blackness' forged an oppositional voice, an anti-progressive writing that was cynical and sometimes nihilistic. This mordant literature formed a dissident tradition in a country noted for its benignly progressive optimism. Like their male predecessors, the female Jeremiahs focus their works on a singular protagonist. Their 'isolatoes', to use Melville's term, are alienated from their community. Indeed, community hardly exists in any meaningful or sustaining way in 'The Yellow Wallpaper', *The Bell Jar* or *Quicksand*. Such works have therefore formed a dissident continuity within women's writing. For, whereas writers from Jewett to Anne Tyler have explored the affective bonds of community, the jeremiad writers have been bitterly anti-communitarian. Whereas a solidly communitarian figure such as Eudora Welty (discussed in the next chapter) discovers in familial and social life inexhaustible fascination (and consolation, too), the anti-communitarian attacks the emotional deformations wrought by society. She then writes a jaggedly expressionistic *cri-de-coeur* to savage the pieties of marriage, home, family.

Jessie Fauset: Internationalism and Hybridity

Jessie Fauset was the first black woman to attend Cornell University. From 1919 to 1926 she worked with the prominent black sociologist and political theorist W. Du Bois as literary editor of his magazine *The Crisis*. She played a major part in the Harlem Renaissance. Fauset's energies were distributed polymathically across a range of activities; she was poet, story-writer, essayist and author of four novels. Her career maps out one trajectory for the woman writer – a pattern seen also in the lives of the Southerners Caroline Gordon and Katherine Anne Porter: the female literary entrepreneur or woman of letters. This entrepreneuralism reflects at least in part the expanded opportunities for women in various areas of literary production: in journalism and, for women like Hurston or Fauset, in academic writing and political commentary. Financial exigency was sometimes responsible for this mobility across a range of types of writing. But the very disparateness or heterogeneity of these writing lives also suggests a pattern of female creativity marked by multiplicity and proliferation; female creativity expands into a range of guises, rather than settling into a monolithic identity.[20]

Jessie Fauset's political journalism was markedly international-ist, developing post-colonial attacks on the imperial pretensions of Europe (notably in an attack on Belgium in her report on the 1921 Pan-African Congress). She voiced hopes that 'We should like to see Liberia while developing creeds and customs which will enable her to cope with foreign methods, stick to her own system of dress and ethics and traditions.'[21] A cosmopolitan critic, Fauset reviewed black Francophone literature; and, like Hurston, she developed an interest in African–American folklore. In 'Dark Algiers the White' (published in *The Crisis* in 1925) Fauset brought these two interests, in folklore and international varieties of black culture, together to create an intriguingly prescient account of ethnographic tourism. A black American in Algiers, Fauset is here entranced by the exoticism of Africa; but she ironically notes the cultural distance between herself and a people of similar skin colour who are far from her own Western identity. Fauset is nimbly alert to gaps of understanding between black America and Islamic Africa, as when she notes her 'tongue-tied Western fash-ion' in the face of the inexplicable. Fauset also anticipates the developing interest of black Americans in Islam, entering a mosque to hear the supplicant 'breathe a prayer to the God who watches alike over East and West' (p. 397). These essays are an early manifestation of a politics of the black diaspora, as they care-fully monitor congruences and differences across African cultures.

The politicised internationalism of Fauset's journalism contrasts with her fiction, which is embedded within the black American experience and, like Larsen's work, moves towards an existential enquiry into racial identity. Like Larsen, she was fasci-nated by 'passing', a topic which provided the dynamic for her most famous novel, *Plum Bun* (1929). But even in a relatively anodyne work such as *The Chinaberry Tree* (1931), largely an exer-cise in hometown nostalgia, there are moments, often slightly surreal or hallucinatory, where the cosy celebration of familial bonding is replaced by a more disorienting sense of the fluidity of identity. At such points the narrative becomes dream-like, as fundamental questions of identity swim up: is my colour really what it seems to be? where do I belong? Thus Laurentine's meeting with the Halloway sisters: 'It was as though she were suddenly seeing herself in a mirror, a self curiously bleached and lightened' (p. 11). Fictions of miscegnation and passing often become catalogues or repertoires of looks and glances since it is in the moment of the look, the instant of recognition, that one discovers innate 'blackness' or 'whiteness' (or, as here, a more disconcertingly hybridised or composite racial being). Thus, when Melissa first catches sight of Laurentine, she sees 'a beautiful deep gold face, suspended apparently without body in the upper half of the screen-door' (p. 16). It is a strange moment, and Fauset points up these moments by giving her heroine the Kafkaesque symbolic name Laurentine Strange (she is daughter of a white gentleman and his coloured mistress). Laurentine's dilemma is the central crisis of many protagonists in Hurston, Larsen and Fauset: to be fated to be a 'beautiful ... face', with one's bodily substance hardly recognised or conceived (the sexuality of the mulatto heroine is the great topic of *Passing, Plum Bun* and *Their Eyes Were Watching God*).[22]

Plum Bun, Fauset's most important novel, creates a more densely textured representation of American society than that found in Nella Larsen's work. Whereas Larsen moves her 'passing' fiction towards psychological fable, Fauset is interested in the social and economic forces that create a context where to pose as a white becomes attractive or even a compulsion. The heroine, Angela Murray, moves to New York, and finds that her light skin enables her to move in white circles; she maintains this fiction within her relationship with Roger Fielding, her all-too-Anglo-Saxon blond lover. The ironies of this situation proliferate. Roger is prone to cast aspersions on the 'coons' while sitting with his arm around Angela. But Fauset is careful to present this fantastically risky gambit as the product of a racial politics inflected by money. Intriguingly, *Plum Bun* was published in 1929, the year of the great Crash, and as if in tune with that event it presents a society where buying and acquisition have become imperatives. Angela had 'learned the possibilities for joy and freeedom which seemed to her inherent in mere whiteness'.[23] This freedom first expresses itself in the shopping trips undertaken by Angela and her similarly light-skinned mother (the darker father and sister are excluded), as they travel into white shops. 'And she began to wonder which was the more important, a patent insistence on the fact of colour or an acceptance of the good things of life which could come to you in America if either you were not coloured or the fact of your racial connections was not made known' (p. 46). The 'good things' are what make passing worthwhile, rather than some abstracted sense of racial hierarchy; one passes to achieve consumerised fulfilment; materialism frames racial identity. The settings of *Plum Bun* encompass an array of environments within this consumerist world: shops, theatres, restaurants.

Fauset is sometimes criticised for fashioning a relatively conservative aesthetic; her social realism has seemed leaden to critics who admire the modernist experimentation of the Harlem Renaissance. Her middle-class fictions have seemed to deny the folkloric and proletarian ideals of the movement.[24] Yet we might see Fauset's social realism as more attuned to the new realities of the American city than such commentary accounts for. *Plum Bun*, with its attention to consumerism (one section of the novel is simply entitled 'Market'), traces a selfhood where consumption and performance have become the constituents of identity. The *social* drive of Fauset's realism enables her to follow this process with particular closeness: we are 'made', in this world, by how others see us; and if they think that we are white, then this is indeed the case. As Angela's mother, Mattie, says: ' "I can't label myself" ' (p. 31).

Fauset's work points to a paradoxical truth, often overlooked in the adverse comments that her work is too middle-class. As in Larsen's fiction, *Plum Bun* incorporates representations of the 'talented tenth', the African–American élite. Angela's sister, in particular, maps out a prototypical life for the urban black middle-class, with her attendances at public lectures, her circle of clever and stylish bourgeois friends. The desire to achieve freedom through passing is, then, itself a sign that a certain amount of freedom has already been gained by these young black subjects. They have left their traditional communities; have often migrated to the anonymous cities; have left family behind (Angela's parents are dead). An amount of autonomy has already been gained by Angela, living in her New York apartment. The power of Fauset's work is its concerted focus on the question, 'What Next?'

But this is also its weakness. As *Plum Bun* evolves, Fauset's plotting becomes more and more dominated by intricate patterns of sentimental revelation and racial discovery. Angela discovers that her 'white' friend, Anthony, also has black ancestry; he is of Brazilian *mestizo* descent. As in Frances Harper's *Iola Leroy*, the 'solution' to one's mulatto identity lies in the serendipitous discovery of a partner who is also half-caste. The latter stages of *Plum Bun* – a sentimental melodrama of racial revelation and romantic fulfilment – echo the late-Victorian narratology of Harper's novel. But Fauset steps back from the explicit didacticism that accompanied this plotting in *Iola Leroy*. *Plum Bun* engineers resolutions via romance and sentimental fulfilment; it lacks a politicised framework that would elevate these happy encounters into a more lasting, and transformational, social vision. In this sense the novel's sub-title, 'A Novel Without a Moral', seems to give the game away. Fauset's title seems to gesture at a modernist refusal to point up explicit 'messages' in fiction; it abjures the explicit didacticism implicit in works like *Iola Leroy*. At the same time, to refute a 'moral' *tout court* might be to sidestep any form of larger ideological commitment. The final question provoked by Fauset's work is what the politics of the black woman's novel would look like, in an age when the preachiness of the Victorian novel was becoming unfashionable. And how to fashion an engaged, political fiction beyond the parameters of didactic 'protest' fiction has been the quest of black women from Hurston to Toni Morrison.

Agnes Smedley's Heterogeneous Socialist Realism

Agnes Smedley's *Daughter of Earth* is a major example of the leftist polemical fiction of the late 1920s and 1930s. Smedley fits alongside Tillie Olsen and Meridel Le Sueur as one of the 'Daughters of the Great Depression', in Laura Hapke's phrase: a radical, an activist, and the creator of explicitly engaged fictions.[25] *Daughter of Earth* was published in 1929, the year of the Crash – the timing adds further symbolic weight to her status as an iconic figure within this group of radical women writers. During her lifetime she was, like Jessie Fauset, a prominent internationalist. She was active in the campaigns for independence in India (incurring the wrath of the British Government); in campaigns for the promotion of birth control; and in the Chinese revolutionary movements of the 1930s and 1940s. Indeed, a long stretch of her life was spent in China, and she produced a handful of books about the Communist struggle there, of which *Battle Hymn of China* (1943) is the best known.

Much of her writing was political reportage, and it is Smedley's deployment of a documentary, reportorial style *within* fiction that creates the complexity of *Daughter of Earth*. This is an angry, rough-hewn book. Smedley steadily accumulates episodes that testify to America's economic and social inequities; the novel follows its heroine, Marie Rogers (a thinly disguised proxy for Smedley herself), from a Missouri farm through Colorado mining camps and on to education and failed marriage in California and New York. The testimonial power of the novel, as it accumulates incidents of material and emotional deprivation, is straightforwardly grounded in personal experience; the force of the novel is directly rooted in an almost-confessional dynamism. One explanation for this highly personalised form of reportage, whereby events in Smedley's own life became building blocks for a semi-fictionalised narrative, would be to see this technique as a typical 1930s discourse used in both male and female writing. The American Communist Party published a 1935 survey, *Proletarian Literature in the US*, which listed Smedley and John Dos Passos, amongst others, as practitioners of 'reportage'; the editors, who included Granville Hicks, argued that this form had come to the United States from the Soviet Union, and had now become a distinctively American style.[26] But such a nakedly personalised form of reportage does present problems: is the story meant to be representative? What is the relationship between the story of a singular woman and the larger historical forces to which Smedley, as a Marxist, attuned herself? *Daughter of Earth* never really 'solves' the question of how an individualised story can be harmonised with Marxist historiography. Instead, it advances on a stylistic level a heterogeneous and divided variety of voices rather than a homogeneous discourse. Smedley employed the familiar trope of the quilt to explain this patchwork technique:

> I recall a crazy-quilt my mother once had. She made it from the remnants of gay and beautiful cotton materials. She also made a quilt of solid blue. I would stand gazing at the blue quilt for a

little time, but the crazy-quilt held me for hours. It was an adventure.

I shall gather up these fragments of my life and make a crazy-quilt of them. Or a mosaic of interesting pattern – unity in diversity. This will be an adventure.[27]

As an encapsulation of the familiar analogy between women's writing and quilting, this could hardly be bettered. The result was an amalgamated or melded fiction: partly autobiographical and partly documentary, intermittently polemical, and a travel journal too. The documentary realism of *Daughter of Earth* is placed in paradoxical conjunction with a more personal and autobiograph-ical mode; the kaleidoscopic fiction that results often seems on the edge of formal dis-integration. The deployment of the patchwork quilt image is also vital because it suggests that the overall aesthetic of *Daughter of Earth* should be seen as moulded by a desire to cleave to *female* traditions. Smedley was working within a stylistic register shaped primarily by men, the reportage of John Reed and the Soviet realists. But she then embedded that language within a narrative whose shaping principle derives from female folk arts.

This is particularly important because Smedley's actual repre-sentation of Marie's mother is of a brutal and temperamental woman. Smedley frames the mother's suffering by noting that she herself was unhappy; but she unsparingly creates a radically de-mythologised mother:

> I remember my mother's thimble taps, and I remember a tough little switch that cut like a knife into the flesh. Why she whipped me so often I do not know. I doubt if she knew. But she said that I built fires and that I lied. What business that was of hers I was unable to see. As the years of her unhappy married life increased, as more children arrived, she whipped me more and more.   (p. 11)

The stark, unadorned, plain style is one of gritty vernacular realism; the subject, that of the embittered relationship between mother and daughter, is an overtly womanly usage of this tech-nique. The larger, poignant paradox of *Daughter of Earth* is that the image of the mother's quilt is the governing metaphor for the novel's form, but that the *actual* mother in the story engenders nothing but conflict. On a formal level the novel posits a womanly, creative genealogy which is a kind of idealised continuity, and is in stark contrast to the realities of the relationship between mother and daughter: the novel adumbrates contradictory models of female lineage – formalistically suggesting kinship even as it creates vignettes of mistrust and violence.

The tensions inherent in Smedley's text are typical of the interwar social problem novel. Although we can, I think, recognise a shared interest in a nexus of questions (of female identity, of the female self 'in' politics), the works of Hurston, Fauset, Larsen and Smedley are varied, and even within the texts there is a notable heterogeneity of tone and register, a paradoxically consistent *inconsistency* across a range of fiction. Critics who search for organic form and artistic unity will not find it in the shifting voices of Hurston's fiction; those who desire a steadily evolving career will not find this model in Larsen's abruptly ruptured writing life. Agnes Smedley's reportage is, likewise, fissiparous; her political fiction wraps a highly personalised record into documentary realism. All of these writers fashioned a range of styles, and the result was a form of politicised novel marked by fissures, ruptures, discontinuity, and by a willingness to 'break', in Hurston's term, across fictional languages.

5

'There are So Many Horrible Examples of Regional Writers, and the South is Loaded'

Eudora Welty, Caroline Gordon, Katherine Anne Porter, Flannery O'Connor[1]

The critics have not agreed with Flannery O'Connor's dismissive joke. For them, rather than 'horrible examples' the South has supplied some of the best of modern American writing. While O'Connor warns of the facile diminution of the area's literature to 'regional writers', critics including Louis Rubin, Richard Gray and C. Hugh Holman discover a richly serious body of conscious artists. They emphasise the centrality of history to the Southern writer; the tragedy at the imaginative heart of this literature; the interest in religion; the attentiveness to the material specificities of life and the suspicion of abstract philosophising. Southern literature seems to possess sufficient coherence as a corpus of work to sustain generalisations such as the comment that these writers 'have tended to depict man's nature as being religious, to view the individual very much as a creature of time and history, to assume the individual's commitment to society and his determining role within it'.[2] One is also struck by the assumption in these critical accounts that Southern writing encompasses both men and women. Caroline Gordon, Katherine Anne Porter, Eudora Welty, Flannery O'Connor: all have featured regularly in critical accounts since the 1950s. Indeed, there is a strong case for suggesting that literary criticism of the South was feminist *avant la lèttre*.[3]

114

These accounts responded to the obvious: Southern writing *was*, to a great degree, home to many fine women writers. Why this should be so is less clear. The folkloric and storytelling traditions of the South are sometimes cited as cultural features which helped to nurture female talent. A more telling cause might be that the historicity of Southern culture, repeatedly highlighted by commentators, chimed with women writers. In the South, accusations that women writers were obsessed with the past were, quite simply, irrelevant. Southern women deployed historical subject-matter because Southern writers, if not the South as a whole, had a historicist ideology. When Caroline Gordon or Eudora Welty wrote about the Civil War in *None Shall Look Back* or 'A Burning', readers might have found fault with their specific representations of the Confederate past; but that these women had a right to such topics was never in doubt. The historical axis of Southern life has provided a kind of covenant between the woman writer and this subject-matter, offering a sustaining legitimacy to her work: to write historically is inevitable and right.

But what of the other part of the equation, the womanliness of Southern women's fiction? To put it crudely: is the Southern woman writer a different kind of writer to her Northern or Western sister? One feature does seem to be important in Southern writing: a wide-ranging and mobile polymathy. The Southern woman writer creates fiction, essays, polemics; her role as letter-writer or journalist is also important. This multi-vocalism and discursive range is not unique to the South, of course (think of Edith Wharton, equally fluent in short and long fiction, and a prolific travel writer too); but it does provide a unifying model for this region. This polymathy created a highly *professional* competence. For instance, Caroline Gordon and Katherine Anne Porter were effectively women-of-letters who worked as journalists, essayists and editors. While O'Connor and Welty were more solidly embedded in fiction alone, their stories cannot be understood without reference to their essays and, as I argue in my discussion of Welty, photography.

This professional, polymathic prolific creativity is important because it cuts against the grain of two familiar stereotypes of the woman writer: the amateur 'lady' novelist, writing partly for pleasure; and the silenced, forgotten and marginalised author. The latter image is often invoked by scholars when they recover forgotten or overlooked texts; critics are driven by a sense that silence, often enforced by neglect, has been the lot of the woman writer. The example of Tillie Olsen stands as testimony to this marginalisation; Olsen's volume, *Silences* (1978), centres on the unjustly silenced female writer. As Carla Kaplan notes, 'Since the appearance of Olsen's *Silences*, feminist criticism has continued to build on this recuperative paradigm of recovering lost, silenced, misunderstood, or devalued women's voices' (and she then cites Virginia Woolf's poignant phrase, the 'infinitely obscure lives' of women).[4]

Southern writers have been misunderstood (but which writer, male or female, is not misunderstood?); they are certainly not 'silent'. Looking at the work of Welty, O'Connor, Porter and Gordon, the reader registers a fantastic *vocalism*. Vocalism in two senses: first, the writer's often prolific ability to give voice to herself across a range of written discourses. The range of accomplishment might, perhaps, have something to do with the gender of these writers. It might be that the shifts between forms of creativity reflect a more mobile, unsettled and flexible model of literary production than that suggested by the received image of the settled (male) writer, ensconced in his study with no distractions. In place of an essentially linear and accretive career (the writer, we often say, develops or deepens or follows a particular thread of creative reasoning throughout an evolving career), these women had careers of multiplicity and division, marked by interruptions and forays into other fields. The Southern writer's vocalism might also emerge from the region's vernacular traditions, its rootedness in oral storytelling and gossip. Certainly, it could be argued that for a writer such as Eudora Welty the culture of the South is primarily spoken, and that the writer's task is to find written forms for stories transferred in conversation.

Eudora Welty: the Buzz of Chat

Eudora Welty's stories seem on first reading to be slight chamber-pieces with little overt significance beyond an acute, beautifully microcosmic observation of Southern manners. Compared with other Southern storytellers, especially a Flannery O'Connor or Caroline Gordon, Welty (1909–) appears unconcerned by the big themes (History, the Idea of the South, Race); but this slightness is itself telling. These are stories in which the authorial point-of-view is marginal or hidden. Often, the story or novel is a tissue or tapestry of voices, and the position of the author remains masked behind a range of other voices which she has given space to. Long stretches of Welty's fiction appear to be dramatic dialogue, with an extremely light or fragile surrounding structure of narrative commentary or explication. A novel such as *Losing Battles* (1970) often seems to lose narrative momentum as the writer's attention is wholly caught up with the task of reproducing the rhythms and diction of Southern speech. There is experimentalism here. Welty's method links her to a mid-twentieth-century, late-modernist fictional school which foregrounded dialogue to create a more 'objective' recording of reality. Technically, her work is akin to that of Christopher Isherwood (who celebrated a fictional 'camera' where the subjective intervention of the writer's consciousness would be restrained, and the putatively 'objective' recording functions of prose would be emphasised) or Henry Green (with his massive blocks of unframed dialogue). Her technique anticipates the hyperbolically profuse dialogues of an avant-garde writer such as William Gaddis. This method can produce an opaque fiction, since the guiding voice of an explicit narrating consciousness is denied us. Lorna Scott Fox has complained that the extraordinary transcription of Southern voices in *Losing Battles* becomes 'an atonal recording of a family chinwag that at times is as oppressive as the real thing'.[5] The minute attentiveness to the cadences of dialect becomes a buzz of chat, usually at the expense of dynamic narrative drive. Sometimes it is difficult to understand what is simply *going on* in a Welty story.

Welty began her career in journalism and photography. Working as a publicity agent for the New Deal's WPA (Works Progress Administration) in the mid-1930s, she travelled through the small towns of rural Mississippi to create a photographic record of this deprived area. Welty's pictures, with their casual, snapshot-like quality, have an engaging simplicity; but, as with the stories, one senses a latent narrative beneath the casual anecdotage. What interests me about these photographs is their intimacy, their recording of daily life in the South and oblique revelation of racial division and massive poverty (Welty sardonically noted that 'The Depression, in fact, was not a noticeable phenomenon in the poorest state in the union').[6] Many photographs are simply entitled 'Home'; the places range from shacks to houseboats to gutted ante-bellum mansions, but all testify to the South's fascination with place and rootedness. Many pictures were also of impoverished African–Americans. Welty claimed that her photography constituted a humanist art of empathy and sympathy; she rejected explicitly ideological readings of documentary photography:

> And had I no shame as a white person for what message might lie in my pictures of black persons? No, I was too busy imagining myself into their lives to be open to any generalities. I wished no more to indict anybody, to prove or disprove anything by my pictures, than I would have wished to do harm to the people in them, or have expected any harm from them to come to me.[7]

Welty's early career as a photographer provides certain avenues into her fiction. As a photographer, Welty followed a peripatetic documentary aesthetic where the casual serendipity of image-making becomes a guarantee of the picture's authenticity. Instead of the stage-managed framing of events, this 'finding' of images, as the photographer travels about, is designed to guarantee deeper truths: an aesthetic of the unwilled and happenstance.

Interviewed about her photography some forty years after the Depression, Welty stated she did not believe that 'a work of art in itself has any cause to be political unless it would have been otherwise. . . . I think a work of art must be moral.'[8] Welty, then, presents the taking of photos as an innocent exercise in sympathy, motivated by desire to 'part a curtain, that invisible shadow that falls between people'.[9] But this desire for understanding, expressed by Welty in warmly emotive terms, often leads in the stories to a contrary realisation: that the human heart contains grimmer sentiments than humanists would hope for. Many of Welty's stories are highly satirical or sour analyses of the fallibilities of humankind, even though the brilliant evocations of speech and manner suggest the local colorist's fondness for community. Welty used the machinery of local color, but her communities are likely to be marked by division, rancour, dissent, envy and even madness. Her introduction to *The Collected Stories* posited a commitment to the richness of community life; her stories 'come from living here – they were *part* of living here, of my long familiarity with the thoughts and feelings of those around me, in their many shadings and variations and contradictions'.[10] Yet humanity in Welty is rarely as sympathetic as these words suggest, and many readers note instead the sourness or even misanthropy underpinning stories such as 'Lily Daw and the Three Ladies' or 'A Piece of News'. Comic vignettes of Southern life, these early tales (from the 1941 *Curtain of Green* volume) are unsparing in their delineation of petty snobbery, latent violence and mutual suspicion.

The tension here is between a form of regionalised sentimentalism and an acute consciousness of grotesque behaviour. The cleverness of Welty's method, though, lies in her refusal to *point up* this polarity. As one reads on in a Welty collection, these divisions or contradictions become gradually clear, but she rarely flags up her intentions. Welty's methodology creates a renunciatory aesthetic, a compositional technique which shuns the overt and explicit in favour of the indirect, implicit or covert. Her 'autobiography' explores this technique, and suggests in its very title her tactful, allusive art. *One Writer's Beginnings* (1984) suggests that Welty is relatively insignificant (*one* writer, as if a host of competing authors stand just off-stage; *beginnings* – we will be told the start of the story and nothing more). Welty here tracks back and forth across her childhood, picking up motifs rather than formally articulating a linear narrative. She then allows the significance of these themes to emerge organically from her reminiscences: the dense weave of memory contains embedded morals, and the biographical act is a meditation allowing latent significances to emerge as if of their own accord. She emphasised the subjective order of experience above objective chronologies:

> The events in our lives happen in a sequence in time, but in their significance to ourselves they find their own order, a timetable not necessarily – perhaps not possibly – chronological. The time as we know it subjectively is often the chronology that stories and novels follow: it is the continuous thread of revelation.[11]

Welty's claim follows a certain strand of modernist narratology which privileged the primacy of subjective experience; formal and objective chronologies fall away (compare Virginia Woolf's statement that time is not like a string of gig lamps). In her stories this meant that Welty relinquished one of the short fiction writer's favoured techniques: the structuring of a tale through a clear tempo until it reaches climax or dénouement. Axiomatic in

American story-writing since Edgar Allen Poe argued that the tale should always aim for the 'singleness of effect', this tectonic principle achieved popular hegemony in the 'O. Henry' style of telling. But climaxes are rare in Welty's fiction. Sometimes, for instance in 'A Still Moment', the critical moment is embedded within the story. Elsewhere, the narrative ordering of events is too complex and knotted for the reader to point with any confidence to where the climax of the story might be. And a story like 'The Burning' is structured around overlapping moments of crisis and closure. The 'difficulty' of such tales lies in the enfolding of a complex narrative pattern with continual suggestions that what is told is, in spite of this formalistic resistance, of outstanding significance. Our lives contain, as she says above, the 'continuous thread of revelation'; what, though, is being revealed?

Narrative complexity and the demands of 'revelation' are demonstrated in Welty's fierce enigma, 'Keela, the Outcast Indian Maiden'. Two white men approach an old black cripple, Little Lee Roy, as he sits on his porch. One tells the other a weird tale: he came across the cripple in a travelling show, where he was disguised as the Keela of the title. The story then tantalisingly tacks towards the subjects of disguise, racial camouflage (a black man pretending to be a native American) and transvestism. Max taunts his friend, Steve, who witnessed this spectacle: " 'Bet I could tell a man from a woman and an Indian from a nigger though" ' (p. 44). Welty concludes with one of the whites thumping the other, as they bicker about the true status of the black (Indian?) man (woman?). The cripple then laughs repeatedly, as he listens to the tale of his own degradation: does this signal complicity or mockery or hysterical resignation? The tonal register of the story seems to be a mixture of all three. Here, Welty constructs a fable about our inabilities to recognise racial essence. The two whites need to be certain of racial and gendered certainties; but the character of 'Keela' (at once nothing and everything: a man and a woman, a native American and an African–American, the confidence (wo)man of the South) mocks this quest for certitudes: the cripple's laughter signifies a conscious delight in the epistemological puzzle he poses his white scrutineers.

Race is never far from Welty's fiction. 'Powerhouse', also from *A Curtain of Green*, is a mirror-image of Zora Neale Hurston's writing from the same mid-century period. Whereas Hurston, a black

writer, adopted and mimed the white language of academic scholarship, the white Welty 'blacks up' in the jazzy, hip slang of the
story. The voice is that of the Harlem Renaissance's modernist
black patois, but there is also a transgressive surplus of explicitly
racial language. Powerhouse is a black pianist:

> Powerhouse is playing!
> He's here on tour from the city – 'Powerhouse and His
> Keyboard' – 'Powerhouse and His Tasmanians' – think of the
> things he calls himself! There's no one in the world like him.
> You can't tell what he is. 'Negro man'? – he looks more Asiatic,
> monkey, Jewish, Babylonian, Peruvian, fanatic, devil. He has
> pale gray eyes, heavy lids, maybe horny like a lizard's, but big
> glowing eyes when they're open. He has African feet of the
> greatest size, stomping, both together, on each side of the
> pedals.   (p. 131)

The passage disorients: it blatantly foregrounds clichéd images
of blackness (the 'African feet of the greatest size') while deriving
its rhythmic intensity from African–American oral traditions. The
nakedness and self-declarative use of racist language is overt
enough to read like a conscious parody of this discourse, as if
Welty were a black writer, parodying a white stereotype of the
black as musically possessed dervish. And the jazzy, slangy
textures of the prose are so brilliantly mimicked that one could
easily be seduced into thinking that this was written from within
African–American culture; it exemplifies what Patricia Yaeger has
called Welty's 'dialogic imagination' – her intertextual re-writing
of other authors.[12] It is a tremendously *knowing* slide between
linguistic registers, miming simultaneously a stereotypical
language of racial cliché and an innovative register of black
expressiveness, while alerting us to the author's game. The paragraph after the one quoted blows open the trick: 'You know
people on a stage – and people of a darker race – so likely to be
marvelous, frightening.' The narrating voice is now *aware* of its
own racial assumptions. In 'Powerhouse' Welty achieved the
'double-voicing' usually found in minority American literatures
which deploy the language of the dominant culture. She then
went further, and built into her prose a kind of verbal nudge, an
elbow in the reader's ribs to alert her to what is going on.
  Several of Welty's stories deal in a condensed and compressed

format with major episodes from American history, particularly the traumatic past of the South. These tales have undertows of political commentary, all the more remarkable given the concision and indirection of Welty's method. They are historical chamber-pieces, glancing tales of major events which shadow forth complex and layered readings of the nation's identity. It would not be going too far to suggest that a trio of tales are as significant for their fictional representations of the South as Hawthorne's short stories were for the imagining of New England's Puritan heritage.

'First Love' appeared in *The Wide Net* (1943); it tells the story of the trial and disgrace of Aaron Burr, the former Presidential candidate who in 1807 led a failed conspiracy to create a secessionist state in the Mississippi valley. Tried for treason, he was found innocent but then drifted away into exile and obscurity (this is the Burr later fictionalised in an eponymous novel by Gore Vidal). Welty's story is based on a fascinating conceit: the story is seen from the perspective of a young boy, Joel Mayes, 'a deaf boy twelve years old' (p. 154). The tale thus turns Burr's great claim to fame, his oratorical skill, into a mystery; Welty sets out to render in fiction a historical figure, whilst depriving herself through the deployment of this protagonist, of a means to illustrate what made Burr significant. When Joel hears Burr and his fellow-conspirators talking, their words remain enigmatic: 'Inside his room was still another interior, this meeting upon which all the light was turned, and within that was one more mystery, all that was being said' (p. 157).

On one level this is a daring technical gambit: how to create a fictional-historical figure, while depriving oneself, as author, of their very words. On another, Welty uses the child's muteness to explore the extraordinary attractiveness of Burr, whose enigmatic power exceeds language itself. At the end of the tale, after his trial, Joel follows Burr onto the Natchez Trail, into disgrace; he forsakes even his family. The final passage is replete with a sense of mysticism and the extraordinary, but also alert to the banality of Burr's escape. 'He had eluded judgement, that was all he had done, and Joel was glad while he still trembled.' Yet Joel walks on, apparently following the lost leader: 'He did not see how he could ever go back and still be the boot-boy at the Inn.' The last sentence: 'He saw that the bodies of the frozen birds had fallen out of the trees, and he fell down and wept for his father and mother, to whom he

had not said good-bye' (p. 168). In its collation of regret, mourn-
ing and melancholically glorious defeat, these sentences form a
compressed reflection on the myth of the South; but the power of
the writing lies in Welty's fastidious and muscular refusal to
confirm this tantalising allegory. This is a parable about the
witnessing of Southern history. The little boy is a silent witness to
events; he remains incommunicado as Burr's conspiracy unfolds.
He is nonetheless swayed by the mystery and pageantry of the
doomed Burr, even as he remains trapped within his own silent
universe. The story thus becomes an indirect and inferential
commentary on the South's famed weakness for pageantry and
martial romance. The boy is entranced by this romanticism; but he
is at the same time utterly isolated, locked in a sealed world of his
own illusions.

Another story deserving close scrutiny is 'A Still Moment'. The
three protagonists are also grounded in historical actuality:
Lorenzo Dow is a Protestant mystic, crying 'I must have souls!' (p.
189); James Murrell, a murderer and aspirant leader of brigand
insurrections; and Audubon, the famous natural historian and
illustrator. Welty builds her story around a trio who incarnate as
'representative men' the key national characteristics of the early
Republic: religious utopianism, wild violence, and the ambiguous
pastoralism of Audubon (caught as he is between wonderment at
the New World's riches and the need to control the environment).
At the end of the tale the murderer, the man-of-God and the naturalist are held together in contemplation of a white heron. It is a
moment saturated with the sublime and a strange sense of manic
collectivism – 'all eyes seemed infused with a sort of wildness' (p.
195). Unusually for Welty she follows her account of each man's
response to the vision of the white heron with a rare example of
commentary on her narrative's significance (its inner, almost allegorical meaning):

> What each of them had wanted was simply *all*. To save all souls,
> to destroy all men, to see and to record all life that filled this
> world – all, all – but now a single frail yearning seemed to go
> out of the three of them for a moment and to stretch toward
> this one snowy, shy bird in the marshes.   (p. 196)

These sentences are notable for their untypical directness and
generalising simplicity; Welty deploys a straightforward authorial

voice, linking three representative Americans (mystic, murderer, naturalist) together on account of their desire for plenitude ('all, all'). Whether or not this is a persuasive fictional parable about the origins of American identity is, perhaps, less important than the manner of its telling; the uncharacteristic forwardness of 'A Still Moment' helps to emphasise just how indirect Welty's stories usually are.

A third and far more characteristically oblique example of her historical chamber-fiction is a story from the 1950s, 'The Burning'. Even given the plaudits granted her work, this piece has attracted fantastic accolades for its impacted, layered and dense narrative weave. As Harold Bloom comments, 'The imagining is almost irrealistic in its complexity of tone and indirect represenation.'[13] This 'irrealistic' technique is striking because 'The Burning' is an historical tale, and the reader anticipates a degree of realism and mimesis in fiction addressing recorded events. Welty fashions an astonishingly fragmented and, on first reading, baffling account of the burning-down of Jackson, Mississippi by General Sherman's troops in 1863. Jackson was Welty's home town, and its razing a notorious event in the War; on personal and cultural levels this narrative is the centre of Welty's historical imagination. The story is told in an extremely elliptical and rapidly shifting manner; significant detail is presented allusively. What seems to happen is this. Two sisters, Miss Theo and Miss Myra, stand in their house as the Union troops arrive. The house is burned. The women escape, along with their slave help, Delilah. Later, they hang themselves from a tree. A young baby, Phinny, perished in the fire; later we discover that this child was begotten by the women's brother, Benton, upon Delilah.

This much is clear: 'The Burning' is a miniature narrative of enormous violence, horror and pain that touches on familiar motifs within the literature of the South. The ruined manse, miscegenation, dynastic downfall – all these topics are glimpsed. As in a great deal of her work, the story is punctuated with frozen tableaux, almost photographic in composition (reminding us of Welty's first profession). These beautiful images, nearly always richly coloured and painterly, are also the enigmas at the centre of her work, both demanding and resisting interpretation. 'The Burning', like 'First Love', adopts a child's perspective to cast naively wondering light on Southern history. Here, the child Delilah looks into an opulent mirror, a surviving relic in the burned manse, and catches an image of Jackson in the old days:

She saw people walking the bridges in early light with hives of houses on their heads, men in dresses, some with red birds; and monkeys in velvet; and ladies with masks laid over their faces looking from pointed windows. Delilah supposed that was Jackson before Sherman came. Then it was gone.   (p. 493)

What is this? A dream? A reflection, perhaps (of a picture also buried in the ruins)? An opulent and comic vision, the still-life captures a poignant sense of loss and the fantastically dream-like world of the ante-bellum South. The scene creates a poetic conceit for the South's past: history as a child's hallucinatory viewing of a wrecked mirror.

Welty's fiction endlessly plays with expectations of what is the fit between 'real life' and the shape or length of a work of fiction. A short story such as 'The Burning' plays a *trompe l'oeil* effect: superficially slight, it contains in elliptical form a massive swathe of history (one might even argue that it touches, with frantic restlessness, on all the major features of the South's history). If the impacted, lapidary stories contain stuff from which longer narratives are often fashioned, then Welty's novels sometimes reverse the pattern. *Losing Battles* (1970) appears to be woven from trivial incidents and defiantly ordinary domestic detail: family reunions, emotional misunderstandings, reminiscences of childhood. This sprawling novel has the scope, not least in sheer number of pages, of an epic. And Welty signals great expectations: the novel is prefaced with a cast list and a map of its setting, suggesting a fictionally constructed domain to place alongside William Faulkner's Yoknapatawpha County. However, while Faulkner's texts repeatedly alert us to their historiographical resonance (a figure like Quentin Compson explicitly meditates on the enduring significance of the Civil War), Welty's Southern epic is shorn of positioning, historiographical voices. Large expanses of the text consist of dialogue with very little framing material:

'I see now what you're dressed up for! You got your husband back,' said the smiling lady, who had the voice of a tease.
'I got him back this morning, Miss Pet.'
'And I hope you were ready for him!'
'Tried to be.'
'How many ladies is it?' Jack wondered aloud.

'This is a busload of schoolteachers, all of them teachers but Miss Pet Hanks,' Gloria told Jack. 'It looks like all the teachers of the Consolidated School System of Boone County. This is the first time any of them's come to see me since I was married.'

His lips moved to her ear. 'Honey, ask those teachers what they want with you now.'[14]

The inconsequentiality and indirection is typical of Welty's dialogue. Conversations overlap and interweave (a commentary on Gloria Short's dress folded into excited speculation about who is on the church bus). As ever, what is being said is less important than the manner of its saying: the expostulations, exclamations, cries and whispers of everyday chat. And there is a great deal of this kind of talk in *Losing Battles* – nearly five-hundred pages of chit-chat.

What might we infer from the excessive normality of the lives represented in *Losing Battles*? The title gestures, pretty directly, to the South's epic past of defeat and loss; but here Welty construes 'defeat' in ways more humdrum and comic. The defeats of *Losing Battles* are the everyday losses of family squabbles or the loss of face in a small community. Welty eschews monumental history, either the grand historical narrative of the Civil War or the more recent loss of the Depression years (the novel is set in the 1930s, although little is made of the economic context – as Welty said, the Depression was business as usual for a State like Mississippi). In place of the great, foregrounded events of history, Welty positions the buzz of quotidian conversation, family squabbles, the warp and woof of normality. *Losing Battles* creates an 'anti-historical' historical fiction; Welty sends out signals that she will portray a climactic and eventful story, but turns away from the past's grand narrative to explore history's forgotten interstices.

Welty's historical writing marks yet another generic modification of local color realism. She shares the colorist's attentiveness to forgotten and marginal details of everyday life: the quotidian is accorded dignity as the novelist finds resonance in the trivial. I think we first see local color taking on this explicitly historiographical significance in Willa Cather's *Death Comes for the Archbishop* (1927). Cather there focused on a major period of American history (the incorporation of the Southwest into the United States), but she dealt with her subject with tactful indirection. Her two protagonists, Fathers Vaillant and Latour, ruefully note that they are on the margins of history rather than at its centre: 'As Father Vaillant remarked, at Rome they did not seem to realize that it was no easy matter for two missionaries on horseback to keep up with the march of history.'[15] What Cather does here is to 'solve' a major problem in women's historical fiction. If a woman addressed important historical matters, it was often the case that these topics would be coded as masculine subjects (as here: war, exploration, politics). Cather's solution was to feed into historical writing the discoveries of local color, especially the principles of Sarah Orne Jewett. Jewett had fashioned an implicatory, indirect art where significance emerges obliquely in scenes of superficial triviality. Cather then embedded this narratology in a range of historical settings, creating a form of local color historicism: the history of the American margins. After Cather, a genealogy runs down through Welty and into Toni Morrison's historical novels – a women's historical fiction energised by a recognition that historical significance can be found in the underside of the past.

The most famous of Welty's novels, *Delta Wedding* (1946), pursues a narrative tactic of sly revelation and obliquely telling detail. This account of a large Southern family in the days running up to a wedding exhibits Welty's recurrent interest in the family, celebrations and rituals, even as it deploys an ambitiously experimental narrative method in a typical conjunction of 'ordinary' topic and strenuously avant-garde technique. *Delta Wedding*'s lovingly textured representation of Southern life (its voices and clothes; the buildings and food of the confederacy) is an example of the folkloric anthropology seen again and again in American women's writings. But in Welty's novel the texture of objects, the smell of cooking – the sheer sensory *ambience* of the South – achieves a monumentality that is almost abstract, as if her quest for detail had become impressionism, and human agency less important than moment-by-moment changes of sight, smell or sound:

> It was a soft day, brimming with the light of afternoon. It was the fifth beautiful week, with only that one threatening day. The gold mass of the distant shade trees seemed to dance, to sway, under the plum-colored sky. On either side of their horses' feet the cotton twinkled like stars. Then a red-pop flew up from her nest in the cotton. Above in an unbroken circle, all

around the wheel of the level world, lay silvery-blue clouds whose edges melted and changed into the pink and blue of sky. Girls and horses lifted their heads like swimmers. Here and there and far away the cotton wagons, of hand-painted green, stood up to their wheel tops in the white and were loaded with white, like cloud wagons. All along, the Negroes would lift up and smile glaringly and pump their arms – they knew Miss Dabney was going to step off Saturday with Mr. Troy.[16]

Scene-setting and picture-painting are taken to an extreme of detail, finesse and sensory plenitude; the image of the cotton wagons 'like cloud wagons' finds aesthetic delight in rural ordinariness. And yet, as in an eighteenth-century landscape image of pastoral labour, the scene is also politically coded. The black labourers' place in this ordered world seems secure, and they appear complicit in the rituals of the field; but still they 'smile glaringly'. The very uniformity of their collective presence ('the Negroes') contrasts poignantly with the minute attentiveness the narrative accords to cloudscape and farm machinery. This is a society where it is important to know that carts are 'hand-painted' but African–Americans are registered en masse as 'the Negroes'. This is a white world, and Welty shows how, for many of her white characters, the labouring and servant class of African–Americans simply register as a collectivised presence, achieving none of the reality, the simple 'thereness', of white society. In its understatement her contrast between the density of the white South and the textural/textual thinness of the African–American world is a telling commentary on the phenomenology of segregation. As Welty's farmers go about their business, their minds are over-stuffed with memory and family folktale; but their workers, immediately around them, signify with nothing like the same density of reference.

As Charles Taylor has argued, questions of multiculturalism increasingly turn on a 'politics of recognition' (the demand for a group to be recognised in and for its own cultural identity); but Welty often imagines a community of 'unrecognition' where one race is largely unknown to the other. Her early photographs of the everyday lives of Mississippi's blacks can be read as attempts to 'recognise' a forgotten culture. And stories like 'Keela, the Outcast Indian Maiden' or 'Powerhouse' might take Taylor's summary of '*mis*recognition' as their motto:

The demand for recognition in these latter cases is given urgency by the supposed links between recognition and identity, where this latter term designates something like a person's understanding of who they are, of their fundamental defining characteristics as a human being. The thesis is that our identity is partly shaped by recognition or its absence, often by the *mis*recognition of others, and so a person or group of people can suffer real damage, real distortion, if the people or society around them mirror back to them a confining or demeaning or contemptible picture of themselves. Nonrecognition or misrecognition can inflict harm, can be a form of oppression, imprisoning someone in a false, distorted, and reduced mode of being.[17]

In Welty's fiction this phenomenology of 'nonrecognition or misrecognition' produces plots which turn on impersonation, imitation and ventriloquism. It can also give rise to moments of great violence, as Taylor's 'form of oppression' is resisted.

In *Delta Wedding* two crucial encounters between black and white crystallise the racial dynamic of the South. Both centre on Troy Flavin, the groom whose wedding is the climax of the novel. Troy occupies a typically Weltyan position of putative centrality and actual marginality; he is the main young male in the book, but hardly figures in the ebb-and-flow of domestic chit-chat. He is the overseer-to-come, the successor to the estate, and the repository of traditional plantation virtues of autocracy and masculine power; but in Welty's re-worked configuration of the Southern household such qualities count for little. When Partheny, one of the serving girls, is slighted by Troy, she mutters: 'dat high-ridin' low-born Mr. Troy' (p. 132). This is one of the few explicit character judgements in the novel, but all the more resonant for its isolated prominence. Having a black character pass judgement on Troy is a quiet, understated but devastating moment: a sudden reversal of established racial pattern. Furthermore, towards the end of *Delta Wedding* there is a remarkable but fleeting moment when the deeper truths of Troy Flavin's character are sensed by a future relative. Shelley walks into Troy's office:

> The green-shaded light fell over the desk. It shone on that bright-red head. Troy was sitting there – bathed and dressed in a stiff white suit, but having trouble with some of the hands. Shelley walked into the point of a knife.

> Root M'Hook, a field Negro, held the knife drawn; it was not actually a knife, it was an ice pick. Juju and another Negro stood behind, with slashed cheeks, and open-mouthed; still another, talking to himself, stood his turn apart.
>
> Shelley ran to Troy, first behind him and then to his side. Wordlessly, he pushed her behind him again. She saw he had the gun out of the drawer.
>
> 'You start to throw at me, I'll shoot you,' Troy said.
>
> Roots vibrated his arm, aiming, Troy shot the finger of his hand, and Root fell back, crying out and waving at him.   (p. 195)

Amidst the preparations for the wedding this is a shocking incident, all the more powerful for its contrast with the celebratory high spirits in the surrounding chapters. Note, too, how Welty heightens the melodrama with her careful attention to the intense colours of the scene (the black 'hands', Troy's red hair, the white of his shirt). The heart of the scene is a bitter, ironic play with the meaning of 'hands': a 'hand' is the colloquial name given to the farmworkers, and it is through the hand that Troy shoots Root. It is an act of retribution that turns on an awful pun; but it also, with characteristic indirection, contains a barbed political critique. For Troy, the 'hands' are just that, pairs of hands; and there is an apt justness in meting out a punishment that will rob Root of that which gives him worth.

The melodrama and violence of the scene, with its awful abruptness out of a 'B' movie, suddenly forces the reader to reconsider the tapestry of quotidian life woven so carefully throughout the preceding pages: which represents the 'truth' of Mississippi life, arbitrary cruelty or the textures of ritualised domesticity? Welty is committed to an aesthetic where such questions will be raised but left with no simple answers. As much as a commentary on the South's sudden brutalities, this episode resonates as illustrative cameo of the divergent ways of men and women. In the most explicit commentary in the novel on what it means to be a man in the Delta, Shelley thinks:

> Running back along the bayou, faster than she had come, Shelley could only think in her anger of the convincing performance Troy had given as an overseer born and bred. Suppose a real Deltan, a planter, were no more real than that. Suppose a real Deltan only imitated another Deltan. Suppose the behavior

of all *men* were actually no more than this – imitation of other men. But it had previously occurred to her that Troy was trying to imitate her father. (Suppose her *father* imitated . . . oh, not he!) Then all men could not know any too well what they were doing. Everybody always said George was a second Denis.

(p. 196)

It is important that this insight should be adduced from the point of view of a character; Welty rarely pins such explicitly didactic commentary to an authorial narrative position. None the less, even with this caveat, the reader senses that with its general-ising power and declarative status, this is one of the book's central statements. And what a radical commentary it is: suspicious of 'authentic' behaviour, alert to the impersonations implicit in social life, sarcastic about the learnt rituals of masculinity. Retrospectively, Shelley's speculations cast a cold light back over the novel. On re-reading, we now see the everyday rituals of the female world, however trivial, as manifestations of a reliably authentic culture; the Southern male's orthodoxies as clichéd reit-erations of a patriarchy. Welty wrote in *One Writer's Beginnings* of the 'thread of revelation' in fiction. In a work like *Delta Wedding* this 'revelation' takes a political form: the unveiling of the deep structures of society in the South.

Katherine Anne Porter and Caroline Gordon: Politics and the Southern Woman

The business, practice and culture of writing is central to the Southern *littérateuse*. Gordon, Porter, Welty and O'Connor worked as editors, journalists and contributors to the literary magazines; they also created an informal literary salon. Porter wrote the Introduction to Welty's *A Curtain of Green*; O'Connor knew and admired Porter and Gordon; Gordon reviewed O'Connor. Years before talk of 'networks', Southern women worked in consort, often commenting on each others' work. The South's famed regionalism granted its writers an intensity of scrutiny, suggestion and criticism usually associated with the salons of Europe. These women also aspired to a masculine ideal of literary vocation – a self-consciously strenuous engagement with the business and practice of writing. Katherine Anne Porter admired men-of-letters such as Cyril Connolly and Edmund Wilson. And she idolised Ford Madox Ford for what she saw as his heroic literary endeavour: 'You will learn from him what the effort really is; what the pains, and what the rewards, of a real writer.'[18]

Katherine Anne Porter (1890–1980) mapped out the vocation of a woman-of-letters. Few would elevate her to the very top division of literary achievement, but her fiction and criticism mark out a formidable professionalism and range. She fashioned a career from a disparate range of activities: journalism, literary criticism, short stories. She was also politically active, writing about the trial of Sacco and Vanzetti, the immigrant radicals who became a *cause célèbre* for the intelligentsia in 1927. It is likely that Porter will increasingly be seen as a precursor to the political women-of-letters of the 1960s such as Susan Sontag and Joan Didion; she also helps to correct the stereotypical image of the late 1940s and 1950s as a period of passive quietude for women.

But her political involvements have proven difficult to encapsulate. In 1948 she gave talks on fascism and attacked Nazi sympathisers; she also praised the 'stylish literary communism' of New York. But she was also anti-Semitic and an outspoken opponent of school desegregation at the end of the 1950s. A recent biography notes her 'deep-seated racism'. A leftist, she never adhered to a conventional socialist ideology. She was drawn to the radical right-wing pastoralism of the Southern Agrarians, the conservative movement centred on Nashville's Vanderbilt University in the 1920s and 1930s (and a group which Caroline Gordon was also associated with).[19]

One might see this ambivalence, if not self-division, as the creative centre of Porter's work. Her literary criticism, for example, is also marked by antinomies, as Porter tacks between divergent and even paradoxical accounts of her favourite writers. The 1952 collection of essays, *The Days Before*, was one of the earliest American attempts to identify a tradition of women fiction writers; she wrote about Stein, Cather, Katherine Mansfield, Welty and Virginia Woolf. Porter identified an emphatically womanly canon. She wrote quizzically, with a mixture of admiration and censure, about her peers. Her collection of 'Three Views' of Gertrude Stein is especially interesting for its tartness and its blending of autobiographical reminiscence and close textual criticism. Collating essays written over twenty years, the essay transcends the narrowly subjective by using the critic's life story as basis for a history of changing taste. The methodology of these essays is to enmesh personal memoir, close textual reading and biographical accounts in a tightly idiomatic prose.

Porter's essays also touch on another topic of recurrent fascination for American women writers: marriage. In 'Marriage is Belonging' (1951) she provided a wry historical perspective on the current marital fervour: 'The Victorian marriage feather bed was in fact set upon the shaky foundation of the wavering human heart, the inconsistent human mind, and was the roiling hotbed of every dislocation and disorder not only in marriage but all society, which we of the past two generations have lived through.' Porter does not deny the centrality of marriage to human experience (how could she: she married four times); but she brings to the debate a wry, cynical worldliness about the wedding fever of the 1950s. 'There is no such thing as perfect faithfulness any more than there is perfect love or perfect beauty. But it is fun trying.'[20] The tone of this commentary is as important as what is said: Porter's ironic view of marriage suggests that even in the heyday of the 'domestic ideology' there were voices looking forward to the scepticism of 1960s feminism.

Porter's fiction rarely features in discussions of American women's fiction; she is a good example of a writer who is ghettoised as a Southern author rather than incorporated into larger patterns of literary history. In part this is an accident of chronology and classification. Two of her collections were published in the 1930s but evinced little interest in the social problems of that decade. Another collection was published just after the war; and the *Collected Stories* finally emerged in the mid-1960s. She seems temporally rootless, lacking a home in a specific decade. The lack of a major novel in her canon of short fiction also means that, unlike Welty or O'Connor, her work lacks the ballast that longer fiction gives to a short-story writer.

It is regrettable that Porter's standing has been hampered by these factors; the stories now seem ready for the readings nurtured by feminist literary criticism over the past two decades. Take the novella 'Pale Rider' (1939). A short account of a newspaper journalist and her fleeting affair with a soldier, this First World War story occupies the fictional space mapped by Hemingway in *A Farewell to Arms*. Porter reverses the pattern of Hemingway's fiction, placing the woman at the centre of the tale and displacing the soldier away from the centre; hers is a female recasting of a typical male narrative. Ironically enough, 'Pale Horse, Pale Rider' (the title comes from an old spiritual) was published in 1939, the start of the next war; but the prevailing tone is one of scepticism towards war and the State's military propaganda. The heroine, Miranda, is urged to buy one of the Liberty Bonds used by the US government to raise capital for its war chest; she is resistant to these entreaties and disorientated by military propaganda:

> Miranda tried not to listen, but she heard. These vile Huns – glorious Belleau Wood – our keyword is Sacrifice – Martyred Belgium – give till it hurts – our noble boys Over There – Big Berthas – the death of civilization – the Boche . . .
>
> 'My head aches,' whispered Miranda. 'Oh, why won't he hush?'[21]

At such moments 'Pale Horse, Pale Rider' is cynical and sceptical; its tone fits with the sarcastic tartness of Porter's journalism. But 'Pale Horse, Pale Rider' is intriguing for its range of tones and its heterogeneous mixture of voices. Alongside social satire sits a more meditative and reflective narrative voice, a poetic rendering of the dreams and wistful memories of Miranda. This is a discourse with its roots in modernism's concern for the interior monologues of the female subject:

> Oblivion, thought Miranda, her mind feeling among her memories of words she had been taught to describe the unseen, the unknowable, is a whirlpool of grey water turning upon itself for all eternity . . . eternity is perhaps more than the distance to the farthest star. She lay on a narrow ledge over a pit that she knew to be bottomless, though she could not comprehend it; the ledge was her childhood dream of danger, and she strained back against a reassuring wall of granite at her shoulders, staring into the pit, thinking, There it is, there it is at last, it is very simple.   (p. 324)

The slight stiffness of Porter's prose is revealing: a modernistic account of inner space is couched in an old-fashioned narrative discourse, marked by a certain over-literalness. One can imagine a writer like Virginia Woolf attempting a much more fully fledged mimesis of what Miranda is thinking, a mimesis where the flow of consciousness would find a syntactical equivalent. Instead, the author is solidly positioned between the reader and the character's consciousness, as if we were still in the late nineteenth century.

Although written in the late 1930s, 'Pale Horse, Pale Rider' deals with an era some twenty years earlier; the other two short fictions in this collection are also historically positioned at the turn of the century. The first story, 'Old Mortality', deals with the young women of a Southern family; Porter directly situates her narrative with datelines: '1885–1902', '1904'. And the second novella, 'Noon Wine', also carries a historical specificity in its title: 'Time: 1896–1905', 'Place: Small South Texas Farm'. The subtext of this trilogy is the social change rippling through American society at the start of the century. Porter's heroines are new women: dissatisfied with established pieties, sometimes wry and cynical, but still fascinated with the romanticised world of courtship. The stories point up a contrast between the heroines' daydreams and a reality that is more disappointing: Miranda's lover, Adam, dies rather pathetically of influenza, not on the battlefield. And the heroine of 'Old Mortality' (also called Miranda, although it seems unlikely that this is the same character recurring), feels that history, particularly the accumulated weight of the Southern past, is too much to bear. Here, Porter presents history as imprisonment or as millstone; the female subject feels the constricting power of the past, and desires escape:

> Her mind closed stubbornly against remembering, not the past but the legend of the past, other people's memory of the past, at which she had spent her life peering in wonder like a child at a magic-lantern show. Ah, but there is my own life to come yet, she thought, my own life now and beyond. I don't want any promises, I won't have false hopes, I won't be romantic about myself. I can't live in their world any longer, she told herself, listening to the voices back of her. Let them tell their stories to each other. Let them go on explaining how things happened. I don't care. At least I can know the truth about what happens to me, she assured herself silently, making a promise to herself, in her hopefulness, in her ignorance. (pp. 224–5)

It is sometimes necessary to be free from the burden of stories; inherited stories can carry their own dead weight of trammelled lives. For Porter's characters it is important to resist these inherited narratives, whether they are tales of the South or stories of masculinity and war.

'Old Mortality' also gave voice, by Porter's creation of Miranda, to the iconic Southern belle. That image of intensely idealised beauty is central to Southern culture but rarely de-mythologised.[22] Porter's belle wants to turn away from this Southern mythology. As she plainly thinks: 'I won't be romantic about myself' – though Porter also suggests that this resistance is itself a form of naivety (Miranda makes promises to herself 'in her ignorance'). In her pragmatic debunking of idealism, Porter articulated an anti-romantic scepticism that other Southern writers have admired. Eudora Welty saw her as a writer who repudiated falsehood. She argued that Porter resisted the Romantic mythology of the South because it was just one of 'those universal false dreams, the hopes sentimental and ubiquitous.' 'They are excoriating stories.'[23]

But Porter's work also charts the seductions of those 'universal false dreams'. In order to excoriate 'the hopes sentimental and ubiquitous' Porter has created fictions which examine why such dreams might be attractive in the first place. 'Flowering Judas', Porter's own favourite amongst her tales, meditates on the allure of radical politics. The tale reflects on a woman's place in revolution. Laura, a young American, works in revolutionary-era Mexico. The alluring political radical, Braggioni, courts her; he is mystified as to why a *gringo*, a *gringita*, would be involved in politics. Laura listens to his awful courtly singing 'with pitiless courtesy'. But while Braggioni is trapped in his own self-love, Laura is equally locked in her delusions: ' "It may be true I am as corrupt, in another way, as Braggioni", she thinks in spite of herself, "as callous, as incomplete".' In the conclusion, an enigmatic dream-sequence brings forward a character, Eugenio, who offers Laura flowers from the Judas tree: 'She saw that his hand was fleshless, a cluster of small white petrified branches, and his eye sockets were without light, but she ate the flowers greedily for they satisfied both hunger and thirst.'[24]

Radical commitment is the subject of 'Flowering Judas'; it is also the target for Porter's mordant scepticism. Porter coolly dissects the personal and potentially selfish reasons for being drawn to revolutionary politics: Eugenio was the lover who lured Laura to Mexico, and then died. It is through symbolism that Porter then wraps together her conflicting interpretations of women-in-revolution. The symbolic eating of the leaves conflates the eroticism, the sheer need, the betrayals and the destructiveness of Laura's politics. Unaccustomed as we now are to such a foregrounded use of a symbolic fictional language, the image of the Judas tree might seem a little arch, a little too *designed*. But we can see it as serving a very pragmatic purpose in Porter's storytelling. She deployed symbols not in order to take refuge from the turbulence of history and politics, but in order to shape her own very divided and ambiguous response to the psychology of radical engagement. Hunger, destruction, eroticism, idealism: it is this uneasy, jostling variety of response that is held together, if only temporarily, in the conclusion to 'Flowering Judas'.

Southern fiction's symbol-making was often blended or melded with other registers or languages: in O'Connor, with a sardonic form of the Gothic; in Welty, with an attentive local color realism. In the work of Caroline Gordon (1895–1981) the symbolic register is grafted on to a form of careful, historicised realism. Gordon's works, from *Penhally* (1931) to *None Shall Look Back* (1937) depicted the South's historical past in a plain, austere, evenly Augustan prose. Her response to the Confederacy's turbulent history is to give form to the inchoate by means of restraint and classicism. Such a stylistic register also enabled Gordon to forge a language of war. The Civil War was the subject, indirectly or directly, of most of Gordon's work. It is at the centre of *None Shall Look Back*, where she answered the question of whether a woman can write about what is reckoned a thoroughly masculine topic by creating a flattened, dispassionate documentary tone:

Forrest's horse had been shot out from under him. A shell crashing through the horse's body just behind the rider's leg had torn the already wounded animal to pieces. The rider, disentangling himself, went forward on foot. He was splashed with blood and his overcoat had fifteen bullets in it, but he was uninjured. Placing his hand on one of the bloody gun carriages he threw back his head and yelled with triumph. His men yelling too gave him back his own name: 'Forrest! Forrest!' Then still hysterical with joy they ran about over the field, gathering up the arms of the enemy's dead and wounded.[25]

How does the woman writer approach, and appropriate, a fictional subject insistently coded as masculine? Gordon's war writing (and there is a great deal of it in *None Shall Look Back*) adopts a terse plainness; it is laconic, factual, unemphatic. Would the unknowing reader be able to detect a signal of the author's gender? Although many of the scenes in *None Shall Look Back* are on the battlefield, they suggest neither an overt feminisation of war (contrast Frances Harper's domestication of conflict in *Iola Leroy*) nor an active mimicry of male discourses of war (contrast Cather's self-conscious goriness in *One of Ours*). Gordon's restraint and cool historicism suggest instead a kind of androgynous classicism.

Gordon's style was a manifestation of her conservatism. *None Shall Look Back* presents the Civil War as horrific primarily because it produced chaos. Gordon's ideal conservative society was marked by order and formalism, manners and restraint. The Civil War is thus represented as less a matter of issues (slavery, abolition) than as an elemental conflict between opposing sensibilities: order versus disorder. In one memorable aside, order and discipline are the virtues of the slaveowner faced with rebellious slaves: 'The problem was to keep them in order. The best way to do that was by disciplining your own thoughts' (p. 134). As Frederick Hoffman has noted: 'For Miss Gordon life needs to move in an orderly fashion from the fixed point of a patterned and naturally pure world toward a more stylized, a more formally ordered world.'[26] Gordon had been associated with the Southern Agrarians, a group of writers and intellectuals whose collection of essays, *I'll Take My Stand* (1930), articulated a distinctive reactionary politics: anti-industrial, anti-scientific, feudal, agrarian, profoundly historicised, keenly aware of the tragic dimensions of human experience (the Agrarians were impatient with what they saw as the naive progressivism and optimism of Northern, Yankee culture). Gordon's fiction bears testimony to these ideas; she was also married to a leading Agrarian, Allen Tate; and conversion to Roman Catholicism in the 1940s might also be seen as further confirmation of her reaction against scientific materialism.

Gordon's work forms part of an intriguing genealogical strand in recent women's writing: an explicitly reactionary female tradition, grounded in a conservative philosophy and often rooted in the South. For Gordon, a sense of place and an instinctive suspicion of disorder underpinned a conservatism that would have appealed to Edmund Burke. In the work of the major figure in this reactionary tradition, Flannery O'Connor, a theological conservatism emerged: O'Connor's fundamentalist Roman Catholicism led in her fiction to ironic satire of modernity and liberal humanism. As Gordon wrote in an admiring review of her fellow Catholic's work:

> In Miss O'Connor's vision of modern man – a vision not limited to Southern rural humanity – all her characters are 'displaced persons,' not merely the people in the story of that name. They are 'off center,' out of place, because they are victims of a rejection of the Scheme of Redemption. They are lost in that abyss which opens for man when he sets up as God. This theological framework is never explicit in Miss O'Connor's fiction. It is so much a part of her direct gaze at human conduct that she seems herself to be scarcely aware of it.[27]

Flannery O'Connor: 'Every Action is Weighted with an Eternal Consequence'

Flannery O'Connor (1925–64) demands an astigmatic reader. With one eye the reader will pay attention to her declarations of Catholicism, and will read her densely symbolic tales for their allegorical deployment of theological axioms. Joyce Carol Oates has recently read the stories in this way: 'Suffused with Catholic ideology, or in any case a passionate wish to believe in Christ and salvation by way of the Roman Catholic Church, Flannery O'Connor is the most visual and relentlessly "symbolic" of writers.'[28] With the other eye the reader will note O'Connor's political and cultural subtexts – the way her stories embody, though often in labyrinthinely complex ways, a distinctive ideology of region, race and political reaction. O'Connor's letters are testament to the depth and strength of her beliefs. 'I take the Dogmas of the Church literally', she wrote in 1957. And in 1958:

> It is simply that the main Catholic concepts are in line with reality – the realization that man is not perfectible by his own efforts . . . the ever present concern with death as the end of

life, that every action is weighted with an eternal conse-
quence.[29]

Many of the stories derive from O'Connor's categorical adher-
ence to the Roman faith. She is fond of dramatic situations which
pitch the supposedly insightful sceptical humanist into fraught
awareness that life contains more mysteries than rationality can
account for. A story such as 'Revelation' (1964) demands to be
read in terms of Catholic eschatology. Mrs Turpin's vision:

> A visionary light settled in her eyes. She saw the streak as a
> vast swinging bridge extending upward from the earth
> through a field of living fire. Upon it a vast horde of souls were
> rumbling toward heaven. There were whole companies of
> white-trash, clean for the first time in their lives, and bands of
> black niggers in white robes, and battalions of freaks and
> lunatics shouting and clapping and leaping like frogs. And
> bringing up the end of the procession was a tribe of people
> whom she recognized at once as those who, like herself and
> Claud, had always had a little of everything and the God-given
> wit to use it right. She leaned forward to observe them closer.
> They were marching behind the others with great dignity,
> accountable as they had always been for good order and
> common sense and respectable behavior. They alone were on
> key. Yet she could see by their shocked and altered faces that
> even their virtues were being burned away.[30]

With its intense, hallucinatory, Bosch-like conflation of the
grotesque and the transcendental, this paragraph encapsulates
O'Connor's almost medieval Catholic mysticism. The visionary,
symbolic writing demands to be read in a theological context,
particularly because its power turns on a typically acute reading
of a philosophical crux (in the purgation even the 'virtues' of the
apparently good will have to be cleansed). And yet, in astigmatic
fashion, the paragraph can be read with the other eye, for its
highly particularised Southern social vision. The revelation is a
sociological one, as Mrs Turpin realizes that her middling good
works will count for nothing in the final moments; even being
able to sing 'on key' will be worthless. The recognition of snobbery and social rivalry in this passage is especially acute: the self-
regard of the lower middle-class, and their dislike of white-trash

(for once, Mrs Turpin sniffs, clean) and blacks (note, in an emphatic phrase, that these are 'black niggers', their coloured alterity attracting Mrs Turpin's attention even here). The 'Catholicism' of this moment, in other words, is profoundly shaped by O'Connor's rendering of a specific local culture, and its attendant stratifications and prejudices. And the final horror of Mrs Turpin's vision is largely dependent on the revelation that in heaven good works might still leave one in the company of white-trash, blacks, freaks and lunatics.

There are increasing signs that critics want to construct secular readings of O'Connor, readings which acknowledge her Catholicism but interpret the stories for a political subtext. O'Connor's work has recently begun to be re-appraised within the context of the Cold War. For Jon Lance Bacon, O'Connor's fiction 'focuses on the cultural climate promoted by the anxiety that Stalin and Sputnik could elicit'. Bacon reads her as a dissenting voice in the 1950s age of affluence: 'She called attention to the discrepancy between an idealized "American way" ... and the social realities produced by this merger of politics and culture.' Certainly, O'Connor's career was overshadowed by the Cold War. In 1960 she received a sorority award at an annual luncheon where the speaker, one Mercer Livermore, talked about her community service 'to the women behind the men behind the missiles' at Cape Canaveral. The *Atlanta Journal* reported Ms Livermore's comment that 'women, over all, are more interested in missiles as an important factor in our American defense than men are'. Such incidents suggest a culture where buffets and bullets could be found in disturbing proximity. Against such a backdrop (anxiety; heightened national security; the commitment to American nationhood in the face of outside threats) O'Connor's quirky, localised, Catholic fictions might seem to constitute an idiosyncratic, if not a dissenting, intellectual position.[31]

These stories work in a multiplicity of ways; densely symbolic and obliquely allegorical, they seem to contain some kernel of truth which is at the same time elusive. Her stories seem simultaneously transparent and opaque. The transparency is inherent in the 'O. Henry' format of the short story: her compact tales have the ostentatious climaxes and reversals-of-fortune demanded of the short story writer who fashions her work for the popular marketplace. Trained at the University of Iowa writing school, and the winner of a large number of story competitions, O'Connor was the very model of the professionalised marketplace author. At the same time, one catches in O'Connor a foretaste of the tricksiness, playfulness and deconstructive energy of the 1960s. She was an architect of bizarre jokes, vertiginous dénouements, paradoxes and teasing symbolism. Her black comedy might remind readers of Ken Kesey, Kurt Vonnegut or Philip Roth. Even the titles of her stories incarnate this darkly playful irony, since they so often mean the very reverse of what they say. Thus, 'A Good Man is Hard to Find', a story about a family's happenstance, fatal encounter with a murderer known as 'The misfit', might be more accurately titled, 'A Bad Man is all too easy to find'.

In her stories O'Connor focused on the South's customs with an anthropologist's eye; her stories are filled with odd turns of expression, slang, rituals, all illustrating the quiddity of a localised culture. The tales are often about enslavement to ritual, about the futile re-enactment of patterns of behaviour which have now become bleached of all meaning. They describe the comedy and tragedy that ensue when her characters find their routines suddenly interrupted or subverted. One early story, 'The Geranium', explores the frustrations borne by an old man who, transported from his Southern home to a bleak New York tenement, relies on the positioning of a flower as a consolatory ritual. Another, 'The Barber', follows the exasperated preparations of a Southern liberal as he awaits the weekly mockery of his redneck barber. And another, 'A Late Encounter with the Enemy', explores the dying thoughts of a Southerner destined to imagine a procession which might be a symbolic vision of a now-lost Southern history. These miniature portraits of tragicomic rituals constitute a radical commentary on the nature of 'Southernness'. O'Connor's South is hardly that of the area's proselytes, the Allen Tates and John Crowe Ransoms who venerated an agrarian, philosophical order beyond Yankee society's industrialised depredations. O'Connor was more interested in white-trash than neo-classicism.

Her readings of the South's racial dilemmas are particularly significant, given that O'Connor's career coincided with the growth of Civil Rights in the late 1950s and early 1960s. Her letters contain some extremely acerbic commentary on these matters. She complained, for instance, about the inclusion of an incident involving segregation and Civil Rights in a story by her friend

Cecil Dawkins: 'It sounds as if these things are dragged in to show where the author's sympathies lie; leave it to the NAACP.'[32] (The NAACP was the National Association for the Advancement of Colored People, the leading Civil Rights group.) Her letters on Civil Rights have a tone of mocking resignation, as when she witnessed a protest: 'We are getting pretty smart here in Georgia and are a heap smarter than they are in Alabama. We just let them niggers ride by and waved at them.'[33] Although the tone is not that surprising – one imagines that ironic capitulation before the tide of history was a fairly common position amongst educated Southerners – the letters do encourage us to look again at the complex representation of race in O'Connor's fiction. Here, the central text is the extraordinary 'The Artificial Nigger'.

Has a story about race ever carried a more provocative title? An elderly man and his grandson (the mother has died – O'Connor's families are typically lopsided or fractured) travel, for the first time, from their rural home to a nearby city. This, like many O'Connor stories, is a trip of revelation; Nelson will see African–Americans for the first time in his life. The day trip moves from awkwardness towards danger. They find themselves in the black part of town. The child runs into an old woman, and in the ensuing panic Mr Head refuses to acknowledge that he is related to the boy. It is only on the way home, when they encounter a weird plaster figurine, that the stand-off between the two travellers is resolved:

> The Negro was about Nelson's size and he was pitched forward at an unsteady angle because the putty that held him to the wall had cracked. One of his eyes was entirely white and he held a piece of brown watermelon.
>
> Mr. Head stood looking at him silently until Nelson stopped at a little distance. Then as the two of them stood here, Mr. Head breathed, 'An artificial nigger!'
>
> It was not possible to tell if the artificial Negro were meant to be young or old; he looked too miserable to be either. He was meant to look happy because his mouth was stretched up at the corners but the chipped eye and the angle he was cocked at gave him a wild look of misery instead.   (p. 268)

In two letters of 1955 O'Connor claimed that she wanted to suggest by the figurine 'the redemptive quality of the Negro's suffering for us all', and that 'there is nothing that screams out the tragedy of the South like what my uncle calls "nigger statuary" '.[34] This is the trenchantly Catholic O'Connor speaking. But there cannot now be many readers for whom the suffering of America's black population is 'redemptive . . . for us all'. What is offensive here is not so much racism as the *utilisation* of others' suffering for one's own spiritual purposes. And yet the story, almost in defiance of its own creator, contains other significances. I am struck by the tale's oblique and sardonic mapping of the phenomenology of racism. When Nelson first sees an African–American, he has to be told that this is a black man ('You said they were black . . . You never said they were tan'). The story analyses the necessity of blackness for the white imagination – necessary for the self-definition and racial solidarity of whites. The reconciliation at the end of the story takes place after a moment of shared, communal racial perception: the two look at the artificial nigger together and for the first time have an emphatically collective response, fostered by this image of darkness. After a series of confused responses in the face of 'real' blackness (misrecognitions, misperceptions), the fake black homunculus, with its blatant expression of misery, provides a simple emblem which eradicates differences: 'The two of them stood there with their necks forward at almost the same angle and their shoulders curved in almost exactly the same way and their hands trembling identically in their pockets' (p. 268). Racial difference is necessary, O'Connor implies, as a dynamic to engender collective identity in the white South. Every paragraph in this story is saturated with references to darkness and blackness, providing an insistent reminder that colour is the very structure of Southern culture. The coda to the story, though, provides a theological framework. Mr Head now feels the 'action of mercy'; the tale follows a pattern of misunderstanding, contrition and, perhaps, redemption. The contemporary reader finds a knotted allegory of racial identity; but O'Connor herself frames race in a theological structure. This, in miniature, illustrates the dilemma posed by O'Connor's work: we extract political, particularly racial and 'Southern', meanings from her work. But such meanings were, for O'Connor herself, framed by larger, transcendental significances.

Joyce Carol Oates noted that O'Connor was the most 'relentlessly "symbolic" ' of writers; but as a symbolist she was not alone amongst the writers of the South. In stories such as 'The Burning' or 'Flowering Judas', Eudora Welty and Katherine Anne Porter also turned their stories into emblematic narratives, with symbolic events at their heart. Symbolism might be thought to mark a retreat from the overtly political writing of the 1930s (a retreat into a hermetic, private, aestheticised writing); but for Welty, Porter and O'Connor the symbolic mode became a pathway *towards* political topics: race, the Civil War, revolutionary commitment. As we shall see in the next chapter, this form of politicised symbolism was then to become one of the dominant modes for women's fiction in the 1940s and 1950s, achieving a broader national currency in the work of Elizabeth Hardwick, Jean Stafford, Jane Bowles and Ann Petry.

6

Dysfunctional Realism

Ann Petry, Elizabeth Hardwick, Jean Stafford, Jane Bowles

The historian Elaine Tyler May describes the immediate postwar period as one dominated by 'The Reproductive Consensus': 'Procreation in the cold war era took on almost mythic proportions.'[1] The baby-boom, the idealisation of the home and childrearing, attacks on feminism: all these features marked a period usually characterised for its reaction against the advances women had made in earlier decades. Despite women's movement into the workplace during the war, 'no general feminist argument was made in justification'.[2] Indeed, the era saw bitter denunciations of feminism. In 1947 *The Modern Woman: The Last Sex*, by Marynia Farnham and Ferdinand Lundberg, argued that female sexuality found its real fulfilment in motherhood. Drawing on (pseudo)-psychoanalytical models and on historical anecdotage, the authors presented feminism as a disaster. Only by active propaganda in favour of the traditional family and sex roles could this dangerous ideology be overcome. The idealisation of home life was central to their programme of re-education. *The Modern Woman* quickly became a popular and influential work.[3]

For literary critics this was a period lacking political bite; fiction had collapsed into a circumscribed attentiveness as writers focused on the private and the ethical at the expense of a broader social vision. Symbolism, irony and psychological realism supplanted the polemics and politicised realism of the 1930s. Chester Eisinger, in what remains one of the few studies of the immediate after-war period, wrote of Robert Penn Warren and Carson McCullers: 'although they show an interest in social issues, they turn away from these issues to find their real center in moral–ethical problems, or in what concerns the inward, private being'.[4] The left-wing commitment of 1930s writers now seemed treacherous.

The 1940s and 1950s did see cultural experimentalism, even radicalism, but this progressive energy was popularly associated with *male* artists. The literary outlawism of Jack Kerouac and William Burroughs; the icon of the teenager in the films of James Dean: various rebels – the 'beatnik', the 'hipster', the 'outsider' – became fashionable during the period. A writer such as Norman Mailer would defiantly stake his claim in 'The White Negro' (1957) to be a rebel. This radicalism now often seems like a romanticised fantasy of individualised self-fulfilment; the rebel was more of a conformist than he imagined.[5] But it was a rebellion which had been given a scholarly stamp of authority, as America's sociologists and political commentators began to identify a malaise in their nation: a stifling conformism. The economist J. K. Galbraith had described the 'Affluent Society' in his 1958 work of that name; but other commentators stressed the debilitating effects of an affluent conformism. Key works included *The Lonely Crowd* (1950), edited by David Riesman; William Whyte's *The Organization Man* (1956); Paul Goodman's *Growing Up Absurd: Problems of Youth in the Organized Society* (1960) and Sloan Wilson's bestseller *The Man in the Grey Flannel Suit* (1957). These works presented a consumerist world where individuals were none the less subordinated; the new suburban dream had stifled America's vibrant individualism.

These arguments concerned men, their working lives and their need to re-establish and re-assert independence. As Barbara Ehrenreich has shown, debates about conformism and rebellion were predominantly arguments about perceived threats to masculine autonomy: a constricting social order was seen to be closing in around the male self. Ehrenreich sees the idealisation of non-conformism as a revolution by American men against the home and its perceived constraints. In place of breadwinning and the family, male intellectuals had begun to valorise 'independence' in ways that excluded women. For the 1950s 'gray flannel dissidents', conformism was the latent psychosocial problem of American life: 'The word was "conformity," and in the fifties "conformity" became the code word for male discontent – the masculine equivalent of what Betty Friedan would soon describe as "the problem without a name." ' After the Beatnik, 'All of America could see that there were men . . . who refused to undertake the support of women and seemed to get away with it.'[6]

Men created a space for heroic, masculine non-conformity;

they interpreted female culture as if it occupied the opposite pole: a conformist, domestic zone of narrowed orthodoxy. This representation was increasingly found in portrayals of the female realm produced by men in the 1950s. Ehrenreich notes the moment in Kerouac's *On the Road* (1957) when Dean Moriarty leaves a group of women, dismissed as a 'sewing circle', to go out onto the road (where he will find the 'ecstatic joy of pure being').[7] Even Miller's *The Crucible*, that iconic testament to the individual's resistance to conformism, had a gendered subtext encoded with the era's sexual politics. The male outsider, Proctor, is pitted against a terrifying establishment made up of young women and their male proxies. Read now, after the Cold War's thaw, the play reveals a world where the real witch-hunt ironically takes men as its quarry, while women create a bleakly conformist society.

The picture of American culture becomes, though, more complex still when we read what women writers themselves were saying at this time. For Jane Bowles (1917–73), Elizabeth Hardwick (1916–) and Jean Stafford (1915–79), all of whom came to prominence in the 1940s, the lives of girls and women had already begun to change radically. The monolithic female culture resented by the male outsiders is belied by works written *within* the womanly world. These writers operated from within the domestic ideology, parodying its assumptions and stealthily subverting stereotyped images of the home and the female self. Their work anticipates the attack by Betty Friedan on the 'feminine mystique'; they slyly constructed stories which, while set within the domestic spaces of the American bourgeoisie, reveal those living rooms and bedrooms to be the site of psychological disruption, excess and a disorientating comedy.

Jane Bowles's *Two Serious Ladies* (1943), Elizabeth Hardwick's *The Ghostly Lover* (1945) and Jean Stafford's *The Mountain Lion* (1947) were works of 'dysfunctional realism': dysfunctional in that home life is now the setting for repeated crisis and breakdown (often envisaged in blackly comic terms); realism in that the fundamental generic code for these writers remains social realism. The experimentalism of Joyce Carol Oates or Susan Sontag remains distant; but their experimental fictions of the 1960s descended from a fiction of the 1940s and 1950s which already presented in nascent form the narrative of crisis captured in Betty Friedan's feminist polemic, *The Feminine Mystique*: a world of domestic 'normality' conditioned by the anti-depressant and the gin bottle, scored by frustration and a bubbling discontent. The dysfunctional realists invoked a familiar world (the female realm of friendship and domestic sentiment), but then undermined it with a creeping disorientation and disturbance. Planted within an established tradition – the novel of manners – these books traced middle-class discontent twenty years before an anatomy of bourgeois disillusion became the foundation for a revitalised feminist ideology. Manners seem to creak and crack under the stress of disruptive behaviour and an incipient madness. Hardwick, Stafford and Bowles were fascinated by psychological anguish: ordinary life is marked (and marred) by incursions of behavioural excess which foreshadow deeper mental crises. Even a work like Ann Petry's *The Street* (1946), on the surface a novel written within the format of social protest fiction, traced a psychopathology of family life: 1940s fictions anticipated that slogan of the 1960s, 'the personal is political'.

Ann Petry's *The Street*, Hardwick's *The Ghostly Lover* and Stafford's early fictions such as *Boston Adventure*, also shared a narrative line: the tale of thwarted or disappointed female ambition. In all these works the young woman is first glimpsed in all her potential and naive hopefulness; the narrative that unfolds is essentially a 'declensionist' plot, as social and emotional pathways to fulfilment are closed down. In this sense postwar fiction continues and deepens the harsh, ironic, even tragic modes seen in earlier writers such as Chopin and Larsen. This might be another reason why 1940s and 1950s fictions have fallen out of critical favour: they proffer few progressive or hopeful resolutions to the heroine's dilemmas – one cannot easily extrapolate an ideology of uplift from these tales of blunted ambition. The last paragraphs and sentences of these novels indicate in outline a grim closure:

> The great brown and copper doors upon which an icy ray of light was shining separated her forever from him and his shelter like the forbidden gates of Eden.   (*The Ghostly Lover*)[8]

> And as the train roared into the darkness, Lutie tried to think out by what twists and turns of fate she had landed on this train. Her mind baulked at the task. All she could think was, it was that street. It was that god-damned street.
> (*The Street*)[9]

> And, as Molly dies at the end of *The Mountain Lion*, Magdalene says in the novel's last sentence: ' "Lord Jesus. The poor little old piece of white trash." '[10]

To regard these women as 1960s feminists *avant la lèttre* would, I think, be a mistake. Jean Stafford was always outspoken in her attacks on the feminist movement, and towards the end of her life produced increasingly irascible articles with titles like 'Don't Use Ms. with Miss Stafford Unless You Mean ms' (1973).[11] Elizabeth Hardwick was at the time sceptical about the programmatic radicalism implied by feminist classics such as De Beauvoir's *The Second Sex* (although she later shifted her ground). Feminist critics who have attempted to assimilate these writers to an overtly radical agenda have faced an uphill struggle, largely because, as Shelley Ratcliffe Rogers notes of Stafford, 'her fictions invite readings which her essays refute.'[12] To a certain extent we have to read for the novelist's *oblique* engagement with a proto-feminist constellation of interests. Moreover, we also have to acknowledge that works of fiction, like *The Mountain Lion*, perhaps create a creative space where the writer engages with her social realities in ways more complex, layered and, indeed, radical than the format of the essay can allow for. The *implications* of the creative text are more politically enriching than the overt message of the essay.

Ann Petry's *The Street*

One of the major genealogies traced in this book has been the fiction of black female agency. From Hopkins and Harper in the 1890s, through to Larsen and Fauset in the 1920s and 1930s, and then on to Hurston, a novelistic line of descent can be followed. All these writers trace the black heroine's attempts to create an autonomous space of self-fulfilment and individual agency, and her resistance to a nexus of social, political and economic forces. For a writer such as Frances Harper, the ideology of 'uplift' would establish both individual empowerment and a cohesive ethnic identity; for other writers, notably Nella Larsen, the specific existential dilemmas of the mulatto heroine undermine this progressive quest. For all of these novelists the entwining of a sentimental plot (the heroine's search for romantic or erotic fulfilment) with a vocational plot (what will she do with her life?) provides a basic narrative grid.

Ann Petry's *The Street* (1946) is important for its place in this genealogy. Her characterology, her analysis of human agency and motivation, derives largely from an earlier tradition of naturalist fiction (itself stretching from Theodore Dreiser to Richard Wright). Human autonomy, in the naturalist scheme, is qualified by environment, society, and inheritance. The individual's self-determinism is compromised by a host of constricting forces, many of them insurmountable but also unknowable until they manifest themselves with irrevocable logic. In an interview in *Crisis*, Petry confirmed this naturalism: 'In *The Street* my aim is to show how simply and easily the environment can change the course of a person's life.'[13] In *The Street* 'environment' is constituted by economic pressure, familial commitment and the failure of society to provide institutional ladders up from poverty. Petry's heroine, Lutie, has integrity and potential; but the forces opposing her are relentless and unstoppable. The title, 'The Street', stands for all those anonymous forces of urban corruption that face American blacks. Lutie tries repeatedly to raise herself and her son up from poverty, but her diligent attendance at evening school is undermined by the need to make money quickly; she begins singing in a nightclub, a job that brings her unwelcome and eventually threatening attention. *The Street* thus becomes a kind of 'anti-dream' fiction, a harsh denunciation of the US's constrictions and depredations. Petry's depiction of a sinister, tentacular, societal repression is grounded in a very specific and explicit account of the economic dilemmas that black women find themselves in:

> Yes. The women work and the kids go to reform school. Why do the women work? It's such a simple, reasonable reason. And just thinking about it will make your legs stop trembling like the legs of a winded, blown, spent horse.
>
> The women work because the white folks give them jobs – washing dishes and clothes and floors and windows. The women work because for years now the white folks haven't liked to give black men jobs that paid enough for them to support their families. And finally it gets to be too late for some of them. Even wars don't change it. The men get out of the habit of working and the houses are old and gloomy and the walls press in. And the men go off, move on, slip away, find new women. Find younger women.   (p. 278)

An early account of Petry's novel, by Robert Bone, attacked its lack of a broader vision of society and its fixation on the

African–American dilemma: 'The trouble with *The Street* is that it tries to make racial discrimination responsible for slums.'[14] But this, surely, is where the novel's power lies: in its re-envisaging of naturalism through a racial prism. *The Street* is a bridge between earlier forms of naturalism and a post-1960s fictional model, such as that found in Toni Morrison's work, where 'racial discrimination' would indeed be seen as entwined with economic oppression.

Petry's is also a robustly direct form of polemic writing which looks backwards to Charlotte Perkins Gilman's analysis of the domestic economy and forward to second-wave feminism's assault on the interlocking of sexual and economic oppression within the home. *The Street* is often read as a female answer to the black 'protest' fiction of Richard Wright: an angry urban realism depicting the vicissitudes of street life, thus calling for a radical transformation of society. But this polemic voice, with its concentration on the domestic oppression of women ('washing dishes and clothes and floors and windows') also establishes a continuum with earlier female writing. The didactic authorial voice looks back to Pauline Hopkins; the materialist account of the home economy looks back to Gilman; and the acidic accounts of the difficulties of black life look back to Larsen. Furthermore, Petry's bitter account of an awesome, relentless socio-economic determinism made *The Street* into another female jeremiad.

The Street interlocks somewhat paradoxical representations of human agency and environmental pressure. Lutie is characterised as a reflective, deeply ethical human being; faced with the corruption of allowing herself to be bought by men who could help her out of financial difficulty, Lutie steadfastly refuses. But the novel presents a society utterly devoid of systems to translate individual moral reflexiveness into broader, collective models of action. *The Street* depicts a radically atomised form of defiance rather than collective action. Lutie feels no solidarity with other African–Americans, except negatively – they are, at least, not white. The honourable heroine has no means to give her integrity a wider, socially sanctioned validity, even though Petry's narrative is constructed to demonstrate that Lutie will maintain her virtue. The resulting deadlock is broken by melodrama. Having positioned her heroine, armed with a scrupulous moral sensibility, in a social context where every choice threatens corruption, Petry finds closure through violence. Tempted repeatedly by the nightclub gangster, Boots, Lutie beats him to death. She then flees to Chicago, leaving her son with the grim future of reform school and inevitable destruction on the streets of New York. Even in her moment of flight, Lutie remains trapped. She traces a design on the window of the train, a 'series of circles that flowed into each other' (p. 312) – a rather clunky symbol of the interlocked systems of deprivation that have brought Lutie to this *dénouement*. The utter negativity of the conclusion is such that she imagines the reform school as a better future for her son than a life with her on the street.

The ending of *The Street* returns us to a conception of female sexuality that is almost Victorian in its melodrama: the defence of sexual integrity is so vital, so central to Ann Petry that she fashions an ending where her heroine preserves virtue at the expense of her son *and* becomes a murderess. *The Street* effectively ring-fences its heroine's sexuality. The pressures mount and mount on Lutie, as her financial dilemmas increase in complexity. Petry reiterates her attractiveness again and again. Yet, in spite of everything, the lady is not for turning into a sexual plaything, even if this means that she will become a murderer. An early reviewer of *The Street* sensed the intractability of the novel's closing sections. Writing in the *New Republic* in 1946, Bucklin Moon complained that after an exciting start he was 'suddenly dumped into a bog of hopelessness that made me, as a reader, flounder rather badly'. He complained that the latter sections of the book were 'banal and contrived', and that Petry had failed to fulfil her promise in the 'fight against racial intolerance and for the logical integration of the Negro into the American life stream'.[15] Petry, as Moon implies, fails to resolve her fiction in a progressive way. Having charted a constricting network of social and economic pressures, Petry can find no way out. Lutie can only resist 'the street', either stoically or through violence; her integrity is founded on dogged resistance. The 'hopelessness' sensed by a reader like Moon is, I think, created by the novel's inability to find a radical and trans-formational vision of what selfhood might be; the novel is at its most naturalistic in its sense of the self as embattled, determined, acted upon.

I can put this another way: *The Street* reads in retrospect like a novel awaiting the feminist theory of the 1960s. Feminism would make the connection between personal, sexual behaviour and an embracing politics of social transformation. In *The Street*, Lutie's sexuality remains a sanctuary, a retreat from the world; a later generation of women would seek to connect sexuality and society in a radical ideology. *The Street* identifies a dilemma – the Gordian knot of deprivation enveloping Lutie on account of her race and gender. It would be twenty years before a politics evolved to provide the unpicking of these threads.

Jane Bowles: Expatriate Satire

Jane Bowles's work was conditioned by expatriatism. Most of her adult life was spent in Tangier, where she lived with her husband, the writer and composer Paul Bowles. Exiled from America, she nonetheless returned to the middle-ground of American society in her one novel, *Two Serious Ladies* (1943), and a number of short stories and plays. *Two Serious Ladies* is a black comedy and a skewed novel of manners located in the bourgeois leisure class. Bowles's settings (a cocktail party, a vacation in Panama) look to the consumerist fictions of Fitzgerald or Hemingway's travel stories; but Bowles pushed the anxieties implicit in tales like *Tender is the Night* or 'Cat in the Rain' towards a surreal and sardonic direction. Bowles's work anticipates that of Sylvia Plath or Joyce Carol Oates; it takes the everyday terrain of feminised leisure (a dinner party, a holiday), and finds there a dark, disorientating comedy. Bowles's mordant satire also foreruns the female assaults on middle-class pieties which were a dominant motif of 1960s fiction. From *Two Serious Ladies* we can trace a genealogy down to Plath's *The Bell Jar*, Susan Sontag's *Death Kit* or Joyce Carol Oates's black comedies of suburbia: a lineage of fractured narratives about disturbed bourgeois life.

Bowles's stories posit a disorienting, comic proximity between the 'ordinary' world and a much more decadent and even phantasmagorically bizarre environment. Hysteria and comic madness break through and break up conventional reality. On a train, one of Bowles's two serious ladies (the title itself a wry gag at the expense of middle-class gravitas) is suddenly attacked. A woman

> gave Miss Goering a smart rap on the ankles. She was quite red in the face and Miss Goering decided that in spite of her solid bourgeois appearance she was really hysterical, but since she had met many women like this before, she decided not to be

surprised from now on at anything that the woman might do.[16]

Here, Bowles takes the over-familiar association between women and hysteria, accepts the cliché, but then turns this assumption on its head by using hysteria to present a skewed, alternative social reality: madness *is* our normality. Such disconcerting interventions are the stuff of Bowles's fiction; but they go beyond mere slapstick to touch on more troubling areas of behaviour. Certain writers – Gilman, Plath, Oates – have created first-person narratives which inhabit and embody the hysterical voice. Bowles's hysterical narratives pursue a different tack. She satirically assumes the ever-present, latent hysteria of 'normal' life.

Mrs Copperfield's sightseeing trip to Panama quickly degenerates into a series of encounters with prostitutes and other social marginalia. The comic pleasure of Bowles's work is that such meetings are negotiated with an equable decorum, as if it were perfectly normal for this married lady to be propositioned by a central American prostitute:

> 'Te-ta-ta-tee-ta-ta,' she said and tapped her heels for a few seconds. She took both Mrs. Copperfield's hands in her own and pulled her off the bed. 'Come on now, honey.' She hugged Mrs. Copperfield to her. 'You're awful little and very sweet. You *are* sweet, and maybe you are lonesome.' Mrs. Copperfield put her cheek on the woman's breast. The smell of the theatrical gauze reminded her of her first part in a school play. She smiled up at the Negress, looking as tender and as gentle as she was able.   (pp. 43–4)

Comedy becomes a means to accommodate madness and puncture the surface of 'normal' behaviour. Alongside their fairly obvious comic effect, such episodes suggest that the even-surfaced and even-tempered tenor of middle-class life rests alongside a realm of bizarre, surreal and even crazy behaviour that might constitute its 'true' reality. Bowles monitors unlikely details, creating an atmosphere of disconcerting incongruity. She runs together banal, everyday facts with wildly assertive authorial commentary: 'The girl had the bright eyes of an insatiable nymphomaniac. She wore a little watch in a black ribbon around her wrist' (p. 101).

The title, *Two Serious Ladies*, gestures towards a propriety and decorum which are endlessly subverted by Bowles's fondness for black jokes, random plotting (a slide from one weird gathering to another) and coded hints at her characters' polymorphous sexuality. *Two Serious Ladies* reads like a camp text, written in a code to appeal to the initiated reader while satisfying the naive reader with a patina of familiarity. Bowles's own bisexuality inevitably inflects our reading of moments like this: her fiction becomes teasingly double-voiced, speaking to both a heterosexual and homosexual readership. With its sudden, fleeting hints of sexual transgression, as when Mrs Copperfield is propositioned by the prostitute, the novel suggests that 'normality', if read correctly, would reveal itself as the very reverse of normality.

Her short stories are equally attuned to moments when normality dissolves into comedy and farce. In 'Plain Pleasures' an innocuous dinner engagement ends in a farrago of drunken recrimination. In 'A Guatemalan Idyll' an American tourist is bedded by a local woman, and then remarks that the experience was 'almost like death itself' (p. 340). In 'Camp Cataract' we glimpse a typical figure, marked by Bowles's interest in crazed gentility: 'Her fragile, spinsterish face wore a canny yet slightly hysterical expression' (p. 359). All three stories are about the middle-class behaving badly; all describe, with great comedy and satire, what might be called 'gracelessness under pressure'. Whereas the traveller of, say, a Hemingway story would exhibit a firm 'grace' as he encounters difficulty, Bowles's ordinary Americans collapse into a manic, graceless panic.

John Ashbery praised Bowles for the poetry of her prose, a poetry co-existing with awkwardness: 'Mrs. Bowles's seemingly casual, colloquial prose is a constant miracle; every line rings as true as a line of poetry, though there is certainly nothing "poetic" about it, except insofar as the awkwardness of our everyday attempts at communication is poetic.'[17] The mimetic immediacy of her dialogue contrasts, however, with the stiffness of her diegetic narrative. Here, Bowles's prose has the slight clunkiness and arthritic formality of translation. It is possible that for Bowles, fluent as she was in her exiled tongues of French, Spanish and Arabic, her native tongue came to be a foreign idiom. Bowles's sentences sometimes have a longwindedness and grammarian's exactitude that in a fussy way suggest comic prissiness. This is then combined with a form of deadpan irony, as bizarre or comic observations are steadily rendered in a flat manner:

> Miss Goering struggled up the hill entirely alone. She kept her eye on the wall of the last store on the main street. An advertising artist had painted in vivid pinks a baby's face of giant dimensions on half the surface of the wall, and in the remaining space a tremendous rubber nipple. Miss Goering wondered what Pig Snout's Hook was. She was rather disappointed when she arrived at the top of the hill to find that the main street was rather empty and dimly lighted. She had perhaps been misled by the brilliant colors of the advertisement of the baby's nipple and had half hoped that the entire town would be similarly garish.   (pp. 131–2)

In its shape and structure *Two Serious Ladies* has a great deal in common with works by other experimental female writers. Like the lesbian modernist, Gertrude Stein, or the folklorist, Zora Neale Hurston, Bowles contructs an inside/outside narrative whose discourse seems to be both within and without its culture. For Hurston, the placing of glossaries and other exegetical anthropological devices within her fiction indicates a certain distance from the reality being rendered. In Stein, an almost clichéd 'womanly' terrain of quotidian domesticity is shaped by an avant-garde syntax which acts to de-familiarise known environments. In both cases, a narrative 'frame' distances a known world. In Bowles's work it is comedy, and particularly a comic voice of ironic bathos, which transmogrify the over-familiar realities of the American middle class into surrealism.

Jean Stafford: *The Mountain Lion* and *A Mother in History*

The paradoxes and contradictions of Jean Stafford's career are bemusing and at times troubling. Increasingly given to intemperate attacks on the women's movement, her writing from the late 1940s through to the 1960s nonetheless traced a developing sense of gender as a cultural construction. A novel such as *The Mountain Lion* (1947) foresaw one of the central arguments of 1960s feminists: that as gendered beings we are made, and that the idea of 'woman' is constructed rather than a natural given or a biological fact. A later work, *A Mother in History* (1966), is equally important as a precursor to the political journalism of writers such as Joan Didion and Susan Sontag; it is a wry, oblique, female perspective on an iconically male event – the assassination of John F. Kenney by Lee Harvey Oswald. Searching for a key to this national trauma, Stafford looked aslant by interviewing not the major male participants but Oswald's mother. Her study adumbrated a form of feminist reportage, an investigation where politics would be seen as if in a mirror, and women not men would take centre-stage.

The *Mountain Lion*, like *The Ghostly Lover*, is a 1940s fiction of fractured adolescence. Stafford depicts the introspective, brooding youth of Molly, a preternaturally talented girl whose fictional sisters are Elizabeth Hardwick's Marian (*The Ghostly Lover*) and Sylvia Plath's Esther Greenwood (*The Bell Jar*). Stafford situates Molly's coming-of-age in a very specific cultural context. Molly and her brother Ralph grow up torn between the aspirational sophistication of their stepmother and the hardy, Western masculinity of their grandfather and uncle. The novel begins as a comedy of misjudgement, as the children try and fail to gauge what is the appropriate behaviour for each environment; it will end in tragedy, as the mythology of the American West, incarnated in the hunt for the mountain lion, leads to Molly's death. Stafford's novel is knowing about the ways that maternal and paternal genealogies, and two forms of America (the East Coast and the West), buffet these children. In particular, Stafford scrutinises the deforming impact a myth of the West has upon the young girl. The children arrive at their Uncle Claude's Colorado ranch, where 'The landscape itself was frightening' and where men live out resolutely masculine routines:

> The men were skillful, good-humored, hard, living within the present time and on a large scale. When they got drunk on a Saturday night, they did so with abandon, behaving exactly as drunk people in the movies did. Their lawlessness seemed natural. It seemed altogether reasonable that they hunted at all times except during the open season when, as Uncle Claude said, 'there was too much danger of getting shot at by them dudes from Denver.'   (p. 97)

It is into this world of almost-mythological masculinity that Molly is initiated; and its casual violence is finally her undoing, as she is mistakenly shot by Ralph when he hunts the mountain lion. The frontier masculinity of Uncle Claude's world appropriates Ralph, and then destroys Molly. As Susan Rosowski notes, 'In *The Mountain Lion* Jean Stafford uses her pen as a divining rod to reveal sources of the psychosexual violence so thinly veiled in formula western fiction.'[18]

Formalistically and tonally, *The Mountain Lion* stands as a good example of what I term dysfunctional realism. It is a crisply lucid and witty study in familial disintegration. The narrative is tightly focused; the Fawcett family occupy centre-stage. Stafford's paragraphs map out a forensically observed, mordant comedy of manners. At the same time, the emotional palette of *The Mountain Lion* is darker, and more disturbing, than my sketch would suggest. The central relationship between Molly and Ralph recalls a theme drawn from Victorian sentimentalism (the close companionship of a brother and sister, as in *The Mill on the Floss*), but Stafford colours their bond as one of suffocating affection and even latent incest, giving way to rivalry. This is a novel about maturation where oncoming adulthood is mapped in terms of foreboding and an almost Gothic intensity. At the moment when he leaves childhood, Ralph reflects on 'his own black, sinful mind', and then he says to his sister, ' "Molly, tell me all the dirty words you know" ' (p. 158).

Stafford's novel deploys the symbolic mode seen in Katherine Anne Porter's 'Flowering Judas': an overt, foregrounded symbolism is used to explore gender politics. Just as the flowering Judas tree indicates the attractions and deceptions of revolutionary politics for a young woman, so Stafford uses the lion as metaphor for the destruction of femininity by a stylised masculine violence. These mid-century fictions are solidly embedded in a fictional discourse where the author looks to such symbols to focus a narrative. The female symbolists developed a narratology which formed a counterpart, a womanly response, to the theories of symbolism explored by male literary critics during the late 1940s and 1950s. Charles Feidelson, in *Symbolism and American Literature* (1953), argued that the writers of the American renaissance (Poe, Emerson, Hawthorne, Melville) constituted an inaugural school of symbolists. Emphasising literary structure, Feidelson contended that these writers created self-reflexive literary artefacts. As later commentators have shown, Feidelson, like many of the 'New Critics', emphasised literary texture and linguistic autonomy at the expense of the political and cultural processes informing a novel or poem.[19] But what evolved in female symbolism was a figurative language used to turn literature back towards such an engagement. While symbolism is sometimes seen as a retreat from the hard facts of politics into a closed literary formalism, for many women writers the symbolic mode provides a discourse for political engagement. Eudora Welty's Confederate mirror in 'A Burning'; the slain baby in Toni Morrison's *Beloved*; Porter's Judas tree; Stafford's mountain lion: in all these instances the complexities of American political history are condensed and then encoded in a figurative, symbolic language. Formalistically, these images act to unify and centre these narratives, providing a structural leitmotif; but they also act as ideological hooks, attaching tales of often great obliquity to the actualities of history.

Novels and films about the assassination of John F. Kennedy have now become the centre of a small fictional and journalistic industry; but in *A Mother in History* (1966) Jean Stafford created an early, female perspective on this iconic event. Stafford went to see the mother of Lee Harvey Oswald, Kennedy's assassin (himself later assassinated by Jack Ruby); she sought the meaning of this event not in male accounts but in conversations with a woman who had found herself serendipitously 'in history'. Stafford's lapidary, ironic account is a witty and conspicuously open-ended womanly perspective on what might be seen as the central male drama of the American century: a woman talks to a mother about her son's execution of the icon, J.F.K. And yet the overall tone is quizzical, wry and understated; the feminisation of this male drama rests in a refusal to engage with the heady drama and portentous signifying that had already begun to gather around the shooting. Stafford hazards no decisive comments on the riddle of the assassination. Even the rather grandiose title becomes a kind of bathetic joke: there is little comment on 'history', and Mrs Oswald's position as a mother is imagined in resolutely ordinary terms from the opening sentence: 'In a tidy, unexceptional little house, on an unexceptional block of similar houses (they were seedy, but they were not squalid . . .).' *A Mother in History* can be read as a work of foregrounded triviality, rather like Stein's *Autobiography of Alice B. Toklas*. The great and notorious men of history or art (Picasso, Gris; Oswald, Kennedy) are placed in flattened vignettes, as the woman writer creates an understated alternative history. The text works by indirection; Mrs Oswald foregrounds her status as a typical mother, endlessly saying things like 'This is motherhood', but the more she claims her typicality the stranger motherhood becomes as a concept.[20] Indeed, the book concludes with a visit to Lee's graveside – on Mother's Day. What does it mean to display one's maternal virtues, asks Stafford, if one's son is an assassin?[21] At such moments, Stafford's work presciently maps out terrain later explored by Joyce Carol Oates and Toni Morrison: a female re-visioning of the mythology of violence in America.

Elizabeth Hardwick: 'Short-Wave Autobiography'

A common fictional code underpins the work of Jean Stafford, Jane Bowles and Elizabeth Hardwick. All three writers are realists whose work is ultimately rooted in a close observation of manners; they monitor the ebb-and-flow of the (largely middle-class) social scene with an attentiveness that would have appealed to Henry James. But in all three writers we see a tugging and stretching at the limits of realism: in Bowles's surreal, madcap scenarios; in Stafford's willingness to interlard her realism with symbolism; and in Hardwick's fractured domestic realism (*The Ghostly Lover*) or her meshing of historical record with a slanted, confessional first-person voice (*Sleepless Nights*).

Elizabeth Hardwick has published two novels: *The Ghostly Lover* (1945) and *Sleepless Nights* (1979). She is well known as a critic, and was instrumental in the foundation of the *New York Review of Books* in the 1960s. As with other women (Caroline Gordon or Katherine Anne Porter), the lacunae in Hardwick's career, and the willingness to work across literary forms, have perhaps hindered valuation of her *oeuvre*. But both of her novels are important works. Hardwick's specific contribution to postwar writing has been a crafted, poetic realism which understatedly engages with questions of great concern to commentators on women's lives. *The Ghostly Lover*, for instance, is a novel about the sentimental education of a young woman; it anticipates by twenty years Sylvia Plath's life of a fragile, talented female subject in *The Bell Jar*. Meanwhile, *Sleepless Nights* is a strikingly refracted account of the relationship between 'real life' and writing, between private and public utterance.

The Ghostly Lover on first reading seems to be written in an overly familiar discourse. Attentive to the textures of social life, set in a politely affluent world, and constructed through restrained and crisp sentences, this is a story of middle-class youth and early womanhood. *The Ghostly Lover* traces the evolving selfhood of Marian, the daughter of eccentric parents; the second part of the novel deals with her first steps towards independence. The ghostly lover of the title is an elusive figure, Bruce, for whom Marian has a shadowy passion (he also pays for her college bills). There is a pervasive sense of unease to the domestic settings; a strand of discomforting, surreal imagery disorders the easy flow of homely information. On the street Marian sees a frozen dog: 'The head of the dog had been smashed and the matted hair of his body was stuck to the pavement' (p. 160). The tight nuclear family is not all it appears; the parents drift away on their own inscrutable and self-indulgent trips. Family is becoming a nexus for discomfort and pained awkwardness. In particular, the usual patterns of women's domestic lives are becoming unstitched: 'In the fragments of her mother's life the future was before her: marriage and motherhood, the intermediate laziness and the early shadow of the precarious tight-rope walk of old age' (pp. 7–8). *The Ghostly Lover* has what I think is a presciently acute sense of gender as a social determinant; it is studded with sentences which one might imagine, out of context, to come from a much later novel. Of a comment by Bruce (the 'ghostly lover'), Hardwick writes: 'He seemed to say, This is what it means for me to be male and you female' (p. 13).

Alongside this foregrounded sense of gendered identity, Hardwick positions a trenchant diagnosis of middle-class female life. First, this is a novel about the youthful female self; it is a novel of maturation and education, and establishes young adulthood as a time of troubling, if fascinating, disturbance. Marian is a young Southern woman (the novel is set in Kentucky), but Hardwick turns the saccharine romanticism associated with stories of the Southern belle towards a knotted psychological complexity. Moreover, as the story unfolds and Marian attends college, Hardwick touches in coded fashion on the sexual politics of the 1940s. Marian attends college, and is paid for by her male bene-factor; but this arrangement does not result in marriage, even if the initial scenario suggests that she will be 'bought'. At this time, as the historian Rosalind Rosenberg points out, two out of three women who entered college dropped out before graduating;

most were married to fellow-students; and higher education was in effect an arena for courtship.[22] Read within this context, Marian's abjuration of marriage and her maintenance of independence (however fragile) take on a proto-feminist significance. For a fictional heroine to attend college, especially with the support of a male benefactor, and *not* to wed at the end of a 1940s novel would have struck early readers as a departure from the usual plot.

Second, Hardwick's bourgeois characters (rather like those of Jane Bowles) are sharply aware of society's falsities; everyday life is imagined as a tissue of insincerity and superficiality. A typical comment on Marian and Lucy: 'But the impenetrable insincerity, as automatic and instinctual as closing the eyelid against dust, threw its weight between them. Even if they might have spoken to each other, there were no words to work with' (p. 95). This comment forms part of an extended reflection on what is called elsewhere the 'papier-mâché reproductions of emotion, constructed only for the occasion but remarkably powerful for all their falseness' (p. 140). The young woman's response to this pervasively unreal society pre-figures the revolt into an often-jarring self-expressiveness that became a hallmark of the 1960s counter-culture: 'She wanted to break though the sighs, the secrecies, the niceties, break through into a coarse, shouting, foul-mouthed world' (p. 35).

Marian's individualised rebellion foreshadowed Hardwick's essays on sexual politics; Hardwick has been more interested in the personal act of revolt than a programme of collective radicalism. Her sexual politics are marked by scepticism and a suspicion of totalising ideology; she is very much the *Partisan Review* liberal, occupying the 'vital center' identified by Arthur Schlesinger and other liberal thinkers. In an interview from 1985 she also gave a quintessentially tentative response when asked about being a woman writer:

> *Interviewer*: Do you think there are special difficulties in being a woman writer?
> *Hardwick*: Woman writer? A bit of a crunch trying to get those two words together . . .[23]

Her review of Simone de Beauvoir's *The Second Sex* (collected in the 1964 volume *A View of My Own*) is as alert to nuances of languages as it is to the political stance of this feminist classic. Hardwick praises her prose's 'nervous, fluent, rare aliveness'.[24] But she also resists de Beauvoir's generalisations and distances herself from the French woman's Utopianism:

> Naturally, it is clear many women do not fit this theory and those who may be said to do so would not describe it in the words of Simone de Beauvoir ... *The Second Sex* is so briskly Utopian it fills one with a kind of shame and sadness, like coming upon old manifestos and committee programs in the attic.[25]

The ironic scepticism about radical leftism, coupled with a stress on individual experience, stake out Hardwick's liberal middle way. She was more comfortable with the radicalism of her fellow-American Mary McCarthy. In an essay of 1961 she compared McCarthy to the nineteenth-century Transcendentalist Margaret Fuller, and praised these women's antinomian independence:

> Both women have will power, confidence and a subversive soul sustained by exceptional energy. A career of candor and dissent is not an easy one for a woman; the license is jarring and the dare often forbidding.[26]

Hardwick's admiration for the individual dissenter, the candid female radical, is embodied in her two novels; each traces a radicalism rooted in the individual's experience. *The Ghostly Lover* (1945) and *Sleepless Nights* (1979), separated by three decades and the feminist movement of the 1960s, pursue very different narratologies but share a focus on individuated experience. In each work the individual female self is foregrounded, and 'society' is represented as the tight knot of family (*The Ghostly Lover*) or a circle of lovers and friends (*Sleepless Nights*).

Sleepless Nights is an elliptical, elusive and allusive text that hovers between fiction and veiled autobiography. The narrator, like the author, is named Elizabeth, but the relationship between author and narrating voice remains opaque. A first-person narrative studded with details which might well be references to the actual experiences of Hardwick, *Sleepless Nights* maps an interzone between the authentic and fictional (just as the title suggests a tormentingly interim space between sleep and waking). Some of the splintered anecdotes of *Sleepless Nights* have the confessional release of a first-person autobiographical account. A sexual life is glimpsed in fleeting references to lovers and to an abortion: 'I have left out my abortion, left out running from the pale, frightened doctors and their sallow, furious wives in the grimy, curtained offices on West End Avenue.'[27] The admission of omission is typical of the narrative strategy of *Sleepless Nights*: a half-candid text, Hardwick's book is revelatory on its own terms, and creates a zig-zagging, meandering confessional mode. It reveals, half-reveals and conceals the inner life: simultaneously.

But the absence of an authorised life story means that the status of these anecdotes remains elusive: how 'true' are they, and do they add up to autobiographical testimony? The conversational lilt of Hardwick's prose presents another problem, seeming to present a foregrounded voice (a presence) while suggesting, in its drift and incompletion, a riddling conversation. 'Real life' is a matter of hints and whispers, of incomplete and enigmatic semi-narratives. My commentary perhaps makes *Sleepless Nights* sound like a modernist text, and indeed its narrative indirection would have been recognised by Gertrude Stein or Djuna Barnes: ellipsis, disrupted chronology, an elusive first-person voice. Hardwick folds this experimentalism together with older and more traditional narrative forms. Parts of *Sleepless Nights* are in the form of letters; elsewhere Hardwick deploys a journal of intimacy which records the conversations of her friends and lovers. Above all, the novel proffers a displaced and indeterminate diary. Genealogically, then, Hardwick's text derives from a point-of-origin in the free-wheeling experiments of Alice James's *Diary* (a similarly multifaceted and poly-generic form of the diary).

Diaries offer to their readers the seductive and potentially transgressive thrill of revelation. Even the most austere of readers cannot help but anticipate (and desire?) telling confession. If *Sleepless Nights* has a central, unifying motif, it lies here: in Hardwick's scrupulous tacking between revelation and suppression. The book's chronology is a private, introverted one (the 'sleepless nights' of the title, with their ambivalent suggestions of insomniac neurasthenia and erotic compulsion); only occasionally do we come across a detailed date or time. 'It is a Friday night, October 1973' (p. 60). Such references are occasionally granted as means for the reader to position herself, but the emphasis on private chronologies seems to be part of a project to allow 'Elizabeth' her own autonomous narrative space. The randomness and apparently inchoate shape allow Hardwick room to control and give form to private female experience. Tonally, too, Hardwick achieves a voice of steady, composed, equable confession; the woman asserting her right to speak of herself in her own way:

> I slept with Alex three times and remember each one perfectly. In all three he was agreeably intimidating, and intimidating in three ways . . . I was honored when he allowed me to go to bed with him and dishonored when I felt my imaginative, anxious, exhausting efforts were not what he wanted. His handsomeness created anxiety in me; his snobbery was detailed and full of quirks, like that of people living in provincial capitals, or foreigners living in Florence or Cairo.   (p. 65; my ellipsis)

Such passages weave together a tone of forthright, brazen confession (the emphasis on how she 'perfectly' remembers these couplings) with an elegant, mandarin wisdom (the comparison that links Alex with 'foreigners living in Florence or Cairo'). The assumed posture of the narrating voice is finely balanced between confessional authenticity and a wry, almost dandyish formality.

What is the difference between a necessary privacy and an indulgent solipsism? The circumstances surrounding the writing of *Sleepless Nights* had raised this question in a dramatic way. Hardwick first revealed work-in-progress from *Sleepless Nights* in 1973, at a time when her former husband, the poet Robert Lowell, was publishing volumes of poetry (*History, For Lizzie and Harriet, The Dolphin*) which used phrases from Hardwick's private correspondence with him. Lowell, Hazel Rowley has argued, appropriated Hardwick's private words; he shifted private experience into the public realm. After studying the drafts of his poetry, Rowley has confirmed that Lowell changed phrases attributed to Hardwick but still presented them in quotation. This might be seen as a 'colonization of her voice'. *Sleepless Nights*, then, works as commentary on Lowell's appropriation of his ex-wife's experiences and writings. It pursues a strategy of oblique revelation as a response to the brutalising candour of Lowell's own work. As Hardwick herself said in a commentary on the material that became *Sleepless Nights*, hers is 'a sort of short-wave autobiography, one that fades in and out'. And the fading out, the silences and gaps in the narrative, are as important as the explicit revelations because they suggest that the autobiographical act is as important for what it does not tell as for what it states explicitly.[28]

What unites all the novelists in this chapter is an intense attentiveness to the dysfuntions (economic, emotional, familial) of everyday life. In a novel such as *The Mountain Lion* or *The Ghostly Lover* or *The Street*, the family is the site of unease, disillusion and even incipient alienation (the youthful subjects of these novels do not really feel themselves to be part of their family). The narrow focus of these realists – their concentration on a handful of characters, often alone or set against a small, disintegrating family – marks a turn away from the more encompassing social realism of the 1930s. Compared to the work of Agnes Smedley, say, this fictional discourse might seem tremendously limited, as the novelist seems to abdicate responsibility for the representation of her culture in a broad sense. Yet the dysfunctional realists can be seen, with hindsight, to have constructed fictions which proleptically anticipate second-wave feminism's cultural agenda. Dysfunctional realism foreshadows a culture where the satisfaction, and dissatisfaction, of the individual self will become politicised. The tensions of family life, the narrowed social construction of womanhood, the attractions and disappointments of education, the superficiality of bourgeois life, the economic cost of sexual integrity: all these motifs can be found in the writing of 1960s polemicists, but all were adumbrated in fictions written by women who began their careers in the 1940s.

7

'What's Happening in America'

Sylvia Plath, Susan Sontag, Joyce Carol Oates

For feminists in the 1960s, to address 'reality' was to engage in revolutionary and revisionist acts of storytelling. The pioneers of second-wave feminism suggested that basic womanly narratives had been obscured; their revolutionary polemics were acts of storytelling and recoveries of undocumented reality. Thus Betty Friedan's *The Feminine Mystique* (1963) unleashed a powerful political energy through its collation of anecdotage, personal memoir and interview. The book originated in a questionnaire Friedan sent to her fellow-graduates in 1957 about education and women's role in society. The finished volume was structured around the freed voices of women, speaking out from the margins to place their angst at the centre of the culture. *The Feminine Mystique* achieved its vital impetus in moments of confession and collective recognition:

> But on an April morning in 1959, I heard a mother of four, having coffee with four other mothers in a suburban development fifteen miles from New York, say in a tone of quiet desperation, 'the problem.' And the others knew, without words, that she was not talking about a problem with her husband, or her children, or her home. Suddenly they realized they all shared the same problem, the problem that has no name. They began, hesitantly, to talk about it. Later, after they had picked up their children at nursery school and taken them home to nap, two of the women cried, in sheer relief, just to know they were not alone.[1]

The form of *The Feminine Mystique* is a *bricolage* of stories rather than a conventional academic argument (with its linear argumentation and appeal to objective facts). Academic conventionalities, indeed, were increasingly seen by feminists as synonymous with patriarchal narrowness, and the personal testimony gained the imprimatur of authentic experience. These forms of personalised, overtly subjective, narrativised argument had a particular force in the United States where, commentators have often claimed, a confessional culture privileged the individual's utterance of her own experience above other forms of authority: 'To live for the moment is the prevailing passion – to live for yourself, not for your predecessors or posterity', wrote Christopher Lasch in 1978.[2] Lasch attacked the 'culture of narcissism', but for feminists storytelling about oneself acted to foster community. Storytelling forged a collectivism where before there had been isolated, silent individuals. Friedan's intertwining of the narrative impulse with a sense of community reminds us of earlier moments in American women's culture (for instance, Zora Neale Hurston's creation of community by folktale and vernacular energy in *Their Eyes Were Watching God*); it also points to an explicitly *politicised* notion of storytelling that has emerged in the past thirty years: the belief that to tell a story might be to effect social change. As the editors of *Radical Feminism* (1973) argued, in a theory of 'Consciousness Raising' based upon sharing experiences through the telling of life stories: 'personal experiences, when shared . . . are political, not personal, questions'.[3]

The 1960s are synonymous with literary radicalism and experimentalism, and especially with a revolt against narrowly prescriptive realism. America's male writers pursued forms of anti-realism, post-realism, the fabular and the fantastic. Donald Barthelme, John Barth, Leonard Michaels, Robert Coover, John Hawkes, Thomas Pynchon and Walter Abish shared an assumption that conventional literary realism had run out of steam. John Barth coined the phrase, the 'literature of exhaustion', to explain the school of writing left after the major aesthetic work of literary realism had been done; the future of writing now had to be experimental and broadly anti-realistic.[4] For a polemicist such as Friedan, however, the transcription of stories from the 'reality' of modern America remained a powerful, indeed revolutionary, act. The urge to tell stories assumes urgency and political pointedness if the tales are untold. Even straightforward domestic tales take on the air of anthropological field research, acquiring the didactic force of 'news from the front'. Familiar storylines and settings – home, family, courtship, marriage – gained an explicit political significance in the 1960s as polemicists and activists told stories about the marginalised reality of American women's lives.

Realism, the telling of stories from 'real life', was felt to be necessary because the actualities of women's lives had been over-looked. Feminists saw one of their tasks as the voicing of narra-tives produced by what has become known as the 'domestic ideology' of the late 1940s, 1950s and the early 1960s. This was a period of idealisation of the family; of marriage at an early age; of women's return to the home after the working years during wartime; of the staggering baby boom which stretched through to the mid-1960s. Meanwhile, men moved out into a surging econ-omy characterised by modern corporations, technology and suburbia. A vast cultural apparatus – of movies, magazines, adver-tisements – emphasised the centrality of the home, and the centrality of women within the home. Anxieties about the Cold War, it is sometimes argued, served to heighten the attractions of the hearthside as an idealised site of security in a threatening world. It was a time, in Elaine Tyler May's words, of 'Cold War – Warm Hearth'.[5]

Betty Friedan presented the feminist as a storyteller who would give voice to the unknown narratives of this apparently satisfied world. In the major female fiction of the era we see an analogous project: to re-present and re-create female realities and, as a corollary, to re-structure the codes of realism as a genre. The experimentalism of a Sontag, Plath or Oates is not 'anti-realist'; nor, however, is realism inhabited or merely received as a form. From 1963 onwards, when Plath's *The Bell Jar* was published in Britain, literary realism was re-formulated and re-configured by America's women in a moment of deconstruction and revisionism that bears comparison with the 'moment' of the 1890s when local color realism and sentimental fiction underwent an analogous process of rapid, heady re-writing. Plath, Oates and Sontag all wrote fictions engaged with the 'domestic ideology' of the 1950s and early 1960s; all placed the typecast motifs of that ideology (idealised marriage, suburban conformity, the 'junior executive' male) into dizzying, shifting fictions. Oates's 'How I Contemplated the World from the Detroit House of Correction and Began Life Over Again', Plath's *The Bell Jar*, Sontag's *Death Kit* – in all three works we see the normalities of the 1950s home and its steady routines subject to satirical, surreal and vertiginous representation. Toni Morrison's first novel, *The Bluest Eye* (1970), also emerged from this cultural context (it begins with an hallucinatory, child's-eye invocation of the home). All these writers work both within and outside the perimeters of 'realism'. Home, marriage, husband: the constituent elements of familiar terrain are here, but the narratives play with these certitudes, through the 'mad' language of *The Bell Jar*, the giddy turns of perspective in Oates's short story, or the dream-visions of *Death Kit*. Just as the late 1890s saw a discursive *bouleversement* (Victorian domesticity and domestic realism changed utterly by Gilman and Chopin), so the 1960s female avant-garde sought, through stylistic and formal experiment, to extend Friedan's methodology by alerting the reader not only to the reality of the feminine mystique but also to the *construction* of that reality.

Neither 'realist' nor 'anti-realist', these works sit on the margin of genres. In places they offer a mimetic representation of contemporary America; but they also tug at generic convention, subverting the frameworks through which that reality is apprehended. A novel such as *The Bell Jar* or *Death Kit* presents its realism in inverted commas, as it were: the reader is alerted to the framing of the narrative (each story is the record of an abnormal consciousness). They present a form of *inflected* realism, a realism marked by lacunae or mixed with the anti-realism of dream or fantasy.

Recent feminist theory has, however, been impatient with realism, preferring a postmodernist model of representation. Postmodernism unsettles a sense of unitary self; it disturbs reified meaning; it is impatient with realism's claims to mimesis. Postmodernism seems to offer a radical and transformational aesthetic to women.[6] In works such as *Death Kit* we catch a taste of this postmodern feminism in a desire to unsettle 'self', 'the real', 'mimesis'. But at the same time, Sontag, Plath and Oates remain trenchantly committed to another principle of realism: a faith in stories and narrative. As with Friedan's tales from the home, a story is felt to contain revealed truth; and the storyteller's art continues to have a transformational, political significance. For these writers, storytelling maintains the radical power described by the Marxist critic, Walter Benjamin, in his essay 'The Storyteller' (1936). Benjamin praised the practicality of storytelling, its ability to contain something useful (a point that would have been understood by Friedan and the editors of *Radical Feminism*). He also contrasted 'information', which is explained to us (is, indeed, 'shot through with explanation'), with 'the story', which leaves the reader to 'interpret things the way he understands them': 'thus the narrative achieves an amplitude that information lacks'. And the storyteller, seen by Benjamin as the fount of a radical and orally based art, draws directly and unashamedly on personal experience:

> Seen in this way, the storyteller joins the ranks of the teachers and sages. He has counsel – not for a few situations, as the proverb does, but for many, like the sage. For it is granted to him to reach back to a whole lifetime (a life, incidentally, that comprises not only his own experience but no little of the experience of others; what the storyteller knows from hearsay is added to his own). His gift is the ability to relate his life; his distinction, to be able to tell his entire life.[7]

For the novelists in this chapter the telling of a story was similarly embedded in the personal. The storyteller, if not telling a directly autobiographical tale, was nonetheless constructing tales of representative lives which had a general, communal and sometimes didactic significance.

Sylvia Plath: the Female Jeremiad of the 1960s

Sylvia Plath's *The Bell Jar* (1963) was published under a pseudonym shortly before her suicide; it is nearly impossible not to read the book as a *roman à clef* reflecting the experiences behind that tragedy. Esther Greenwood, a bright student from an elite women's college, has won a journalism contest; the prize, a trip to New York, takes her into the world of blandly consumerist women's magazines. Poised between studenthood and adult life, Esther is baffled and frightened by the divisive paths offered her; intellectual gifts lead only towards a staid, altogether traditional career as housewife and mother. Gradually, the narrative shifts from social satire towards a dream-like account of Esther's breakdown. The reader realises that Esther's heightened, ultrasensitive responses are as much a signal of encroaching illness as of precocity. Hospitalised, she descends downwards into electro-convulsive therapy, ludicrous sessions of analysis and, in conclusion, fragile renewal.[8]

The Bell Jar was one of the most important women's novels of the 1960s, and deserves its iconic status for three reasons. First, it can be read as an intertextual work which radically updates the narrative of confinement and hysteria inaugurated by Charlotte Perkins Gilman in 'The Yellow Wallpaper'; Plath's novel is one of the 'hysterical' tales that have featured so strongly in US women's narrative. But it also foreshadows a very particular fascination, nurtured in the counterculture of the late 1950s and 1960s, with marginality, madness and the paradoxical lucidity of those condemned as insane. The Bell Jar rests alongside Ken Kesey's One Flew Over the Cuckoo's Nest (1962) and classic radical studies of the societal oppression of the 'mad' such as R. D. Laing's The Divided Self (1965). It is worth noting that the first American edition of The Bell Jar claimed in its cover notes the authority of actual experience for Plath's book; the account of breakdown was 'completely real and even rational'.[9] Second, Plath establishes a hip, funny, slangy first-person voice, appropriating the heightened first-person voice of American fiction from Huckleberry Finn through to Holden Caulfield in J. D. Salinger's The Catcher in the Rye. Esther is a sister to Holden: brilliant, witty, disintegrating.

Third, and most significantly, Plath's novel crystallised a cultural moment in the early 1960s: the revelation of the 1950s domestic ideology as a 'false consciousness' that oppressed women psychologically even as it proffered a cornucopia of consumer goodies within the shrine of suburban homelife. The Bell Jar was published in the same year as The Feminine Mystique. Friedan's polemic witheringly lambasted the entrapment and nullity of suburban domestic life. Her vignettes of bourgeois desperation, emotional desolation and affluent anxiety are hauntingly congruent with Esther Greenwood's world. Friedan summed up the nightmare as 'Progressive Dehumanization: The Comfortable Concentration Camp'.

What must it have been like to read Friedan's work alongside its echoing fictional counterpart? Unfortunately, Plath's book was only published in Britain in 1963, and the American edition had to wait for eight years (the near-biographical references to people still alive had raised legal difficulties). British readers of Friedan and Plath might have recognised a common terrain in both works. Esther Greenwood, whose name is all too redolent of sentimental Victorian heroines, moves in a world hardly changed since the late nineteenth century: the women's college, home-making, a cult of marriage. She is awarded her literary prize by *Ladies Day*, a journal whose title echoes that of actual genteel publications such as *Ladies Home Journal*. The young prizewinners attend elaborately arranged meals, shrines to the feminine mystique; Plath, in her relentlessly satirical attack on the domes-tic ideology, turns food into debauchery, as Esther gorges on a still-life of rich delicacies. Faced with banquet tables laden with 'yellow-green avocado pear halves stuffed with crabmeat and mayonnaise, and platters of rare roast beef and cold chicken, and every so often a cut-glass bowl heaped with black caviar', Esther makes up her own sickening sandwiches.[10]

> Under cover of the clinking of water goblets and silverware and bone china, I paved my plate with chicken slices. Then I covered the chicken slices with caviar thickly as if I were spreading peanut-butter on a piece of bread. Then I picked up the chicken slices in my fingers one by one, rolled them so the caviar wouldn't ooze off and ate them.   (p. 28)

A ladylike fastidiousness sits alongside a vulgar gluttony: Esther picks up her food delicately, but only to satiate her raven-ous appetite. In its disturbing conflation of gentility and barbarism, this passage is typical of the novel's invocation and revocation of what is 'proper' behaviour for a woman. Plath's descriptions of intense corporeality are another means to examine the social construction of femininity; the sweating, wounded body of *The Bell Jar*, with its endless malfunctioning, rebukes the sanctification of woman. Plath's accounts of vomit, haemorrages and wounds (a relentless flow of dirt and fluids) still shock. Even Esther's treatment, to cure a complaint as intangible as depres-sion, is rooted with extreme crudeness in an electro-convulsive assault on the body.

The sheer physical immediacy of Esther's experience contrasts with her cerebral ambitions. She hopes to be a writer, but fails to get on a writing course. (That one needs to be taught to create, is another wry comment on the endlessly controlled and systema-tised world in which Esther lives.) Her mother proffers advice to take another course, in shorthand. Instead of her own creativity, Esther is encouraged towards a servile copying-out of male discourse. There is, intriguingly, a model of female authorship in the novel. Philomena Guinea has provided the money for Esther's scholarship. Her name echoes Virginia Woolf's collection of essays, *Three Guineas* (1938), locking *The Bell Jar* into an inter-textual field of other accounts of female creativity; but it also carries the blunt connotation of money. After all, it is scholarship money – the guinea – which makes Esther grateful to her bene-factor. Philomena's prose represents sentimentalism bleached of all meaning; it is a desiccated popular form as abhorrent to Esther as the shorthand course offered by the other woman in her life, her mother.

The masculine world grants Esther no outlet for her creativity; but models of female creativity are hardly exemplary, either. This is the entrapment symbolised in the novel's title, the bell jar Esther imagines descending upon her. The jars work somewhat mechanically as a symbol of Esther's problematic sexuality, but more intriguingly they hint at the aborted creativity of a woman whose writing is a mechanical reproduction of male discourse or a mining-out of clichéd female genres. Esther is excluded from the authority held by the men in the novel (authority repeatedly figured as scientific or medical knowledge); and the popular arts of the female novelist are utterly consumerised. The final bleak-nes of *The Bell Jar* lies here: in the discovery of a barren and evis-cerated female literary tradition.[11]

bell hooks, African–American feminist, complained that the model of oppression outlined by Friedan concentrated exclusively on white middle- and upper-class women. Ethnic and working-class women, hooks points out, have never had the privilege of even thinking about rewarding work; economic necessity propelled them into available jobs, heedless of such abstractions as 'job satisfac-tion'.[12] Plath's novel makes this very narrowness of social experi-ence into a strength. She deconstructs the straitened class basis of Friedan's book by sheer excess: *The Bell Jar* reveals the class-bias of middle-class feminism by turning Esther's narrative into solipsism. The introversion and self-obsession of Esther's tale can be read as a form of ironic exposé; Plath creates a first-person narrator who unwittingly reveals the solipsistic individualism of middle-class life. For Esther's problem is partly that class and upbringing mean that she has seen very little of the world. The 'bell jar' is also the confine-ment created by middle-class expectations, the ghetto of life struc-tured by the middle-class feminine mystique.

Yet in spite of all this topicality and specific social reference, *The Bell Jar* is in one way a familiar book. In its basic polemical configuration *The Bell Jar* is a jeremiad, a cry of complaint and warning against the current state of women's lives. The jeremiad is a recurrent mode for American women; it encompasses 'The Yellow Wallpaper', Nella Larsen's work, Sontag's *Death Kit*; Toni Morrison's *Beloved*. All of these works attack a particular social structure (Victorian marriage, post-emancipation black bourgeois life, slavery), not on the basis of broad or abstract ideological argument but through localised illustrations of how society has deformed intimacy between individuals. In Plath's work this jeremiad is directed against naively optimistic 1950s pop psychology, with its problem pages, sub-Freudian analysts' couches and naive faith in the talking cure; a harsher, technological psychiatry, Plath suggests, is the deep structure of the touchy-feely world. *The Bell Jar* suggests, in its resonant title, a world beyond intimacy; the self is cut off from contact with others, sealed off (a sense of claustrophobia, literal and metaphorical, is one of the novel's main motifs). How intimacy could be reconstituted, re-formed and revitalised became, in the aftermath of Plath's novel and the onset of the women's movement, one of the major questions facing the writers of the 1960s.

Susan Sontag: Voice, Ventriloquism, Silence

Susan Sontag (1933–) has forged a protean body of work: as a cultural and political essayist (*Illness as Metaphor*, *On Photography*); as novelist (*The Benefactor*, *Death Kit*, *The Volcano Lover*); and as dramatist (*Alice in Bed*). Her writing life is polymathic and restless; Sontag has followed Virginia Woolf to develop a writing that crosses borders, merges genres and deconstructs received literary conventions. Life and writing feed off one another, interweaving in ways that ceaselessly modify each polarity in this dualism: Sontag's bout of cancer inspired the essays in *Illness as Metaphor* (1978): biography as medical history and cultural criticism. This heterogeneity resists simple summary or totalising judgement; Sontag creates a female literary self continually displaced across a variety of discourses and topics. Although she describes herself as a feminist, Sontag is keen to emphasise individualism and personal autonomy above the claims of collective political action.

Asked in an interview, 'Do you think of yourself as a feminist?' Sontag replied: 'That's one of the few labels I'm content with. But even so . . . is it a noun? I doubt it.'[13] She has been a very political animal (campaigning against the Vietnam War in the 1960s and on behalf of Sarajevo during the recent Bosnian conflict), but her political engagement remains of her own devising and marks out a highly individualistic internationalism (Sontag's Europhilia turns her towards that continent as much as her homeland).

Her 1969 collection of essays, *Styles of Radical Will*, touched on two themes which animate much of her later work. In 'The Aesthetics of Silence' (1967), she called for a writing more responsive to the flexibility and non-linearity of human speech:

> If written language is singled out as the culprit, what will be sought is not so much the reduction as the metamorphosis of language into something looser, more intuitive, less organized and inflected, non-linear (in McLuhan's terminology) and – noticeably – more verbose. But, of course, it is just these qualities that characterize many of the great prose narratives of our time. Joyce, Stein, Gadda, Laura Riding, Beckett, and Burroughs employ a language whose norms and energies come from oral speech, with its circular repetitive movements and essentially first-person voice.[14]

Voice has been at the heart of Sontag's work: her own distinctive voice as an essayist; the assumption of different voices when she composes fiction ('But writing is impersonation');[15] the construction of an elaborate polyphony in *The Volcano Lover*. *The Benefactor* (1963) was written in the first-person voice of an elderly French man. The prose mimes a fastidious tone, and its locutions shape a speaking voice:

> If only I could explain to you how changed I am since those days! Changed yet still the same, but now I can view my old preoccupations with a calm eye. In the thirty years which have passed, the preoccupation has changed its form, become inverted so to speak. When it began, it grew in me and emptied me out. I ignored it at first, then admitted it to myself, then sought consolation from friends, then resigned myself to it, and finally learned to exploit it for my own wisdom. Now, instead of being inside me, my preoccupation is a house in

which I live; in which I live, more or less comfortably, roaming from room to room.[16]

The Benefactor and *Death Kit* (1967) are exercises in ventriloquism: a giving voice, within the syntactical constraints of written English, to the more random patterns of spoken language. In *Death Kit*, by extensive mining of the resources of free indirect discourse, and by configuring her narrative to the weird morphology of dreams and hallucinations, Sontag fashioned a remarkably non-linear storyline. And in both novels the female author uses the adoption of a first-person voice to enter the world of a male character.

Sontag's relationship to masculinity is intriguing. Although she declares her feminism, Sontag's essays often involve not the exploration of a womanly sphere but the identification of radical genealogies incorporating both men and women. In 'The Aesthetics of Silence' she adduces a range of examples from the avant-garde arts, scrupulously drawn across the gender line: Samuel Beckett and John Cage, but Gertrude Stein and Laura Riding too. The 'styles of radical will' mentioned in the title occupy a range of modalities, political and cultural; but they are never exclusively female and they are, these 'styles', self-consciously pluralist. This cultural pluralism is the second motif in Sontag's work. It entails her re-definition of male cultures from a woman's perspective, rather than the excavation of overlooked female traditions. Moreover, the centrality of *culture* to all that she does, means that even when writing about a more straightfor-wardly political subject, say the Vietnam War, Sontag tends to construct her arguments around cultural observation. 'Trip to Hanoi' (1968) grew out of an anti-war journey to the North Vietnamese capital, but it evolves into a meditation on the cultural differences between Asia and the Western order of things; political reportage mutates into a semiotic account of the signs of the foreign.

'What's Happening in America' (1966), a piece about the unfolding turmoil of the 1960s, also demonstrates her willingness to defend popular and folk culture; she has written on photography, rock and film, as well as cleaving to a high avant-garde tradition. Sontag has always sought to dissolve boundaries; impatience with static oppositions between high and low art-forms, between pleasure and seriousness is a constant. Her most famous essay, 'Notes on Camp' (1964), described the camp work of art as one where questions of 'seriousness' were open to a heady displacement: what was trashy might now acquire weight and significance, while overwhelmingly serious works of art mutate suddenly into campy excess. Sontag also said of *The Benefactor*, 'I thought I was telling a pleasurably sinister story that illustrated the fortune of certain heretical religious ideas that go by the name of Gnosticism'.[17] Her comment's combination of a populist aesthetic ('a pleasurably sinister story') and recondite reference ('Gnosticism') is a typical trespass across the border between low and high cultures. I would see these mappings as a continuation of American women's ongoing project to defend folk and popular art, and to weave those forms into elite culture. Sontag, like other women writers from Cather to Morrison, has sought to enrich the novel by attentiveness to vernacular and popular media. Whereas these earlier authors drew on folk-arts such as oral storytelling or quilt-making to provide inspiration for, and analogies to, their art, Sontag's interests lie in contemporary popular media: photography, film, rock. These forms are populist, 'lowbrow' to some: the woman writer continues to expand the stock of written modes by drawing on demotic forms.

Her 1967 novel *Death Kit* was in part an Americanisation of the European existential novel. As with the fiction of Sartre or Camus, the interiority of the self – its crises, compulsions, dreams – is placed at the centre of a tightly focused, cribbed and confined narrative. At the very end of the book the phantasmagoric and hallucinatory tale is revealed as the last delirium of 'Diddy', a middle-class junior executive who is passing away in his hospital bed after a suicidal overdose; the novel is literally his 'death kit', the last assemblages of consciousness. As Liam Kennedy has noted, this is a sustained exercise in the creation of 'interiority', the inward meditations of a consciousness *in extremis*; it is 'an extraordinary exacerbation of consciousness . . . a treatment of the prison-house of consciousness'.[18] The exploration of Diddy's consciousness involves a stretching and tearing of the reader's sense of what is or is not 'real'. This self-conscious puzzle of a novel, structured around strange journeys and happenstance encounters, upsets the causalities and linearities associated with 'realism'. Sontag re-draws the lineaments of verisimilitude. Given details of reality position the reader in a recognisable environment (New York, a train journey, a works conference); but jagged melodrama tests feasibility. At the start of the novel Diddy leaves a train, frustrated at its delay, and kills a workman on the track; at the end of the novel, as the narrative becomes more surreal, he seems to kill the victim again. Until one realises that this is an interiorised, delirious narrative, the connections between events remain fraught and their plausibility questionable. Most strikingly, Diddy conducts a long, erotic, sentimental relationship with a blind girl, an affair by turns touching, macabre and unbelievable. Generically, *Death Kit* sits alongside other 1960s fictions of disorientation: as in *The Bell Jar* or Joyce Carol Oates's work of this time, a quotidian reality is at once granted and knocked askew; a deranged narrative consciousness scrambles the fictional discourse.

Nevertheless, *Death Kit* is rooted in familiar terrain, the suburbia of commuter trains, business meetings and corporate life. Sontag's novel occupies the same middle-class, suburban space as John Updike's Rabbit novels, Joseph Heller's *Something Happened* or John Cheever's stories: the world of the man in the grey flannel suit, the archetypal junior executive. The protagonist, Diddy, works for a microscope firm; he incarnates the skilled, technological modernity of the 'American high' of the 1950s and 1960s. Sontag positions in this familiar territory (an encapsulation of J. K. Galbraith's 'affluent society') a masculine crisis. In fact, *Death Kit* might be read as a woman's appropriation of a typically male subject of this era: the psychic crisis of the American executive. As we saw in the previous chapter, this had become a favoured topic for sociologists keen to demonstrate the baleful impact of mass consumer society on the individual (a male subject in works such as Sloan Wilson's 1957 study, *The Man in the Gray Flannel Suit*). The disintegrating self of *Death Kit* is a more extreme instance of this crisis than anything imagined by a male writer. Diddy, the man in the grey flannel suit in terminal crisis, is a surreal and hyperbolical vision of the masculine agony diagnosed by the sociologists of the 1940s and 1950s. Sontag replaces the complacent age of affluence with an alternative, bourgeois dystopia. Diddy is 'a mild fellow, gently reared in a middle-sized city in Pennsylvania and expensively educated'. He is the 'sort of man it's hard to dislike, and whom disaster avoids'. But:

> Diddy, not really alive, had a life. Hardly the same. Some people are their lives. Others, like Diddy, merely inhabit their

lives. Like insecure tenants, never knowing exactly the extent
of their property or the lease will expire. Like unskilled cartog-
raphers, drawing and redrawing erroneous maps of an exotic
continent.[19]

The grim, black joke hidden in the novel, a joke only revealed
in the final pages, is that this sense of listless unease is even more
serious than we might have expected: Diddy is the 'organisation
man' who has become so ill-at-ease that psychic disintegration
has led him to suicide. In its tracing of bourgeois breakdown and
affluent anomie, *Death Kit* is a complementary novel to *The Bell Jar*
(both novels carry in their titles hints of the extinction that threatens their highly educated, supposedly 'fulfilled' protagonists).

Each of Sontag's novels is a sustained meditation on genre;
each radically re-embodies a specific novelistic mode. Whereas
Death Kit appropriates European existentialism to critique the
social construction of American masculinity, *The Volcano Lover*
(1992) politicises that most bland (and 'feminine') of genres, the
historical bodice-ripper. Sontag here paints a broad canvas, pictur-
ing Revolutionary-era Europe during the Napoleonic Wars, while
focusing her narrative on the romance between Emma, wife of Sir
William Hamilton, and Lord Nelson. As melodramatic epic and
grand narrative of love and war, the subject-matter could hardly
be bettered; the fate of nations, political upheavals and intimate
passions are all present in a novel repeatedly signalling parallels
with the world of grand opera. Generically, *The Volcano Lover* is a
historical romance, written to a formula that Cooper or
Hawthorne would have understood; it is grounded in actualities
but then imaginatively expands upon history to create a
fictional–historical space. *The Volcano Lover* is both fact and fiction,
history and romance. Sontag also deploys romance in a more
popular sense: a record of high emotion, especially sexual
passion. Her historical romance thus presents an oxymoronic
combination of political history (revolution, war) and a record of
intimacy or passion.[20]

Sontag's configuration of historical forces is dialectical, and
takes its structure from the opposition of progressives and reac-
tionaries at a moment of political transformation. She opposes the
Enlightenment's rationalism to Royalist reaction. *The Volcano Lover*
fashions a specific, late eighteenth-century world in order to cast
light on the era's paradoxical mixture of rationalism and cruelty.

Central episodes are set in Naples and Sicily in the aftermath of Napoleon's incursions across Europe. The central conflict is between on one side the liberals and Republicans, who try to set up their own radical city-state, and the reactionary Bourbon dynasty (aided by the British). Sontag records the terrible revenge exacted by the monarchists as they punish the radicals: 'Setting an example meant being merciless – the Cavaliere knew that'.[21] In these passages Nelson is repeatedly and ironically referred to as 'the hero', as Sontag carefully positions the Admiral in conjunction with the harsh punishments he orders.

There is a further dialectic incarnated in the very character of Sir William Hamilton. As connoisseur, antiquarian and scholar, he embodies Enlightenment values: a spirit of disinterested enquiry and scientific scepticism (Sontag repeatedly emphasises Hamilton's atheism). But his is a profoundly de-politicised intellectualism; Sontag represents Hamilton as a dilettante, a man whose scepticism has not evolved towards political free-thinking. When the Revolution unleashes its ferocious energies, Hamilton firmly renounces the political libertarians (even though he is sickened by their excessive punishment, too). He thus becomes a kind of composite or median figure, a representative man who enfolds in his leisured personality the intellectual advancement of the Enlightenment and the barbarism of the old order. He is a scientist but also a reactionary, a lover of Italy who rejects the nation's republican nationalists. He occupies the contested middle-ground of political progress, where advancement and reaction war with one another.

Given Sontag's leftist sympathies, and her early readings in Marxist theory (to which she ironically refers in 'Trip to Hanoi'), it seems likely that this representation is indebted to Georg Lukács's famous commentary on Sir Walter Scott's heroes. Lukács, working within a Marxist critical tradition, saw the historical novelist as a structural analyst of deep historical forces and a cartographer of class struggles. He read the *Waverley* novels as representations of a conflict between the outdated Highland clans and the Lowland Scots/English, a conflict between attractive antiquity and the unattractive but inevitably successful forces of progress. The hero, in Lukács's scheme, tends to sit in the middle of the historical dialectic, neither a reactionary nor a progressive. He is 'always a more or less mediocre, average English gentleman', and this average and middling representativeness embodies the *zeitgeist*. He possesses a 'certain moral fortitude and decency which even rises to a capacity for self-sacrifice, but which never grows into a sweeping human passion, is never the enraptured devotion to a great cause'.[22] Sontag represents Sir William Hamilton in just such a de-mythologised manner; he is the middling hero, a man sceptical about the 'great cause' of revolutionary politics in exactly the way Lukács describes.

Sontag, like Toni Morrison, has taken to heart the words of another European Marxist, Walter Benjamin. Benjamin's dictum that every record of civilisation is also a record of barbarism underpins both *Beloved* and *The Volcano Lover*, records of past civilisations that are essentially atrocity exhibitions. *The Volcano Lover*'s account of Lord Nelson, for instance, is trenchantly anti-heroic, recording his fiercely punitive reaction against the radicals, and his narcissistic dreams of his own heroism. As an exploration of British imperial cruelty, *The Volcano Lover* has parallels with earlier American attacks on Old World autocracy, notably Herman Melville's *Billy Budd* and Alice James's swipes in her *Diary*.

The Volcano Lover's prose is digressive, essayistic, polyphonic. The onward rush of historical melodrama, propelled by an urgent narrating voice, is diffused into a slower, reflective and multi-voiced narrative. In place of the compulsive, narrow questioning of popular fiction ('what happens next?') Sontag expands her paragraphs into ruminative philosophical queries:

> The human imagination has always been entertained by the fantasy of biological misalliances, and by the reality of bodies that don't look as bodies are supposed to look, which can endure ordeals bodies are not supposed to be able to endure. Painters loved to invent such creatures when they had the pretext. Circuses and fairs display them: freaks, mutants, odd couples, animals doing stunts that violate their nature. The Cavaliere may not have been familiar with Bosch and Bruegel on the subject of hell or the torments of Saint Anthony, but he had seen somewhat less inspired depictions of those anatomical assemblages called demons or monsters. Were it only a question of these freakish beings in every corner, the contents of the prince's lair would not have been so original. Even more astonishing was the profusion of whimsical, threatening – no, freakish – objects.   (p. 247)

The voice is relaxed, expansive, speculative, fond of synoptic analyses; it is, in other words, the voice of the essayist. Tonally, the register here is not unlike that of Sontag's own essays; but it also reminds us of the digressive and discursive asides of eighteenth-century philosophical fiction (Voltaire, Diderot, Sterne). Sontag thus tries to answer the question of how we voice historical fiction by pitching her narrative in a rhetoric both antiquated and modern.

Although most of the novel is conducted in the third-person (Sontag's essayistic voice), she shifts towards a polyphonic model as the book progresses. She concludes with a collage of first-person monologues or voices, as if deploying operatic arias (Sontag has noted that 'Opera is one of the inspirations of *The Volcano Lover*').[23] The novel closes with the voice of Eleonara Fonseca, a revolutionary poet executed by the monarchists. Her paragraphs are a powerfully direct indictment of Hamilton and Nelson; they create a sudden, undercutting movement, revealing the novel's cynosures in an altogether harsher light. Sir William Hamilton, she says, was nothing but 'an upper-class dilettante'. And in the last paragraph Fonseca stakes her claim for a female revolutionary spirit:

> Sometimes I had to forget that I was a woman to accomplish the best of which I was capable. Or I would lie to myself about how complicated it is to be a woman. Thus do all women, including the author of this book. But I cannot forgive those who did not care about more than their own glory or well-being. They thought they were civilized. They were despicable. Damn them all.   (p. 419)

Sontag's work often concludes with abrupt reversals or *peripeteia* (in *Death Kit*, for example, the revelation that the narrator is on death's cusp). Here, she inverts the pattern of our sympathy by creating antipathy in place of the cosy admiration engendered by historical fiction (with its heroes, heroines and tapestries of great events). And as with *Death Kit*, Sontag concludes by sundering the contract that makes the novel a 'realistic' representation. 'Including the author of this book': the character talks about the novelist who has created her. It is a moment of solidarity between female character and female author, and might be seen as Sontag's feminist version of those moments in the European avant-garde tradition (say, in a play by Pirandello or Brecht) where realist convention is actively subverted: a character steps to the front of the stage and points up the drama's artifice.

This, then, is historical fiction underwritten with a strong political imperative: the parade of glamorous figures from the past is placed in context, situated in an ideological framework, returned to judgement. Polyphony becomes a means to liberate the voices of history, and also a way to involve those voices in a more active, engaged interrogation of history. The freeing of the female poet's voice also breaks with the Lukácsian model seen earlier in the book. *The Volcano Lover* begins with a third-person narrative where characters embody encoded historical forces; but it ends with the direct intercession of a first-person female voice. As Sontag says, 'Ending with Eleonora, and her denunciation of the protagonists, is as far as you can get from the point of view with which the novel starts.'[24] It is as if Lukácsian historiography is finally acknowledged to be itself only a partial historical representation; the writer now has to turn to other, overlooked (female) voices, which are admitted directly into the text. What Sontag does here is, in effect, to feminise a leftist theory of historical fiction: an older model of historical dialectic is superseded by a form of politics of the personal – a woman's outcry against political iniquities. The novel, published in the early 1990s, becomes a form of delayed meditation on themes associated with the 1960s, themes Sontag herself addressed in pieces such as 'Trip to Hanoi'. Revolution, power, the legitimacy of violence, the place of women in history: these motifs – recurrent themes in Sontag's work – are addressed through historical fiction's refractory prism. At the end of the novel, Sontag positions an explicitly *female* revolutionary voice. Whereas 'Trip to Hanoi' saw Sontag chafing against the received ideology of revolution (she regretfully notes how little conventional Marxist ideology means to her), in *The Volcano Lover* Sontag finally but powerfully identifies the woman's voice in revolution.

Joyce Carol Oates: 'Notes on Failure'

Joyce Carol Oates (1938–) is famously (and tiresomely, in her own eyes) renowned for her fascination with violence; critic after critic enquires after her un-ladylike intrigue with mayhem, injury and murder. In a review essay on Oates's recent work, Sally Robinson confesses herself puzzled by the novelist's lurid fictions – 'except to say that Oates's voyeuristic imagination, like Hitchcock's perhaps, inevitably seeks out the shocking and sordid'.[25] Her recent explorations of boxing and its masculine culture have hardly failed to dampen down this interest. *On Boxing* (1987) is one of the quirkiest keys to a novelist's work in recent years. The essay pans out into a cultural mapping of her preoccupations: masculine crisis, physical and mental extremities, the thin line between 'ordinary' and pathological behaviour. Oates's fascination with the boxer can also be seen as a gambit whereby she alludes to, and then re-writes, an iconic subject in America's masculinist literary tradition; she annexes the sacred literary territory where the American male writer explores sport, masculinity, violence. *On Boxing* alludes to Mailer and Hemingway, but chastises their writings for imprecision. 'Hemingway never wrote about boxing with the sympathy or perception with which he wrote about bullfighting.' Meanwhile, 'Mailer cannot establish a connection between himself and the boxers'.[26]

On Boxing is a work of appropriation and re-writing; its power lies in Oates's anthropological and mythographic analyses of what constitutes 'maleness'. She tellingly draws on an essay by the anthropologist Clifford Geertz to illuminate the rites of sport in America, explaining that boxing is central to American masculinity. 'As the bloody, repetitious, and ephemeral cockfight is a Balinese reading of Balinese experience, a story Balinese tell themselves about themselves, so too is the American boxing match a reading of American experience, unsentimentalized and graphic.' Early twentieth-century women such as Willa Cather and Zora Neale Hurston were drawn to the discoveries and discourses of anthropology; Oates re-directs their womanly anthropology towards the rituals of the male world. And what she finds at the centre of boxing is a brutal, elemental, archaic and artistic sport which tells us about civilisation itself: 'to write about boxing is to be forced to contemplate not only boxing, but the perimeters of civilization – what it is, or should be, to be "human" ' ('Foreword'). For the male sports fan, Oates's account of the obsessive culture of sport evokes jostling feelings: admiration in the face of her forensic anthropology; discomfort because one recognises certain truths while resisting her typecast generalities.

Would her essentialism be tolerated if it was directed towards women's sub-cultures? Boxing represents 'man's greatest passion – for war, not peace'; 'Boxing is for men, and is about men, and *is* men.'[27] The problem with such confident generalisations is that they carry in their syntax the form of facile reversibility: that boxing 'is men', and therefore man 'is' boxing.

Her enquiry leads to speculation about 'a sport of crisis': the crisis of masculinity staged in the boxing ring. Boxing might seem to be a gladiatorial, neo-Darwinist celebration of success, but for Oates it is equally a drama of failure: 'Failure, hurt, ignominy, disgrace, physical injury, sometimes even death – these are facts of life, perhaps the very bedrock of lives, which the sports-actor, or athlete, must dramatize in the flesh; and always against his will.'[28] Failure interests Oates. Just as she is drawn to the other side of the boxing contest, the defeat and decline of the vanquished, so she has written of the importance of failure to the writer. 'Notes on Failure' (1982) would, read in isolation, be an essayistic *jeu d'esprit*, a witty survey of the paradoxical need of the writer to *fail* in many literary endeavours. But placed alongside *On Boxing* and the fiction, it reads like a programme for the creative and imaginative potential of the gloomier side of experience: failure, disillusion, disappointment and abjection. Oates describes the varying states of negativity afflicting the writer: 'indecision, frustration, pain, dismay, despair, remorse, impatience, outright failure'. For 'it is perhaps not failure the writer loves, so much as the addictive nature of incompletion and risk'.[29] These meditations on the morbid end of the emotional spectrum, and the writer's need for creative abjection, have been extended by essays on Gothic fiction, which Oates has a particular liking for. She praises Mary Shelley and Robert Louis Stevenson in particular. Their splicing together of gloomy atmospherics with speculative theorising (the two elements then embedded in the popular Gothic genre) has clear echoes in Oates's own work.[30]

Oates's work can be read as an extended meditation on the themes condensed in *On Boxing* and 'Notes on Failure': male crisis and failure; 'hurt, ignominy, defeat'; the underside of the American culture of success. Again and again in Oates's work the central protagonist is a failing male, a man in crisis, the guy on the ropes. Often these figures ought to be successes; they are the scions of affluent families, born into suburban ease and privilege. The Oates fictional cosmology is akin to that created in David

Lynch's movies: a suburbia cast in a Gothic light, the setting for almost cartoonish instances of violence and an abiding sense of societal dysfunction. In *Expensive People* (1968), a first-person tale of a young, disaffected son and his bizarre parents, Oates turned to the familial breakdown and neuroses of *The Catcher in the Rye* and *The Bell Jar*. *Expensive People*, like a great deal of Oates's work, reads as if it were a palimpsest text, where traces of earlier, usually male, narratives are discernible. *Expensive People*'s plot about adolescent male breakdown reminds us of Salinger's classic; but there is much robust satire in the manner of Sinclair Lewis, and the Michigan setting is carefully chosen to allow for lampoons of Midwestern vulgarity. And then there is a black comedy and verbal tricksiness that echo Vladimir Nabokov. As allusive text, a self-conscious collage of different voices, *Expensive People* seems to herald the new 'knowing', self-referential and witty aesthetic championed by Sontag; but in a Preface to a recent edition of the novel, Oates also emphasised its documentary value by stressing realism: 'the descriptive scenes bear witness to a greedily appropriated authentic landscape, that of Birmingham/Bloomfield Hills, Michigan'.[31]

These comments twist our reading of *Expensive People* still further, by slighting the novel's ludic qualities at the expense of its classic realist status and its rootedness in the 'authentic' world. Oates remembers her novel, and encourages us to read it in terms of social realism. Such hermeneutic twists and turns are very much part of the experience of reading Oates; the reader is kept on her or his toes, especially in the kaleidoscopic fictions produced in the late 1960s. The stories in *The Wheel of Love* (1970) deconstructed the conventions of the short story: chronology and the assumed fixities of point-of-view are re-ordered to create splintered, vertiginous tales. These stories also bore the impress of the cultural chaos of the era; many bear refracted witness to Vietnam, Civil Rights and the increasing polarisation of US society. Tonally, Oates captures the sourness of a period when idealism was turning to disillusion. Thus the formalistic dis-integration of 'How I Contemplated the World from the Detroit House of Correction and Began My Life Over Again' (1969) seems to have a mimetic function; the disorienting narrative gives shape to a world losing coherence. This story presents a jagged, fractured narrative, purportedly the 'Notes for an Essay for an English Class'. As either class assignment or the crazy experiment of a disturbed narrator, the story has a cloudy and mutable origin. Ordinary details of character-description (height, physical aspect) are given, but granted the reader in a teasing, scrambled manner. Formal section titles ('Characters', 'World Events', 'Events') act to 'dis-integrate' the story by breaking up narrative into its structural components (Oates might well have been influenced by literary criticism's turn towards structuralism at this time). Above all, 'How I Contemplated the World' plays with perspective; it conflates third- and first-person narrative viewpoints to create a sense of being within and without its protagonist:

> The girl (myself) is walking through Branden's, that excellent store. Suburb of a large famous city that is a symbol for large famous American cities. The event sneaks up on the girl, who believes she is herding it along with a small fixed smile, a girl of fifteen, innocently experienced. She dawdles in a certain style by a counter of costume jewelry. Rings, earrings, necklaces. Prices from $5 to $50, all within reach. All ugly too.[32]

'How I Contemplated the World' actively demands the participation of the reader in the construction of its meaning. On another interpretative level, the story is more conventional; it is placed in a tradition the reader recognises. This story of the home, framed in a jagged first-person narrative and uttered in a skittering, helter-skelter, edgy voice, takes us back to the neurotic discourses of Gilman and Plath. This is a voice whose pain is suggestively adumbrated in elliptical sentences; and as with 'The Yellow Wallpaper', the word 'home' chimes through the prose as both comfortable nest and frightening prison:

> I weep for all the money here, for God in gold and beige carpeting, for the beauty of chandeliers and the miracle of a clean polished gleaming toaster and faucets that run both hot and cold water, and I tell them, *I will never leave home, this is my home, I love everything here, I am in love with everything here. . . .*
> I am home.   (pp. 188–9)

Oates's chosen fictional subject has been the disestablishment of middle-class certainties, the unmaking of suburbia. Works such as *Expensive People* or 'How I Contemplated . . .' are blackly comic, violent melodramas set in the context of the highly affluent, cultured middle class; it is rather as if Edith Wharton's fiction, also solidly ensconsed in the homes of the bourgeoisie, was being re-written in the light of Philip Roth's infamous speech from 1960, 'Writing American Fiction'. Roth notoriously opened his discussion with an account of two recent murders in Chicago and asserted that 'the American writer in the middle of the twentieth century has his hands full in trying to understand, describe, and then make *credible* much of American reality. It stupefies, it sickens, it infuriates. . . .'[33] Roth's commentary provides a clue to the violence in Oates's work. It is not violence *per se* that is important to her; it is how we understand violence that is her great topic. Just as *On Boxing* creates a cultural, literary and anthropological scaffold to place around the ring – an interpretative apparatus to decode brutality – so the fiction seeks a formalistic model to represent or embody the ways in which we as individuals or as a culture might make sense of what 'stupefies . . . sickens . . . infuriates'.

There are satirical and comic potentialities in Oates's conjunctions of class and crisis; she usually exploits them to the full. *The Assassins* (1975) deals with the Petrie family, whose son, Andrew, a prominent and gifted politician, has been murdered. The Ivy League world of the East Coast elites is shown to be riddled with corruption and depravity; the book, published in the wake of Watergate, has a keen sense of public life's decadence. The didactic thrust of the novel is channelled through bizarre comedy, satire and mockery. Andrew, as he emerges through his brother's memories, is a parodic extreme of the Ivy League hero or an adolescent counterpart to Norman Mailer's all-American existential hero, Rojack, in *An American Dream*. Oates is surely lampooning the heroes of Mailer and Hemingway when she describes this young boy, aiming for high office, training himself in the boxing ring. The first section of the novel is narrated in the first person by the brother, Hugh Petrie, whose feckless career as a cartoonist contrasts with the high politics and Machiavellian machinations orchestrated by Andrew. Hugh provides another opportunity for Oates to construct a comic portrait of the American male. Hugh, like Richard Everett in *Expensive People*, is an aesthete, an indolent solipsist trapped in a fantasy life (every third page seems to be a visit to his analyst). As in *Expensive People*, this is a portrait of the artist as a sad case; but these representations of masculinity have, too, a larger significance in Oates's work. Across the range of her fiction, the comic representation of male crisis is a recurrent motif. Oates's fiction, with its caustically comic portraits of male failure, sketches out a feminist fiction whose subject is less the development of female stories than the deconstruction of male stories. And the main tone or tenor of these narratives is comic, a Nabokovian laughter in the dark aimed at the crashing failures of her male protagonists. Thus the iconic representativeness of masculinity in her work: languid aesthete; Machiavellian politician; boxers; doctors.

The shift between an ostensibly 'male' area of thematic concern and subject-matter with a more immediate 'female' signature has recurred throughout Oates's career. The zig-zagging, consciously disorienting pattern of her work amplifies on a larger scale the shifting, restless patterns of her short fiction. It also fits with her desire to slip out of accepted formulations of what a female writer should or should not be doing. I think we see this impatience (or is it even scorn?) for received categories in her often-quoted attack on the labelling of women writers: 'a women who writes is a writer by her own definition; but she is a *woman* writer by others' definitions'.[34] Even the interpretation I have established so far (Oates as the explorer of masculine crisis and abjection) has to be qualified in the light of her more recent fiction. Oates has turned more and more to the representation of women *in extremis*. *The Rise of Life on Earth* (1991) and *I Lock My Door upon Myself* (1990) focus in part on embattled and threatened women.

Oates has used the Gothic, as did her mentors Charlotte Brontë and Mary Shelley, to examine the way we live now. *The Rise of Life on Earth* is not only one of the harshest and bleakest of her works but also a meld of Gothic violence, social criticism and documentary reportage from the American margins. A short, stabbing life story, it recounts the upbringing of Kathleen Hennessy, her abuse at the hands of her father and her attempts to find solace in a nursing career. Exploited by a young doctor, she becomes pregnant and drifts towards the horrific 'solution' to her many problems. Undoubtedly, this is a melodramatic work which never fails to lay its detail on thick (but as D. H. Lawrence observed, a novel succeeds despite the author laying it on thick). Oates creates extreme vignettes of child abuse and self-abasement, and opens up a sentimental chasm between the wretchedness of Kathleen's life and the naivety of her dreams. The novella works because we recognise that the melodramatic excesses are grounded in social realities; the Gothic, for all its hyperbole, becomes for Oates a form of social realism. The everyday reality of urban Detroit – Oates's sometime home, and the setting for much of her work – *is*, she implies, modern Gothic.

The title, however, points to another generic root. The 'rise of life on earth' is a phrase heard by the young doctor in one of his classes:

> at U-M where he'd done his undergraduate work too preparing singlemindedly through the semesters for medical school in the prestigious school in which Larry Abbot had distinguished himself and there came the précis 'The Rise of Life on Earth' seemingly both idea and actual glimpsed phenomena-flood as the chemical yielded mysteriously to the biological, Earth acquiring life, heat, volition, a central nervous system, out of primary water–ammonia–hydrogen–methane arose organic compounds of amino acids, mononucleotides, sugars, how then did these evolve into the long polymer chains required for life, how then when such forms are known to be unstable and vulnerable to solar ultraviolet rays and to water yet the chains did evolve, millions upon millions of years and how then did such inanimate material self-reproduce, replicate, what then is the principle of the organic, why then evolution shifting from the chemical to the biological, what destiny?[35]

The novella, which is very much about procreation and extinction, takes this passage as its governing or framing commentary: 'what destiny?'. The epic, affirmative process of evolution is ironically counterpointed against the squalid self-destruction that marks human behaviour. Oates here takes the reader back to an earlier phase in American writing, the neo-Darwinism that underwrote the naturalism of Theodore Dreiser or Stephen Crane. For the naturalist writer, adoption of a Darwinist paradigm led to emphasis on the determining power of environment and circumstance; we see the model underpinning stories such as Crane's *Maggie: A Girl of the Streets* or Dreiser's *Jennie Gerhardt* – both cautionary tales of young women broken by societal circumstance. *The Rise of Life on Earth* is another tale of life on the margins, another female urban tragedy. Oates continues the ongoing womanly debate with the legacy of naturalism (see my discussions of Ann Petry and Toni Morrison for further discussion of this topic). She underscores naturalism's assumptions by stressing the overwhelming power of social circumstance; but she also emphasises gender as a determinant in this matrix of the ineluctable. Kathleen is an almost archetypal abused girl: ugly, powerless, buffeted by the powerful men in her life (father, lover). Her own futile revenge (secretively murdering patients in her care) is a Gothic, naturalistic reckoning: the last throw of the dice for a powerless woman.

Oates's re-working and cross-fertilisation of genres creates a hybrid: a feminised naturalist-Gothic novella. Generic transformations are absolutely central to the genealogy of women's fiction. American women have revised and modified familiar genres in three main ways. First, they have hollowed-out or deconstructed genres, reducing a literary form to a basic configuration or its constituent elements. Charlotte Perkins Gilman distilled the whole span of nineteenth-century sentimental writing to its spare essentials: man, woman, marriage, house. 'The Yellow Wallpaper' created a minimalist domestic realism later used by Stein in *Three Lives* or Cather in *The Professor's House*. These spare, lean fictions strip out the encumbrances of domestic realism to leave, in Cather's telling phrase, a 'novel démeublé' – an 'unfurnished' novel. A second generic transformation is the whole-scale feminisation of a genre usually associated with male writers. The appropriation of the Western and its male iconography in Jean Stafford's *The Mountain Lion* is a good example. The third tactic is to overwrite and overdetermine the major features of a genre, creating a surfeit or plenitude of familiar generic motifs. Oates's Gothicism might be a good example of this. The method can lead to parody or to what seems like outbidding, as the woman writer seems to go one further in deploying the dominant motifs of a genre. *The Bell Jar* is an instance of this; Plath pushes the tale of youthful crack-up and doomed promise, inherited from Fitzgerald and Salinger, towards an extreme configuration. Instead of Fitzgerald's 'neurasthenia' (in *Tender is the Night*) or the romantic anomie of Holden Caulfield, Plath posits psychosis, savage depression, the full-scale medicalisation of the gifted youngster. Similarly, Oates's novella is a much more bloody, intense and grim narrative than its literary forebears.

If we turn back to the criticism produced in the 1960s we find a useful term to describe these female fictions of modified and re-constructed realism. Robert Scholes's *The Fabulators* (1967) described a fiction of 'fabulation'. Rooted in the fable (Scholes cited Aesop), this fiction would exhibit a 'delight in design' and 'pleasure in form'; but it would also contain allegorical and didactic elements. Scholes thought that 'fabulation' could be used to explain what was going on beyond realism; it would mean a 'less realistic and more artistic kind of narrative'.[36] He cited William Golding and Vladimir Nabokov as fabulators. There are naturally gaps between Scholes's 'fable' and the works I have been describing; Sontag, Oates and Plath can be seen as satirists, and Scholes omits satire from his palette of fabular tones. But many of the key elements are here: design, pleasure, a degree of anti-realism, all edged with didacticism. Plath, Sontag and Oates have all worked as fabulists. What is *The Bell Jar* if it is not a fable about the frustrations of a young woman within a hollowed-out women's culture? And what is Sontag's *The Volcano Lover* if it is not a fable about political violence and a woman's role in revolution?

8

Fictions for the Village

Toni Morrison, Maxine Hong Kingston, Cynthia Ozick

The fiction of the past quarter-century has seen a resurgence of the fascination with community which has been a leitmotif in American women's narratives. Just as earlier periods of cultural transformation witnessed a flowering of fictions with fresh notions of community at their centre (for instance, during the breakdown of Victorian certitudes in the 1890s), so this period (1970–95) can be described as a phase of radical communitarianism. For writers such as Cynthia Ozick, Toni Morrison and Maxine Hong Kingston the novelist remains a storyteller (all three are indebted to the folkloric modernism of the 1920s and 1930s); but the relationship between storyteller and community has become more complex, and sometimes fraught. For the communitarians, storytelling is complicated by the interplay of the imagined communities addressed by the writer. The communitarian writes for a readership of women, for her own ethnic or cultural 'village' (in Morrison's term); but these authors also claim a national significance for their stories, addressing fundamental national subjects (migration, race, cultural pluralism). In writing about the structures of community (the lore of Judaism, say, in Ozick's Puttermesser stories) these authors provide local fictional templates for a conceptualised understanding of what culture is and how the individual situates herself within cultures. Communitarian fiction meditates on the meaning of 'culture' itself.

The communitarians have continued and deepened the interest shown by earlier writers in the vernacular. The forging of a new language, rather than an ironic re-capitulation of earlier modes, is seen in the communitarian's desire to weave oral textures into prose; their prose is stippled with the traces (rhythms, idioms and motifs) of an ethnic vernacular culture. The communitarian tries to catch the elusive discourses of a culture, the spoken language that normally lies beyond writing since it is too fleeting or too trivial to catch the writer's ear. Maxine Hong Kingston adopts the Chinese term, 'talk-story', to denote a story-telling technique which blends narrative, family anecdote and gossip within a loose, episodic fictional structure. And Toni Morrison brings fiction close to oral traditions by incorporating the rhythms and recursive patterns of spoken language into her prose. At the same time the communitarian writer has begun to sense that the vernacular mode is not always a guaranteed route for the writer to represent a culture. For Cynthia Ozick, what she calls 'aural culture' is inevitably tainted by the degradations of modern media (particularly, television); she looks wistfully back to a golden age when writing rather than speech remained the cultural standard. In Toni Morrison's prose, one hears the rhythms of the 'speakerly text' while noting the intensely worked, crafted, attentive inscription of her novels as *written* artefacts. This exchange between the written and the spoken has become a major dynamic in works such as Morrison's *Beloved* and Ozick's *The Messiah of Stockholm*.

To term these writers 'postmodern', as sometimes happens in the criticism, is to misjudge, even if slightly, their representations of community and culture.[1] The keywords we associate with literary postmodernism ('surface', 'play', 'pastiche', and especially 'irony') imply a knowing, sly re-assemblage of past cultures. The literary postmodernist is an ironic pasticheur poised at the exhaustion of cultural advancement, attuned to the shifting surfaces of style as she plays with a back-catalogue of earlier discourses. But the communitarian has a much more urgent need to re-connect with past cultures and traditions; and her sense of style is much more akin to high modernism's need to 'make it new'. Whereas the postmodernist has an almost imperial attitude towards the cultural past (seeing it as a repository of available discourses), the communitarian always senses the strangeness or even unknowability of the past. The need to explore and then recover an opaque past underpins Toni Morrison's *Beloved*, Maxine Hong Kingston's *The Woman Warrior* and Cynthia Ozick's *The Messiah of Stockholm*. Here, the past is imagined in all its alter-ity, as a strange and ghostly world; the communitarians share an urgent, partly didactic desire to unpack the meaning of that world. As Caroline Rody has said of Toni Morrison, 'the burden of communicating an authentic truth remains'.[2] What the 'authentic truth' of communitarian fiction might be, is the subject of this chapter.

Toni Morrison: Fiction for the Village

The imagined community of readers and listeners is for the female writer a more problematic audience than it would be for a male writer: writing out of a 'minority' culture, the female author must decide how to pitch her voice. Does she address an imagined community of other women? For male readers and critics the assumption that a woman writes for other women has often been felt to invalidate the currency of a female work (hence, the use of male pseudonyms by Victorian writers such as the Brontë sisters); the argument, of course, is never reversed. But male critics have been unforgiving when they sense that a woman writer is getting too close to *their* imagined audience. Hence, the sense of trespass when Willa Cather wrote about war or Joyce Carol Oates writes about boxing. A critical double-bind can be seen here: to address the local female community is to be accused of narrowness or slightness; but to address a reading community including men is to mime a language which can never, in actuality, be a woman's.

Those female writers from distinctive ethnic and cultural backgrounds discover that the issue of voice has been further complicated by the expectation that the writer speaks on behalf of a race, religion or area. Continually, the woman writer finds herself in a position of fraught mediation: between the local and the general, the minority and the majority, the regional and the national. And women writers have thus evolved complex strategies of address, often embodied in layered and double-voiced narrative tones which can speak both within and without the minority culture.

Toni Morrison (1931–), whose receipt of the Nobel prize in 1993 confirmed her as the pre-eminent American writer of our age, has shown in interviews a fascination with this question of audience:

> I write what I have recently begun to call village literature, fiction that is really for the village, for the tribe. Peasant literature

for *my* people, which is necessary and legitimate but which also
allows me to get in touch with all sorts of people.[3]

Morrison here re-formulates one of the early feminist models of
women's culture: that it is a 'minority' culture with its own
vibrancy and independence, intersecting with mainstream
culture at certain points (like a Venn diagram of overlapping
circles, with areas of separation and shared territory). Morrison,
in her stress on the autonomous power of African–American and
female cultures, stresses the independent energies of a 'minority'; but she believes that cultural transmission is possible,
indeed desirable, beyond the perimeters of the author's local
'village'. The authorial reach beyond the minority is here
couched in plainly humanistic terms – 'to get in touch with all
sorts of people'. Alongside this humanism rests an urgency, a
politicised compulsion to write a peasant literature 'which is
necessary and legitimate'. Even here, in Morrison's careful
choice of the word 'legitimate', one senses the fraught mediation
I discussed above. There is the fear that to speak from the village
is to court illegitimacy by addressing topics unrecognised by the
larger society.

Morrison's 'village literature' takes as its great theme the idea
of *protection*, particularly the African–American family's efforts to
offer emotional and physical sanctuary against slavery or
economic deprivation. She claimed to write 'for the village, for the
tribe'; but in her fiction the sense of community adumbrated by
these words is continually threatened and disrupted. *The Bluest
Eye* (1970), her first novel, established a paradigm of endangered
security on its very first page. An excerpt from what seems to be a
children's primer is quoted repeatedly in different syntactical
configurations. The opening sentences embody a sturdily basic,
childish syntax:

> Here is the house. It is green and white. It has a red door. It
> is very pretty.

Which then moves into a mimetic representation of a faster,
breathless movement:

> Here is the house it is green and white it has a red door it is
> very pretty

Which then becomes frenzied and, in its unpunctuated rush, meaningless:

Hereisthehouseitisgreenandwhiteithasareddooritisverypretty[4]

The running together of the words suggests a heady, speeded-up, increasingly desperate replay of a moment of childhood innocence. The novel culminates in an act of incest; the opening passages become, when read again, a cruelly ironic overture to a narrative of despoiled childhood. This frenetic sentence, with its broken-down syntax succeeding a childlike representation of domestic bliss, stands as the representative grammar of Morrison's work: the movement from a quiet, edenic stasis to kinetic frenzy is the fundamental pattern of her work. Her protagonists are cast out from the still securities of childhood, home and family into the turbulence of history (the colossal economic and social forces that shatter the lives of Morrison's African–Americans). Here, at the start of *The Bluest Eye* (the start, in fact, of Morrison's career *tout court*), she presents a powerfully miniaturised introduction to that movement from 'Home' to the disintegration of the home and all it stands for, which is the foundational structure of her career.

Centring on a poor, ruptured family in mid-twentieth-century Ohio, *The Bluest Eye* also introduced the dialectic between genres underpinning Morrison's work: it is an extended experiment in storytelling technique, conducted with modernist brio, and a return to the sentimental tradition's terrain (the lives of girl and women). In *The Bluest Eye* a strenuously modernist form features a polyphonic, temporally discontinuous narrative studded with unreliable narrators and poeticised monologues which reveal a character's interiority. At the same time, Morrison chronicles the girlhood bonding and friendships of Pecola and her peers; the novel is positioned in the female world of love and kinship discussed in my first chapter. Even though the novel is set in the 1940s, and deploys a battery of experimental techniques, it returns to – and in so doing revises – the sentimental tradition's emphasis on home, family and the community of women. Morrison's fiction has evolved through a dialectic between modernist national epic (epitomised by William Faulkner's work, though as we shall see, Morrison also resists this comparison) and the older forms of national epic inaugurated by Harriet Beecher Stowe. In bringing together nineteenth- and twentieth-century forms, popular and modernist narrative techniques, she has attempted on a grand scale nothing less than the reconciliation of America's divergent fictional traditions.

Morrison imbricates into her text the distinctive voices and tones of earlier traditions. For example, she adopts the trenchant, historicised didacticism of late-Victorian African–Americans such as Pauline Hopkins or Frances Harper by deploying polemical reflections on race. Take *The Bluest Eye*'s account of the Whitcombs, a mulatto family:

> They transferred this Anglophilia to their six children and sixteen grandchildren. Except for an occasional and unaccountable insurgent who chose a restive black, they married 'up,' lightening the family complexion and thinning out the family features.
>
> With the confidence born of a conviction of superiority, they performed well at schools. They were industrious, orderly, and energetic, hoping to prove beyond a doubt De Gobineau's hypothesis that 'all civilizations derive from the white race, that none can exist without its help, and that a society is great and brilliant only so far as it preserves the blood of the noble group that created it.' Thus, they were seldom overlooked by schoolmasters who recommended promising students for study abroad. The men studied medicine, law, theology, and emerged repeatedly in the powerless government offices available to the native population. That they were corrupt in public and private practice, both lecherous and lascivious, was considered their noble right, and thoroughly enjoyed by most of the less gifted population.   (p. 133)

The passage's sarcasm, explicit political commentary and generalising authority are redolent of *Iola Leroy* or *Contending Forces*. The passage also recalls a tactic used by Harper and Hopkins: the deployment of white racial theory, in all its stark brutality, so as to reveal the deep structures of racial ideology. The mocking quotation of De Gobineau echoes some of the discussions of pseudo-scientific racial theory that are prominent in *Iola Leroy*'s attack on institutionalised racism. Even as it fashions a complex narratology, *The Bluest Eye* encompasses robustly direct and straightforward paragraphs with a forthright political intent.

Reading through the pages of almost any of Morrison's works, one notes her heterogeneous registers: poeticised (and sometimes italicised) monologue; an experimental prose poetry that might be indebted to Gertrude Stein; expository historical narrative; polemic commentary; variation between first- and third-person point of view. I would see this visible, overt, foregrounded sense of discursive transition as Morrison's main genealogical link to her African–American forebears. It is not the adoption of a single model of writing – say, vernacular modernism – which links Hurston to Morrison; it is a shared sense of writing as mobility, as a transition *between and across* styles and discourses (what Hurston termed 'the break').

The power of Morrison's work lies not only in its engagement with these major questions of literary history but also in an engagement with history itself. Each of her novels represents a major 'moment' in the history of the African–American community, as Susan Willis has noted: 'The temporal focus of each of Morrison's novels pinpoints strategic moments in black American history, during which social and cultural forms underwent disruption and transformation.'[5] In what is widely felt to be her greatest novel, *Beloved* (1987), Morrison represents the primal scene of black experience: the implosion of the African–American family under slavery. She begins:

> 124 was spiteful. Full of a baby's venom. The women in the house knew it and so did the children. For *years* each put up with the spite in his own way, but by *1873* Sethe and her daughter Denver were its only victims. The grandmother, Baby Suggs, was dead, and the sons, Howard and Buglar, had run away by the time they were *thirteen* years old – as soon as merely looking in a mirror shattered it (that was the signal for Buglar); *as soon* as two tiny hand prints appeared in the cake (that was it for Howard). Neither boy waited to see more; another kettleful of chickpeas smoking in a heap on the floor; soda crackers crumbled and strewn in a line next to the doorsill. Nor did they wait for one of the relief *periods*: the *weeks*, *months* even, when nothing was disturbed. No. Each one fled *at once* – the *moment* the house committed what was for him the one insult not to be borne or witnessed a *second time*.[6] [italics added]

The paragraph scatters a confetti of dates and numbers but the figures do not add up to a clear, linear history. The italicised dates and temporal phrases demonstrate the extensive deployment of chronological terms; but the periodicity is obliquely rendered so that 'history' emerges as complex, enfolded, fragmented. A date is given, '1873', but is then placed alongside a host of other measurements of time. History is envisaged in terms of its basic building blocks (temporal measurement); but simultaneously, as the reader attempts to relate each detail to another (where is the beginning?), history becomes bristlingly difficult, fiercely demanding interpretation.

The articulate energy of Morrison's syntax moves restlessly between 'subjective' and 'objective' history: the precise point of view shifts to and fro, oscillating between the third-person and the subjective thoughts of individual characters. Her extended use of free indirect discourse creates a narrative which wraps together tightly the narrating voice and the perspectives of her characters. The development of free indirect discourse is sometimes seen by literary historians as an index of slippage from the moral certitudes associated with 'traditional' omniscient narration towards moral relativism; authority itself seemed to slip into an ambiguous space between narrator and character. For Morrison, though, free indirect discourse serves less as a means to complicate the moral function of fiction than as re-assertion of solidarity between author and character; she creates a grammar of hybridity where narrator and character speak together.

A former literary editor by profession, Morrison writes prose with a pointilliste elegance; her sentences display an exacting usage of varying syntactical pattern and punctuation. Each sentence carefully traces a different shape; there are continual modifications of syntax and ceaseless turns in the grammatical architecture of the prose (note the use of parenthesis, colon and semi-colon in this short passage). But it is also a prose which mimes the mixture of ellipsis and declarative directness found in oral expression: '124 was spiteful. Full of a baby's venom', 'No'. The distinctiveness of Morrison's prose lies in this larger variation, between the written and the spoken, betweeen an intricately wrought written technique and the robust immediacy of oral speech.

In a wider sense, too, *Beloved* encompasses both written and spoken historical narratives. Morrison was inspired by the story of Margaret Garner, a slave whose escape from her master in Kentucky in 1856 ended tragically; cornered by her pursuers, she killed her daughter and was attempting to slaughter herself and the other children as she was re-captured. An anecdotal shard from the fringes of history, Garner's story was reported in papers of the time but also has the condensed, parable-like force of folklore. Moreover, in *Iola Leroy*, Frances E. W. Harper's classic black woman's novel, Garner's story is fleetingly mentioned in a conversation: 'that slave mother who took her four children, crossed the Ohio River on the ice, killed one of the children and attempted the lives of the other two'.[7] When Morrison used the story of Margaret Garner she constructed a complex intertextual web by referring to the authenticated records of history (newspaper reports), the folkloric mythology of African–America and the written fictions of other black women. Garner's story has a resonant indeterminacy; it emerges from a multiplicity of sources at the same time – an indeterminacy that Morrison's narrative, with its conflation of history and superstition, explores.[8] And one might read this indeterminacy as part of a larger strategy in *Beloved*: the careful articulation of a layered, imbricated, complex relationship between the late twentieth-century black writer and her culture's past. As a 'talking cure' the novel resurrects and exorcises a massive historical trauma; but it is also written out of a 'poetics of absence' which endlessly reminds us of the sheer alterity of that past and its irredeemable loss.[9] At times *Beloved* reads like the poetic transcription of a dream of history; at others the sheer materiality and plenitude of the past is bodied forth in minute detail. History is 'produced' through the author's exhaustive recuperation of the past even as history's otherness turns this solidity into something dreamlike.

Beloved presents a black counter-family, a fractured and surreal counterpoint to the conventional nuclear family. Sethe, her daughter Denver, and her slain child Beloved, occupy centre stage; a drifting array of men, many outcast or broken by slavery or the Civil War, drifts on the edge. This female-centred family can be seen as Morrison's commentary on one of the major debates in African–American history: whether the black family was irredeemably shattered by the transition from Africa into slavery, or whether currents of familial bonding subsisted within an oppressive social system. Morrison entwines these polarities in her complex narrative. Certainly there is no traditional family as such in the novel. Paul D remembers meeting 'four families of slaves who had all been together for a hundred years' (p. 219); he 'watched them with awe and envy' (p. 219). In this world the strange ménage of Sethe and her daughters might be seen as normal; but Morrison never fails to underwrite the strong emotive bonds between her 'de-familiarised' characters. This is a world pulsing with familial emotion.

To read *Beloved* within the context of recent historical work on slavery is to realise the sophistication of Morrison's fictional analysis of the black family. Peter Kolchin notes that 'The establishment of slavery in America entailed the destruction of families, as Africans – mostly young men – were torn from their loved ones at home and placed among strangers.' The new slaves 'often lived in sex-segregated barracks'. And yet, in spite of the disruption of slave sales ('in the upper South about one first marriage in three was broken by forced separation'), a kind of family life evolved:

> Families provided a crucial if fragile buffer, shielding slaves from the worst rigors of slavery. . . . A new African–American family structure took root in the eighteenth century and spread throughout the South, along with slavery, in the nineteenth. Those families were not, of course, untouched by slavery. Even under the best of circumstances, slave families lacked the institutional and legal support enjoyed by those that were free, and in extreme cases masters could not only hinder but prevent the development of normal family relations. . . .[10]

Beloved is sited in the historical matrix described by Kolchin: the black family is there but it is a 'fragile buffer'; and Morrison takes as her topic one of Kolchin's 'extreme cases' where the master acts to 'prevent the development of normal family relations'. The novel, then, emerges from a deliberately double-voiced reading of black history. It represents the quotidian realities of family life under slavery: absent men, a loosely matriarchal family, the family as buffer. It also embodies the extremity of the Margaret Garner story: the tearing of the family by oppression, punishment and infanticide. In this sense, *Beloved* presents a knotted, complex version of the historical debate, suggestively entwining both apocalyptic and progressive readings of the black family. While Morrison's novels often turn on incidents of extraordinary grimness (*The Bluest Eye* concludes with the incestuous birth of Percola's child, engendered by her own father; *Paradise* centres on a violent assault on a female commune), she testifies to the African–American maintenance of alternative families.

Morrison has claimed that her work is tragic, noting in an interview: 'I write what I suppose could be called the tragic mode in which there is some catharsis and revelation . . . my inclination is in the tragic direction.' In another interview she was asked specifically about her indebtedness to 'Greek tragic patterns' and, replying that she was a Classics minor as a student, talked at length about tragedy, community and order. She had noticed correspondences between the Greek chorus and 'what goes on in Black churches and in jazz'. Both involved reiteration of communally engendered stories:

> They were community property or they were family property and anybody could elaborate on them or change them or retell them. You heard them over and over again. And there was some quality in them that was stark. There was probably also catharsis in the sense of a combination of the restoration of order – order is restored at the end – and the character having a glimmering of some knowledge that he didn't have when the book began. . . . a lot of people complain about my endings, because it looks like they are falling apart. But something important has happened; some knowledge is there – the Greek knowledge – what is the epiphany in Greek tragedy. But in addition to that, it's community oriented, all of this because the door is left open. I don't shut doors at the end of books.[11]

What is interesting about this comment is Morrison's interest in the ameliorating, progressive and civic aspects of tragedy. Her definition of tragedy is strictly in accord with Aristotelian theory, stressing both structural elements (the 'revelation' on which the plot of the tragedy often turns) and the benign emotional effects claimed by Aristotle for tragedy. Morrison finds in Greek tragedy an exemplary aesthetic: communal, civic, cathartic; and also formally complex – 'order' is restored but there is also an openness. Intriguingly, Morrison couples formalistic shape (the sense of a novel's ending) to what we might call fiction's civic responsibility: her fiction is 'community oriented' *because* 'the door is left open'. I think she means by this that a certain irresolution or formalistic indeterminacy (a lack of rigid closure) allow the reader space to imagine different endings and varied conclusions. In terms of reader response, the 'open door' of the Morrison conclusion encourages interpretative participation, fostering a hermeneutic communality between author and reader. Stories, Morrison suggests, are not fixed by set endings. Different conclusions are possible; one can envisage a multiplicity of endings, and this is to keep alive the possibility of a transformational politics since the story of the *polis* is told in a variety of ways.[12]

Not that this combination of open form and weighty political significance does not, at times, lead to Morrison's conclusions becoming frustratingly elusive. The meshing of closure and openness is certain to produce riddling and paradoxical final pages, as the novel pulls in two ways. Morrison says, 'There is a resolution of a sort but there are always possibilities.'[13] In *Beloved* the conclusion takes the form of an enigmatic poetic coda 'about' the ghost of the dead child. On one level these pages mark a general movement out of the chaos of the main narrative towards peace and resolution. The Civil War is over; Paul D and Sethe have found domestic calm and, however tentatively, are looking forward to the future ('We need some kind of tomorrow'). The spirit-child appears to be exorcised, erupting 'into her separate parts, to make it easy for the chewing laughter to swallow her all away' (p. 274). The general stillness is akin to the post-traumatic quietude which descends at the end of Greek or Shakespearean tragedy. But there is still the 'open door' Morrison talked of. First, the haunting by Beloved might carry on, as the family occasionally sense another ghostly face in a familiar photograph. Second, Morrison shifts our attention away from the story of Beloved to the question of the transmission of that story. 'It was not a story to pass on', she writes, 'This is not a story to pass on' (p. 274). A form of meta-fictional commentary, the conclusion points to its own transmission, its status as a story that ought not to be passed on. Yet, of course, the story has been passed on; not only has it been passed on, it has also become a written narrative. *Beloved*'s conclusion achieves, on a tonal level, the stillness of resolution; but with a self-conscious twist it also produces an 'open door' by turning our focus onto the narrative's transmission and its indeterminate status. This conclusion hovers ambiguously between a written narrative (now passed on to its readers) and an oral tale (with the superstitious injunction that it is not to be passed on to new listeners).

Transmission is central to Morrison's body of fiction: the recovery and transmission of oral narratives from the past into a written present, but also the transmission of motifs, tropes and even syntactical structures from earlier writers. One can identify traces of authors as various as William Faulkner, Gertrude Stein, Zora Neale Hurston and Frances Harper; but to find a way to describe these references, while avoiding mechanical talk of 'indebtedness' or 'echoes', proves difficult. Morrison herself is impatient with comparative exercises, seeing this as demeaning her individual achievement: 'I am not *like* William Faulkner.'[14] The problem for literary criticism is that Morrison works on a broader canvas, and much more complexly, than a model of influence predicating a single channel of transference from author to author. And while it is always possible to spot allusions to earlier authors, decoding the significance of such references is less easy.

For Morrison's is an allotropic intertextuality. The basic pattern of her relationship to earlier writers remains constant: through allusion and creative re-writing she pays homage to her forebears, forging unexpected networks of writers. She inflects this basic pattern with distinctive configurations as she engages with different writers; her intertextuality is marked by formalistic and technical range. At various points the reader catches a trace of an image, a syntactical resonance from an earlier writer; or we sense the shadow of an almost-recognisable plot-line falling across the page of the Morrison text. For example, Morrison's major female predecessor, as a female re-maker of the basic sentence, is Gertrude Stein; in both writers a restless energy breaks apart and re-forges elementary syntax. Morrison shares with Stein an interest in repetition and incantation, and a fascination with the music inherent in even the simplest sentences. And that passage from the start of *The Bluest Eye*, with its re-writing of a child's primer, is indebted to Stein's experimentally infantile language in works such as 'Tender Buttons' and 'Pink Melon Joy'. There are echoes, too, of Stein's *Three Lives* in the plot of *Beloved*: the commitment to the tragedies of ordinary and marginal life; the attentiveness to the hallowed moments of everyday female experience.

Morrison draws on, and then re-draws, the texts of male and female *and* black and white forebears. Her importance as a creator of national epics lies partly in this comprehensiveness: her ability to allow divergent and often contradictory literary examples to speak together through her own prose. But it is her re-mapping of black traditions which is especially significant. As Henry Louis Gates, Jr, has recently noted, Morrison can be understood as a

writer who combines the naturalism of earlier black writers such
as Richard Wright (note her tragic sense of the ineluctable, deter-
minist power of social forces) with the 'lyrical, quasi-autobio-
graphical modernism' of Zora Neale Hurston. Morrison creates 'a
new form, which we might think of as a lyrical super-natural-
ism'.[15] And even within this African–American field, her engagement with a black female tradition remains, naturally, more
poignant than these other intertextual engagements. Above all,
her use and revision of motifs from Zora Neale Hurston's work
deserve attention.

Beloved deploys an image central to *Their Eyes Were Watching
God*: the tree. Hurston had used the image of the tree to embody
in vernacular symbolism Janie's sense of self. 'Janie saw her life
like a great tree in leaf with the things suffered, things enjoyed,
things done and undone. Dawn and doom was in the branches.'
The gestation of spring, and the particular example of a blossom-
ing tree, are fairly standard images for stirring sexuality; but
Hurston invigorates these tropes with a heavy sensuality and a
microscopically detailed attentiveness:

> She had been spending every minute that she could steal from
> her chores under that tree for the last three days. That was to
> say, ever since the first tiny bloom had opened. It had called
> her to come and gaze on a mystery. From barren brown stems
> to glistening leaf-buds; from the leaf-buds to snowy virginity of
> bloom. It stirred her tremendously. . . . She saw a dust-bearing
> bee sink into the sanctum of a bloom; the thousand sister-
> calyxes arch to meet the love embrace and the ecstatic shiver of
> the tree from root to tiniest branch cramming in every blossom
> and frothing with delight. So this was a marriage!
>
> [my ellipsis][16]

For Hurston the tree is imbued with an orgasmic sensuality;
but in *Beloved*, where the tree is equally central to the heroine, it
takes on other significances. For Hurston the tree is the tree of life;
for Morrison the tree is part of the iconography of black suffering
– the lynching tree. Sethe has a bizarre pattern of wounds on her
back in the shape of a tree, marks of a whipping that precipitated
her flight from slavery. The scar is that of a 'chokecherry tree.
Trunk, branches, and even leaves.' When Paul D first put his arms
around her, she 'knew, but could not feel, that his cheek was

pressing into the branches of her chokecherry tree' (pp. 16–17). The tree was recognised and named by the strange, white waif, Amy, whom Sethe met during her escape:

> A chokecherry tree. See, here's the trunk – it's red and split wide open, full of sap, and this here's the parting for the branches. You got a mighty lot of branches. Leaves, too, look like, and dern if these ain't blossoms. Tiny little cherry blossoms, just as white. Your back got a whole tree on it. In bloom. What God have in mind, I wonder. I had me some whippings, but I don't remember nothing like this.   (p. 79)

Hurston had transformed the lynching tree into an erotic emblem. Morrison's description looks back to the moment in *Their Eyes Were Watching God* when Janie's sexuality burst into flower; here, too, there is an acute sensory detail. But Morrison recovers the buried significance of the tree, allowing it to function as symbol of pain and eroticism, as an emblem of what America does to its blacks and what in fleeting moments can be recovered by the African–American for her own fulfilment. The chokecherry tree, then, is imagined in a profoundly genealogical way; its significances reveal themselves slowly, as we look back to how an earlier writer used the tree in her own fiction of the black female subject. Fittingly, too, this image is itself a *form* of genealogy: a tree that suggests continuities and further creativity ('it's red and split wide open, full of sap').

Morrison is the most genealogical of writers: not only in her re-writing of earlier authors' favoured images, but also in her self-conscious gift of her own language to writers yet to come.

Maxine Hong Kingston: the 'Talk-Story' of Chinese America

Maxine Hong Kingston's *The Woman Warrior – Memoirs of a Girlhood Among Ghosts* (1976) extends and deepens the project undertaken by earlier women writers such as Willa Cather: the fictional representation of a bilingual, bicultural community in all its shifting, exhilarating complexity. As we saw earlier, Cather's *My Ántonia* created an open, episodic form to accommodate the new stories of the recent immigrants; the novel then becomes a tapestry of tales, a mosaic of anecdotes, memories and folk stories.

This, Cather implies, is one of the ways the migrant experience has transformed American culture: the American story is diversified into *stories*, and the evolving 'trans-national America' becomes a palimpsest of overlapping languages and conversations. Kingston extends Cather's technique. *The Woman Warrior* is woven together from many examples of 'talk-story' – a sort of conversation that is also a form of reminiscence and storytelling. The text, a hybrid of gossip, fable and autobiographical memoir, brings together material from the Old World of China and the New World of California. Kingston's narrative, for instance in the section entitled 'White Tigers', cuts abruptly from fiction (the account of a mythological swordswoman) to fact (life as a Chinese–American girl). The technique of rapid-crossing and juxtaposition creates a collage of voices; the mythic and literal, Chinese and American intermingle and weave together.

Kingston's book bears witness to Elaine Showalter's recent account of the hybridity which often marks women's writing: 'such writing is always double-voiced, what Henry Louis Gates, speaking of Afro-American literature, calls "two-toned", or Rámon Saldívar, speaking of Chicano literature calls "the dialectics of difference", or Naomi Schor, speaking of women's literature, calls "bitextual" '.[17] The hybrid work that results, the 'double-voiced' or 'bitextual' work, moves between cultural spheres, being both within and outside the dominant culture. *The Woman Warrior* is a hybrid or bitextual work not only in its imagining of cultural anthropology but also in its generic configuration. Strictly speaking, this is an autobiography; but discussions of the book occur largely in accounts of American fiction. Kingston stretches autobiographical discourse to breaking point. The development of the writer from girlhood to adulthood provides the loosest of plots; the reader often searches in vain for concrete details of chronology and place. It is the memories and tales of the Chinese homeland which are frequently foregrounded in place of the expected curve of a life-story: the book has its roots in that real life, but the overall effect is to show how ordinary lives are endlessly created out of stories.

As a work about storytelling and self-representation, *The Woman Warrior* is studded with parable-like tales about language, but for Kingston there are *two* languages. A major achievement of *The Woman Warrior* lies in Kingston's embedding of the insights of linguistic theory – particularly about language-learning and biculturalism – within everyday domestic scenarios. At one point Brave Orchid, the mother, cuts through her daughter's tongue because she believes this will quite literally 'free' her speech:

> 'I cut it so that you would not be tongue-tied. Your tongue would be able to move in any language. You'll be able to speak languages that are completely different from one another. You'll be able to pronounce anything. Your fraenum looked too tight to do those things, so I cut it.'[18]

Speaking, voices, tongues: Kingston interprets migrant experience as a journey across linguistic boundaries as much as the literal crossing of geographical space. She has said of her Chinese heritage that 'The culture was handed down orally. It wasn't necessary to be literate.'[19] The entry into America is thus seen as an initiation into a new way of talking. (One might contrast the *written* cultural identity of Jewish immigrants, as witnessed in Mary Antin's pride in her English compositions or, as we shall see, in Cynthia Ozick's suspicion of 'aural culture'.) For Kingston, acculturation is a process of oral transformations. 'Once a year the teachers referred my sister and me to speech therapy, but our voices would straighten out, unpredictably normal, for the therapists' (p. 155). And:

> Most of us eventually found some voice, however faltering. We invented an American-feminine speaking personality, except for that one girl who could not speak up even in Chinese school.   (p. 155)

The startling premise of *The Woman Warrior* is that for the Chinese community America is a land of 'ghosts' – their word for the Westerners. The Chinese homeland remains substantial, while experiences in the United States are bizarre, dreamlike or surreal. Kingston's account of migration and Americanisation is unusually powerful for not tracing the complete assimilation of the Chinese to American ways. The so-called 'New World' remains just that: new, mysterious, strange. When characters do become 'American' there is a process of disorienting transformation, a re-birth as the migrant's former life becomes as insubstantial as fiction. Kingston is fascinated by the fictionality of lived experience; family members insistently tell themselves stories and narrativise their lives as if they were characters in a novel:

It's as if I had turned into a different person. The new life around me was so complete; it pulled me away. You became people in a book I had read a long time ago.   (p. 139)

But in a novel where ongoing dialectics (between authors, between the real and the imagined) play such a central role, it is almost inevitable that *The Woman Warrior* cannot come to a rest at this point. After the renunciation of ghosts, the story turns back to superstition: the final paragraphs tell another Chinese tale, signalling at the end of this novel of immigration and assimilation into modernity a return to Asia's ancient rituals. In the to-and-fro between cultures there can be no final resting place. The conclusion of *The Woman Warrior* is open-ended: these complexities are brought into some sort of harmony but not into an utterly final resolution. Kingston finishes her autobiographical fiction (her fictional autobiography?) committed to an ongoing, dialectical negotiation between China and America: 'I continue to sort out what's just my childhood, just my imagination, just my family, just the village, just movies, just living' (p. 183). By this interplay between fiction and fact, America and China, Kingston moves towards a reading of culture as *hybridised*. Certain Chinese–American critics have attacked Kingston for failing to portray the unique reality of their community; but the conclusion to *The Woman Warrior* suggests that a specific culture is always in dialogue with others, and that cultures are formed by exchange. *The Woman Warrior* represents less a 'translation' of Chinese culture into English than the formulation of a new cultural artefact, neither irreducibly Asian nor fully American; the text occupies a borderland, a liminal space between the two worlds.[20]

Kingston produced her first 'novel' after two works of putatively non-fiction, *The Woman Warrior* and *China Men* (although these ostensibly biographical works were preoccupied with stories, storytelling and a sense of the pervasive fictionalisation of real life). *Tripmaster Monkey* (1989) is a woman's re-writing of the grand male narratives of America. Wittman Ah Sing, the protagonist, is named with comic inaccuracy after Walt Whitman, the founding father of American verse; and his louche student days in San Francisco during the 1960s are played out in the shadow of Kerouac and the Beatniks. *Tripmaster Monkey* thus becomes a picaresque novel about literary ancestry; the ancestor worship of *The Woman Warrior* is developed into a fiction about literary self-definition within a masculine tradition. One could imagine the slipperiness and instability of the protagonist generating a bleakly surreal meditation on the radical instability of the American character; but *Tripmaster Monkey* is too comic and optimistic to become an Asian–American *Invisible Man*. Kingston opts for a tumbling trawl through the absurdities of California in the 1960s. In interviews Kingston has talked about this book as being more 'American': 'In *Tripmaster Monkey*, I work a lot more with American rhythms, and directly with American language that I speak.'[21] Her use of historical and recognisably European literary codes such as the picaresque confirms this Westernising process. It suggest also the flexibility of the relationship between 'village' and nation, even within the career of an individual author. At the end of *The Woman Warrior* Kingston imagined the exchange between Asia and America as an open-ended dialectic. And this dialectic has proven to have a larger significance in her work; at certain points she gravitates more towards the American or Western pole of her hybridised imaginative world. Whereas Morrison saw the 'village' of her community acting as her audience, with the implication that her stories would then resonate beyond the *ethnos*, Kingston envisages an open-ended dialectic between communities (with no final resolution of the cultural exchange).

Cynthia Ozick: 'What Literature Means'

'For me, with certain rapturous exceptions, literature *is* the moral life', claimed Cynthia Ozick in 'What Literature Means' (1982). The forthright morality claimed by Ozick, and the trenchant didacticism of the essay title, are typical of her sense of art and its purposefulness. In an age increasingly suspicious of art's pretensions to teach the reader, Ozick, even in the apothegmic tone of her critical writing, continues with a defiant sense of literature's moral purpose:

> And the writers who insist that literature is 'about' the language it is made of are offering an idol: literature for its own sake, for its own maw: not for the sake of humanity.
> (*Literature is for the sake of humanity*)[22]

Hers is a passionate claim for the importance of art, staking a claim for literature as heightened humanist endeavour. However, Ozick's aesthetic, specifically her meditations on literature's purpose and the status of the writer, are as much inflected by her Jewishness as by a powerful humanism. Ozick's impassioned plea for literature's value derives from an anxiety about the place of creative writing within Judaic culture. Is the artist, in creating a fictional world and devoting herself to her own writing, creating a kind of false idol? It is intriguing that Ozick has accused literary postmodernists of a form of idolatry. Ozick has sometimes seen art as a transgressive practice, both because it appropriates creation to humankind and because, in literature, boundaries, notably between 'right' and 'wrong', become blurred. Morality under Rabbinical law is predicated on strict demarcation of boundaries; but the artist tends to want to cross borders, to explore the forbidden zones of experience.[23] Ozick's critical language is suffused with religious terminology, as she tries to bring Judaism into a meaningful relationship with literary art. For instance, 'What Literature Means' constructs an argument about 'redemption' as a purpose of art ('the sense of possibility ... of deliverance'). And in interviews Ozick has talked extensively about her beliefs, and has highlighted various pathways between Hebraic culture and the practice of modern literature (she notes, for instance, how the term 'Midrash', used for exegesis of Biblical texts, has now become a term in critical hermeneutics).[24]

In interviews Ozick has also attacked what she sees as fashionable multiculturalism (again, on grounds that it fails to discriminate, that it does not demarcate cultures). We need to be careful in positioning her as an 'ethnic' writer since Ozick is sceptical about this kind of vocabulary. Nonetheless, there are congruences between Ozick's anxious meditation on the Jewish artist and Toni Morrison's discussion of the 'village' of African–American writing. Both writers repeatedly reflect on the complex interchanges and exchanges between a 'minority' *ethnos* and a broader American culture. For Morrison, the implied audience for her work is the area where this interchange finds its focus. For Ozick, the disjunction she senses between Hebraic morality and an increasingly secularised national literature is the focus. But the major differences between Ozick and Morrison lie in their contrasting ideas about written and spoken cultures. For Toni Morrison, as for many black writers, to engage with one's culture is to articulate the vernacular; African–American writing mediates between speech and writing. Ozick, though, is impatient with oral cultures. Her essay, 'The Question of Our Speech: The Return to Aural Culture' (1984) mourns the passing of the great age of mass literacy when print culture held sway. Ozick associates TV, film and even phone technology with a cultural diminishment; people talk and watch, rather than read and write. She believes in the primacy of written expression because in reading she discovers a uniquely imaginative, even mysterious, experience.[25] Ozick's faith in the supremacy of written, print culture is another manifestation of Hebraic culture in her work; devotion to books and to the written word is essentially scriptural. Her suspicion of 'aural culture' reflects long immersion in the fundamentally written nature of Jewish lore. Jewish–American writing has, in fact, produced many attempts to represent this culture's vernacular energies (think of Philip Roth's or Saul Bellow's first-person narrators); but Ozick has rarely attempted to represent the *sound* of Jewish America. To come to Ozick after reading in the male Jewish–American tradition one immediately notes the lack of an idiomatic, conversational buzz. Her narrating voice is characteristically rather flat and even-toned, as if eschewing the demotic vigour and oral immediacy found in books such as *Humboldt's Gift*.

Ozick's work has also been marked by a desire to move away from the social realism which has been such a recurrent feature of male Jewish–American writing. She has both courted and refuted the archetypal scenarios associated with Jewish–American fiction: the conflict between Jew and Gentile; assimilation; the place of religious observance in an overwhelmingly secular society. A story like 'Levitation' (1976) begins in a very straightforward way, addressing directly the cultural dilemmas of a Jewish husband and his gentile wife:

> A pair of novelists, husband and wife, gave a party. The husband was also an editor; he made his living at it. But really he was a novelist. His manner was powerless; he did not seem like an editor at all. He had a nice plain pale face, likable. His name was Feingold.
>
> For love, and also because he had always known he did not want a Jewish wife, he married a minister's daughter. Lucy too had hoped to marry out of her tradition. (These words were hers. 'Out of my tradition,' she said. The idea fevered him.)[26]

In its flat and almost schematic mapping of this hybridised marriage, Ozick sets up a 'problem fiction' familiar from earlier forms of Jewish fiction (this is a scenario out of Bernard Malamud or early Roth). What interests me here is the nearly parodic realism of the prose: simple detail, a bare rendering, clipped lucidity. Ozick then works as a fabulist, gradually insinuating marvels and mysteries into her deliberately flattened prose. In 'Levitation' she superimposes a fantastic conclusion on her social realist text. At a party, as the Jews become more heated in their discussion of race and cultural identity, their theorising causes them to levitate above the dull conversations of the Gentiles; Lucy imagines the room rising:

> She craned after it. Wouldn't it bump into the apartment upstairs? It was like watching the underside of an elevator, all dirty and hairy, with dust-roots wagging. The black floor moved higher and higher. It was getting free of her, into loftiness, lifting Jews.   (pp. 15–16)

The sense of fantastic disturbance is close to that of Franz Kafka: a surreal conjunction of the ordinary and the fantastic, encased in a relentlessly urban setting (the room akin to 'the underside of an elevator, all dirty and hairy'). Ozick deploys such magical episodes as a means to reflect on the fraught relationship between Jews and the larger culture. For Ozick, fantasy provides both an escape from, and a form of exhilarating, comic solution to, the question of how Jews and Gentiles might relate.

In *The Messiah of Stockholm* (1987), her best-known recent work, Ozick moves with often quite vertiginous rapidity from realism to fantasy, and in particular from a comedy of banal normality to a light, dizzyingly fabular mode. Lars Andemening, a Swedish book reviewer, believes himself to be the lost child of the martyred Polish–Jewish author, Bruno Schulz (who was killed by the Nazis). The opening scenes, like those of the stories in *Levitation*, create a comedy of office life: the petty squabbles of a trio of literary journalists. Lars, though, has more eccentric, even visionary beliefs; he believes in a lost genealogy which ties him to this perished literary icon. *The Messiah of Stockholm* displays, again, Ozick's fascination with the practice of writing, and her impassioned commitment to literature's transcendentalism (the 'possibility of deliverance' offered by writing). A reviewer of fiction,

Lars reads, translates, writes; the novel is set in an intensely writerly world of newspaper offices and bookshops. And out of this attentiveness to the textures of the literary life Ozick constructs a fable about literary remembrance. Lars finds the 'original' manuscript of Bruno Schulz's *The Messiah* – a moment of cultural recovery akin to Morrison's recuperation and renewal of black oral narratives:

> But there on the table lay the scattered *Messiah*. Retrieved. The original. *The Messiah*, spread out in its curiously rapturous Polish for anyone's bare blink. The original! Recovered; resurrected; redeemed. Lars, looking with all his strength, felt his own ordinary pupil consumed by a conflagration in the socket. As if copulating with an angel whose wings were on fire.[27]

The nonchalance of Ozick's narratives, as they incorporate fantasy into steady social realism, are redolent of Morrison's reconfiguring of realism in *Beloved*. For both novelists, elements of the fantastic and the visionary are allowed to rest alongside and within reality. Such elements of the fantastic and magical are also found in Kingston. For all three writers, in spite of their very real cultural differences, to be what used to be called a 'hyphenate American' is to envisage community as in part a mystical construct. Ghosts, visions, the fantastic: all three writers are *magical*, in the sense that they envisage community as predicated on acts of enchantment. And all three writers favour a kind of ordinary magic, where the fantastic (the ghost of *Beloved*, acts of levitation, the ghosts of white America) are embedded in a remarkably ordinary, even banal world.

This, then, is a further turn in what I have called the radical communitarianism of recent women's writing: that community is imagined not in terms of a secular *ethnos* but as a magical or fantastic web of belief. The village is sometimes marked by a vernacular culture (Kingston and Morrison), or is sometimes predicated on a written body of law and lore (Ozick). But for all three writers the hybridised culture is shaped by acts of enchantment or magic. Toni Morrison recalled in a 1986 interview:

> I grew up in a house in which people talked about their dreams with the same authority that they talked about what 'really' happened. They had visitations and did not find that fact

shocking and they had some sweet, intimate connection with things that were not empirically verifiable. It not only made them for me the most interesting people in the world – it was an enormous resource for the solution of certain kinds of problems.[28]

These contemporary women writers are continuing to develop insights first realised in earlier fictions. In the work of a Sarah Orne Jewett or Zora Neale Hurston, 'community' was increasingly seen in anthropological terms. The intense materialism of Victorian realism gave way to an apprehension of social interconnection in terms of folklore, ritual and storytelling (hence, the emphasis on vernacular traditions, and the meditations on supposedly trivial activities such as cooking). At the end of the century the folkloric and anthropological foundations of American women's fiction have been widened to incorporate the magical beliefs of a community. The magical realism of these writers lies not so much in the use of surreal or magical literary devices to illuminate everyday realities, as in the recognition that reality is in itself rooted in magic, superstition, myth: the foundational structures of community are non-empirical.

Notes

Notes to the Introduction

1. Two biographies encapsulate the impact of feminism on the critical study of American women's writing: Sharon O'Brien, *Willa Cather: The Emerging Voice* (New York and Oxford: Oxford University Press, 1987) and Cynthia Griffin Wolff, *A Feast of Words: The Triumph of Edith Wharton* (New York: Oxford University Press, 1977). Wolff, for instance, argues that Wharton had been emotionally starved as a child, and that her 'feast of words' provided compensation for this trauma. Both Wolff and O'Brien write a feminist psychobiography of their subject.
2. On the various paradigm shifts in American literary studies see Philip Fisher, 'American Literary and Cultural Studies since the Civil War', in Stephen Greenblatt and Giles Gunn (eds), *Redrawing the Boundaries: The Transformation of English and American Literary Studies* (New York: MLA, 1992), pp. 232–50. Nina Baym's essay 'Melodramas of Beset Manhood – How Theories of American Fiction Exclude Women Authors' remains the classic feminist attack on the theoretical structuring of the American canon (see Elaine Showalter (ed.), *The New Feminist Criticism* (London: Virago, 1986), pp. 63–80).
3. Elaine Showalter, *Sister's Choice: Tradition and Change in American Women's Writing* (Oxford and New York: Oxford University Press, 1994), p. 146.
4. Annette Kolodny, 'A Map for Rereading: Or, Gender and the Interpretation of Literary Texts', *New Literary History*, **11** (1980), pp. 451–67. Two other important essays on this subject are: Carla Kaplan, 'Reading Feminist Readings: Recuperative Reading and the Silent Heroine of Feminist Criticism', in Elaine Hedges and Shelley Fisher Fishkin (eds), *Listening to Silences: New Essays in Feminist Criticism* (New York and Oxford: Oxford University Press, 1994), pp. 168–94; Deborah McDowell, ' "The Changing Same": Generational Connections and Black Women Novelists', *New Literary History*, **18** (1987), pp. 281–302.
5. Alice Walker, 'Dedication' to *I Love Myself when I am Laughing: A Zora Neale Hurston Reader*, ed. Alice Walker (New York: Feminist Press, 1979), p. 2.
6. Susan Sontag, 'Note on the Play', *Alice in Bed* (New York: Farrar, Straus & Giroux, 1993), p. 116.
7. Ibid., p. 117.
8. My discussion here is indebted to Elaine Neil Orr, *Subject to Negotiation: Reading Feminist Criticism and American Women's Fictions* (Charlottesville, Va., and London: University Press of Virginia, 1997).

Orr calls for 'a criticism of negotiations, a form of work that emerges where feminist readers and intellectuals argue for productive relations at the crossroads of difference and opposition' (p. 2).

9. Gillian Beer, '*The Waves:* "The Life of Anybody" ' in *Virginia Woolf: The Common Ground* (Edinburgh: Edinburgh University Press, 1996), p. 77.

10. Willa Cather, *On Writing,* with a Foreword by Stephen Tennant (1949; New York: Alfred A. Knopf, 1968), p. 12.

1 'Sickbed Deathbed Birthbed'

1. Susan Sontag, *Alice in Bed* (New York: Farrar, Straus & Giroux, 1993), p. 40.

2. T. J. Jackson Lears, in Richard Wightman Fox and Lears (eds), *The Culture of Consumption: Critical Essays in American History, 1880–1980* (New York: Pantheon Books, 1983), pp. 3–4. T. J. Jackson Lears, *No Place of Grace: Antimodernism and the Transformation of American Culture, 1880–1920* (New York: Pantheon, 1981), pp. 47–58, 'A Psychic Crisis: Neurasthenia and the Emergence of a Therapeutic World View'. Christopher Lasch, *The Culture of Narcissism: American Life in an Age of Diminishing Expectations* (New York: W. W. Norton, 1978) – Lasch primarily discusses postwar American life, but it is clear that he regarded the end of the nineteenth century as the point when narcissism and its attendant therapies first emerged. See his discussion of the waning of the Protestant work ethic (see pp. 52–63).

3. Cited in the 'Introduction' to *The Diary of Alice James,* ed. and with an Introduction by Leon Edel (Harmondsworth: Penguin, 1964), p. 15. Future references in the text are to this edition.

4. Ernest Hemingway to Edmund Wilson, 25 November 1923, *Selected Letters, 1917–1961,* ed. Carlos Baker (New York: Scribner's, 1981), p. 105. I discuss Hemingway's response to Cather in my *Willa Cather in Context: Progress, Race, Empire* (London: Macmillan, 1996), pp. 4–5.

5. Toni Morrison, interview with Tom Le Clair, in Le Clair and Larry McCaffery (eds), *Anything Can Happen: Interviews with Contemporary American Novelists* (Urbana, Ill.: University of Illinois Press, 1983), pp. 252–61 at p. 253.

6. Rosa Braidotti, *Nomadic Subjects: Embodiment and Sexual Difference in Contemporary Feminist Theory* (New York: Columbia University Press, 1994).

7. Kristin Boudreau, ' "A Barnum Monstrosity": Alice James and the Spectacle of Sympathy', *American Literature,* **65** (1993), pp. 53–67 at p. 56. See also Mary Cappello, 'Alice James: "Neither Dead nor Alive" ', *American Imago,* **45** (1988), pp. 127–62. Cappello persuasively argues that James used a kind of comic indifference to her fate to create imaginative freedom.

8. Julie Bates Dock, ' "But one Expects That": Charlotte Perkins Gilman's "The Yellow Wallpaper" and the Shifting Light of

Scholarship', *PMLA*, **111** (1996), pp. 52–63, discusses the fraught textual history of Gilman's story, and argues that many modern editions do not use the most authoritative 1892 *New England Magazine* text. All my quotations are from the Oxford Classics edition, which does use this text: *The Yellow Wallpaper and Other Stories*, edited by Robert Shulman (Oxford: Oxford University Press, 1995). All quotations in my text are to this edition.

9. William Davitt Bell (citing Henry James and William Dean Howells), *The Problem of American Realism: Studies in the Cultural History of a Literary Idea* (Chicago, Ill.: University of Chicago Press, 1993), pp. 175–6.

10. Recently, however, critics have offset Gilman's radicalism by arguing that her politics of colour and race were reactionary. Elizabeth Ammons in *Contending Stories: American Women Writers at the Turn into the Twentieth Century* (New York and Oxford: Oxford University Press, 1992), pp. 34–43, argues that the polemic power of 'The Yellow Wallpaper' is limited by the very specificity of Gilman's focus on a white, middle-class heroine. My discussion of Sylvia Plath's *The Bell Jar* deals with a later version of this argument (bell hooks's attack on 1960s middle-class feminists). Susan S. Lanser makes the depressing suggestion that the horror of 'yellow wallpaper' is largely produced by end-of-century racial typecasting: 'Feminist Criticism, "The Yellow Wallpaper," and the Politics of Color in America', *Feminist Studies*, **15** (1989), pp. 415–41.

11. Willa Cather, 'Preface' to *The Best Stories of Sarah Orne Jewett* (1925), reprinted in *The Country of the Pointed Firs and Other Stories* (Garden City, NY: Doubleday, 1956), p. 11. Another version of this essay, which omits the quoted sentences, was published in Cather's 1936 collection, *Not Under Forty*.

12. Jane Tompkins, *Sensational Designs: The Cultural Work of American Fiction, 1790–1860* (New York and Oxford: Oxford University Press, 1985), p. 124.

13. Carroll Smith-Rosenberg, 'The Female World of Love and Ritual: Relations between Women in Nineteenth-Century America', *Signs*, **1** (1975), pp. 1–29.

14. Sarah Orne Jewett, *The Country of the Pointed Firs and Other Stories* (London: Penguin, 1995), p. 92. Future references in the text are to this edition.

15. 'Jewett is both more "modern" (in her concern with circuits and exchange) and more "nineteenth-century" (in her religious belief and didacticism) than any turn-of-the-century local colorist is conceived to be' (June Howard, 'Unraveling Regions, Unsettling Periods: Sarah Orne Jewett and American Literary History', *American Literature*, **68** (1996), pp. 365–84 at p. 379).

16. Marilyn Sanders Mobley, *Folk Roots and Mythic Wings in Sarah Orne Jewett and Toni Morrison* (Baton Rouge, La., and London: Louisiana State University Press, 1991). She discusses the griot figure on pp. 79–82.

17. Ann Douglas, 'The Literature of Impoverishment: the Women Local Colorists in America, 1865–1914', *Women's Studies*, **1** (1972), 2–40.

18. Elaine Showalter, 'The Awakening: Tradition and the American Female Talent', in *Sister's Choice: Tradition and Change in American Women's Writing* (Oxford and New York: Oxford University Press, 1994), p. 67.
19. Review reprinted in *The Awakening* (New York and London: W. W. Norton, 1994), 'Contemporary Reviews', pp. 164–5 at p. 165. Future references to *The Awakening* are to this edition, and are given in the text.
20. Helen Taylor, 'Walking through New Orleans: Kate Chopin and the Female Flâneur', *Symbiosis*, 1 (1997), pp. 69–85 at p. 70. Taylor sets Chopin in the context of the cultural typecasting of New Orleans.
21. Rod Edmond, *Affairs of the Hearth: Victorian Poetry and Domestic Narrative* (London: Routledge, 1988). Edmond usefully summarises Victorian British domestic ideology, but also suggests that writers challenged this as often as they conformed to it. It is worth noting that a recent collection of short stories by Joyce Carol Oates, stories dealing with the aberrations of the home and domestic catastrophes, is simply entitled *Heat* (1991).
22. Per Seyersted, *Kate Chopin: A Critical Biography* (Oslo: Universitetsforlaget, 1969) pp. 25–6 details Chopin's interest in European writers including de Staël and Brontë.
23. Jonathan Little, 'Nella Larsen's *Passing*: Irony and the Critics', *African American Review*, 26 (1992), pp. 173–82 at p. 173. Little, like me, reads Larsen as an ironist rather than an affirmative or progressive writer.
24. A range of commentaries on the ending of *The Awakening* are included in the Norton critical edition. They include George M. Spangler, who sees suicide as a capitulation to sentimental conventions; Cynthia Griffin Wolff, who reads Edna's decline in psychoanalytical terms of neurotic collapse; and, above all, Chopin's biographer, Per Seyersted, who interprets self-destruction as an act of obdurate heroism. Suzanne Wolkenfeld (pp. 241–7) provides a useful overview of this dispute.
25. Pauline E. Hopkins, *Contending Forces: A Romance Illustrative of Negro Life North and South* (New York and Oxford: Oxford University Press, 1988), p. 13. Future references in the text are to this edition.
26. Siobhan Somerville also contends that there is a subtextual theme of 'female homoeroticism' (see her 'Passing through the Closet in Pauline E. Hopkins's *Contending Forces*', *American Literature*, 69 (1997), pp. 139–66).
27. Pauline Hopkins, *Of One Blood: Or, the Hidden Self, The Magazine Novels of Pauline Hopkins* (New York: Oxford University Press, 1988), pp. 440–621. The novel was also reprinted recently as *One Blood* (London: X Press, 1996). Susan Gillman, 'Pauline Hopkins and the Occult: African–American Revisions of Nineteenth-Century Sciences', *American Literary History*, 8 (1996), 57–82, makes the case that Hopkins 'accomplished a tremendous amount of African–American cultural work' (p. 70).
28. Richard Yarborough, 'Introduction' to *Contending Forces*, p. xxxvi.
29. The illustrations are reprinted in the Oxford University Press text of *Contending Forces*.

30. Frances E. W. Harper, *Iola Leroy or Shadows Uplifted* (London: X Press, 1997), p. 40. Future references in the text are to this edition.
31. John Ernest, 'From Mysteries to Histories: Cultural Pedagogy in Frances E. W. Harper's *Iola Leroy*', *American Literature*, **64** (1992), pp. 497–518, discusses the novel as a prime example of the cultural work achieved by African–American writers at the turn of the century. Harper, he notes, aims for moral uplift 'by engraving upon readers' hearts images representative of a transcendent standard of thought and of action' (p. 509).
32. Elizabeth Young, 'Warring Fictions: *Iola Leroy* and the Color of Gender', *American Literature*, **64** (1992). pp. 273–97, describes the novel as a domestic, feminized vision of war: 'Harper embeds the war in a narrative trajectory of maternal quest and reunion, simultaneously feminizing war narrative and using this literary form to represent the importance of maternal and familial structures in the black community' (p. 274).
33. The subject of the mother in American women's fiction remains relatively unexplored; work so far concentrates on psychoanalytical rather than cultural–historical readings. See the 'Introduction' to Brenda O. Daly and Maureen T. Reddy, *Narrating Mothers: Theorizing Maternal Subjectivities* (Knoxville, Tenn.: University of Tennessee Press, 1991), pp. 1–18.

2 Re-making the Home

1. Randolph Bourne, 'Trans-National America', *Atlantic Monthly*, **118** (1916), pp. 86–97 at p. 96.
2. F. Scott Fitzgerald, *The Great Gatsby* (London: Penguin, 1990), p. 29.
3. Thorstein Veblen, *The Theory of the Leisure Class* (1899; New York: B. W. Huebsch, 1918), p. 179.
4. Charlotte Perkins Gilman, *Women and Economics: A Study of the Economic Relation between Men and Women as a Factor in Social Evolution*, ed. Carl N. Degler (1898; New York: Harper Torchbooks, 1966), pp. 93–4.
5. H. L. Mencken, 'Introduction' to *In Defence of Women* (1918; London: Jonathan Cape, 1927), p. 16. Future references in the text are to this edition.
6. Jayne L. Walker, *The Making of a Modernist: Gertrude Stein from 'Three Lives' to 'Tender Buttons'* (Amherst, Mass.: University of Massachusetts Press, 1984), p. xi.
7. Shari Benstock, *Women of the Left Bank: Paris, 1900–1940* (London: Virago, 1987), p. 163.
8. Gertrude Stein, *Three Lives* (1909; reprinted Harmondsworth: Penguin, 1979), p. 3. Future references in the text are to this edition.
9. Gertrude Stein and Leon M. Solomons, *Motor Automatism* (1896; reprinted with an introduction by Robert A. Wilson, New York: Phoenix Book Shop, 1969), p. 21.

10. Gertrude Stein, *Narration: Four Lectures*, with an introduction by Thornton Wilder (Chicago, Ill.: University of Chicago Press, 1935), p. 8.
11. Gertrude Stein, *Gertrude Stein's America*, ed. Gilbert A. Harrison (Washington, DC: Robert B. Luce, 1965), p. 34.
12. Gertrude Stein, *The Autobiography of Alice B. Toklas* (1933; London: Penguin, 1966), p. 39. Future references in the text are to this edition.
13. Willa Cather, interview with Flora Merrill for the *New York World*, 19 April 1925, reprinted in L. Brent Bohlke (ed.), *Willa Cather in Person: Interviews, Speeches and Letters* (Lincoln, Neb.: University of Nebraska Press, 1986), p. 77.
14. Rachel Blau DuPlessis, 'For the Etruscans', *The Pink Guitar: Writing as Feminist Practice* (New York and London: Routledge, 1990), pp. 1–19 at p. 8. Elaine Showalter surveys the quilt aesthetic in 'Common Threads', *Sister's Choice*, pp. 145–75.
15. Edith Wharton, *The Touchstone* (1900) in *Madame de Treymes and Others: Four Short Novels* (London: Virago, 1984), p. 82.
16. Elaine Showalter, 'The Death of the Lady (Novelist): Wharton's *House of Mirth*', *Representations*, **9** (1985), 133–49 at p. 147. Another study of this 'transitional' Wharton is Gloria C. Erlich, 'The Female Conscience in Edith Wharton's Shorter Fiction: Domestic Angel or Inner Demon?', in Millicent Bell (ed.), *The Cambridge Companion to Edith Wharton* (Cambridge: Cambridge University Press, 1995), pp. 98–116.
17. Henry James's 1912 comment on Wharton serves as the starting-point for Stuart Hutchinson's essay 'From *Daniel Deronda* to *The House of Mirth*', *Essays in Criticism*, **XLVII** (1997), pp. 315–31. Hutchinson unfavourably contrasts Wharton's sense of character and moral choice to her forebear's.
18. Edith Wharton, *The Custom of the Country* (1913; London: Everyman, 1993), p. 27. Future quotations in the text are to this edition.
19. Edith Wharton, *The Age of Innocence* (1920; London: Everyman, 1993), pp. 46–9.
20. Harold E. Stearns, 'The Intellectual Life', in H. E. Stearns (ed.), *Civilization in the United States: An Inquiry by Thirty Americans* (1922; Westport, Conn.: Greenwood Press, 1971), p. 135.
21. Guy Reynolds, *Willa Cather in Context*, pp. 37–45.
22. Two examples of this feminist criticism include the aforementioned essay by Gloria Erlich, 'The Female Conscience in Edith Wharton's Shorter Fiction', and Rhonda Skillern's 'Becoming a "Good Girl": Law, Language, and Ritual in Edith Wharton's *Summer*', also in *The Cambridge Companion to Edith Wharton*, pp. 117–36.
23. Edith Wharton, *Summer* (1917; London: Penguin, 1993), p. 5. Future quotations in the text are to this edition.
24. *A Backward Glance*, cited and discussed by Dale M. Bauer, *Edith Wharton's Brave New Politics* (Madison, Wis.: University of Wisconsin Press, 1994), p. 31.
25. Jonathan Raban discusses these books, and their projection of a dangerously idealised rural life, in *Bad Land: An American Romance*

(London: Picador, 1996), pp. 34–40.

26. Dale M. Bauer, *Edith Wharton's Brave New Politics* (Madison, Wis.: University of Wisconsin Press, 1994), constructs a more upbeat reading of Charity's desire in a chapter, '*Summer* and the Rhetoric of Reproduction', although her phrasing indicates the strain of holding this argumentative line: 'Lest I sound too celebratory in this reading of Charity's desire . . .' (p. 48).

27. Mary Antin, *The Promised Land*, edited and introduced by Werner Sollors (1912; New York and London: Penguin, 1997), p. 1. Future quotations in the text are to this edition.

28. For a detailed review of this life, see Werner Sollors's excellent Introduction to the Penguin edition, pp. xi–lvi.

3 Modernist Geographies

1. Willa Cather, *Not under Forty* (London: Cassell, 1936), p. v. The major example of a critical reading of Cather as nostalgist is Granville Hicks's attack, 'The Case against Willa Cather' (1933), reprinted in *Willa Cather and her Critics*, ed. James Schroeter (Ithaca, NY: Cornell University Press, 1967), pp. 139–47.

2. Edna Ferber is now forgotten, but in her day she was an important popular writer; her work illustrates middlebrow taste. Two of her novels served as the basis for theatrical and then cinematic productions (*Show Boat*) and Hollywood movies (*Giant*).

3. Randolph Bourne, 'Trans-National America', *Atlantic Monthly*, **118** (1916), pp. 86–97.

4. For a reading of Cather that links her sense of nation and community to her sexuality (a rich source of comparison with Stein), see Christopher Nealon, 'Affect-Genealogy: Feeling and Affiliation in Willa Cather', *American Literature*, **69** (1997), pp. 5–37. 'Cather assembled a lesbian strategy for imagining an America in which feeling, not family, would be the basis of affiliation' (p. 11).

5. Donald Sutherland, 'Willa Cather: the Classic Voice', in *The Art of Willa Cather*, ed. Bernice Slote and Virginia Faulkner (Lincoln, Neb.: University of Nebraska Press, 1974), pp. 156–79. See also John H. Randall III, 'Willa Cather and the Pastoral Tradition', in *Five Essays on Willa Cather: The Merrimack Symposium*, ed. John Murphy (North Andover, Mass.: Merrimack College, 1974), pp. 75–96. For a tougher analysis of Cather's classicism see Walter Benn Michaels, 'The Vanishing American', *American Literary History*, **2** (1990), pp. 220–41. Michaels relates Cather's classicism to a 1920s emphasis on the classics as a means to promote national identity and therefore resist the destabilising effect of mass immigration.

6. Joseph Farrell, 'Walcott's *Omeros*: the Classical Epic in a Postmodern World', *South Atlantic Quarterly*, **96** (1997), 247–73. This issue of *SAQ*, 'The Poetics of Derek Walcott: Intertextual Perspectives', contains numerous articles which usefully trace a postcolonial intertextuality.

7. Willa Cather, interview with John Chapin Mosher in The *Writer* (November, 1926), reprinted in L. Brent Bohlke (ed.), *Willa Cather in Person: Interviews, Speeches and Letters* (Lincoln, Neb.: University of Nebraska Press, 1986), p. 94.
8. Sharon O'Brien's chapter, 'Every Artist Makes Herself Born', in *Willa Cather: The Emerging Voice* (New York and Oxford: Oxford University Press, 1987), pp. 403–27, is the major statement of this thesis.
9. Willa Cather, *On Writing*, with a Foreword by Stephen Tennant (1949; New York: Alfred A. Knopf, 1968), pp. 30–2.
10. Willa Cather, 'The Novel Démeublé', in *Not under Forty*, pp. 47–56 at p. 53. Future page references to this essay are given in the text.
11. One might, for example, contrast Cather's comment to this: 'I can take any empty space and call it a bare stage. A man walks across this empty space whilst someone else is watching him, and this is all that is needed for an act of theatre to be engaged' (Peter Brook, *The Empty Space* (London: MacGibbon & Kee, 1968), p. 9).
12. For a discussion of the debate about Cather's anti-Semitism see Guy Reynolds, *Willa Cather in Context: Progress, Race, Empire* (Basingstoke: Macmillan, 1996) pp. 22–4.
13. Willa Cather, *The Professor's House* (1925; London: Virago, 1981), pp. 12–13. Future references in the text are to this edition.
14. Willa Cather, *Death Comes for the Archbishop* (1927; London: Virago, 1981), p. 5. Future references in the text are to this edition.
15. Willa Cather to Dorothy Canfield Fisher (7? April 1922), Dorothy Canfield Fisher Collection, Bailey/Howe Library, University of Vermont.
16. Edward A. and Lillian Bloom, 'The Genesis of *Death Comes for the Archbishop*', *American Literature*, **26** (1955), pp. 479–506.
17. For a number of essays that bring an 'ecopoetic' criticism into focus, see the pieces in *Studies in Romanticism*, **35** (1996), 'Green Romanticism', edited by Jonathan Bate.
18. Hermione Lee, *Willa Cather: A Life Saved Up* (London: Virago, 1989), p. 5.
19. Annette Kolodny, *The Land before Her: Fantasy and Experience of the American Frontiers, 1630–1860* (Chapel Hill, NC: University of North Carolina, 1984).
20. Willa Cather, *The Song of the Lark* (1915; revised edition, 1937; London: Virago, 1982), pp. 371–2. Future references in the text are to this edition.
21. Rebecca West, 'The Classic Artist', *The Strange Necessity* (1928; London: Virago, 1987), p. 215; Ellen Moers, *Literary Women* (London: Women's Press, 1978), p. 258.
22. Daniel Joseph Singal, 'Towards a Definition of American Modernism', *American Quarterly*, **39** (1987), 7–26 at pp. 17–18.
23. Annette Kolodny, *The Lay of the Land: Metaphor as Experience and History in American Life and Letters* (Chapel Hill, NC: University of North Carolina Press, 1975), pp. 4–6.
24. Willa Cather, *O Pioneers!* (1913; London: Virago, 1983), p. 309.

25. Lewis Mumford, 'The City', in Harold E. Stearns (ed.), *Civilization in the United States: An Inquiry by Thirty Americans*, pp. 3–20 at p. 3.
26. Blanche Gelfant, *The American City Novel* (Norman, Okl.: University of Oklahoma Press, 1954); Cecelia Tichi, *Shifting Gears: Technology, Literature, Culture in Modernist America* (Chapel Hill, NC: University of North Carolina, 1987).
27. Carolyn Allen, *Following Djuna: Women Lovers and the Erotics of Loss* (Bloomington, Ind.: Indiana University Press, 1996), p. 2.
28. Dianne Chisholm, 'Obscene Modernism: *Eros Noir* and the Profane Illumination of Djuna Barnes', *American Literature*, **69** (1997), 167–206 at pp. 170–1.
29. Djuna Barnes, *Nightwood* ('The Original Version and Related Drafts', Normal, Ill.: Dalkey Archive Press, 1995), p. 1. Future references in the text are to this edition.
30. Gertrude Stein, 'Tender Buttons' (1911), in *Look at Me Now and Here I Am: Writings and Lectures, 1909–45* (London: Penguin, 1971), p. 188. Future references in the text are to this edition.
31. Wayne Koestenbaum, 'Stein is Nice', *Parnassus*, **20** (1995), pp. 297–319 at p. 299. Koestenbaum's piece is one of the best accounts of Stein, not least because it eschews academic conventionalities in favour of lateral thinking about Stein's *oeuvre*.
32. Gertrude Stein, 'Geography' (1923), in *A Stein Reader*, ed. Ulla E. Dydo (Evanston, Ill.: Northwestern University Press, 1993), pp. 467–70 at p. 467. 'Geography' is a key term in Stein's middle period. Thus *Geography and Plays* (1922).

4 The Interwar Social Problem Novel

1. Catherine Gallagher, *The Industrial Reformation of English Fiction: Social Discourse and Narrative Form, 1832–1867* (Chicago, Ill.: University of Chicago Press, 1985). The other classic discussion of this topic is Raymond Williams's 'The Industrial Novels', in *Culture and Society* (1958; London: Hogarth Press, 1987), pp. 87–109.
2. Women were central to these projects; *American Speech* was edited by Willa Cather's friend, Louise Pound.
3. Franz Boas, 'Preface' to *Mules and Men* (1935), reprinted in Harold Bloom (ed.), *Modern Critical Views: Zora Neale Hurston* (New York and Philadelphia, Penn.: Chelsea House, 1986), p. 5.
4. Zora Neale Hurston, 'Characteristics of Negro Expression' (1934), reprinted in *The Sanctified Church* (Berkeley, Cal.: Turtle Island, 1981), p. 49.
5. *The Sanctified Church*, pp. 56–9.
6. Zora Neale Hurston, *Jonah's Gourd Vine* (1934) in *Novels and Stories* (New York: Library of America, 1995), pp. 3–171 at p. 29. Future references in the text are to this edition.
7. Houston A. Baker, Jr, *Blues, Ideology, and Afro-American Literature* (paperback edition; Chicago, Ill. and London: University of Chicago Press, 1987), p. 58.

8. Zora Neale Hurston, *Their Eyes Were Watching God* (1937; London: Virago, 1986), p. 243. This edition reprints the text of the 1937 J. B. Lippincott first edition, as does the Library of America collection, *Novels and Stories*. Future references in the text are to the Virago edition.

9. Alice Walker, 'Foreword' to Robert E. Hemenway, *Zora Neale Hurston: A Literary Biography* (1977; London: Camden Press, 1986), p. xii.

10. Emily Dalgarno, ' "Words Walking without Masters": Ethnography and the Creative Process in *Their Eyes Were Watching God*', *American Literature*, **64** (1992), 519–41 at pp. 520, 525. Dalgarno studied the manuscript in the Beinecke Library, Yale University; a scholarly edition of the novel, complete with textual criticism of the manuscript, has not yet appeared.

11. Henry Louis Gates, Jr, *The Signifying Monkey: A Theory of African–American Literary Criticism* (New York and Oxford: Oxford University Press, 1988), p. 183.

12. In fact, Gates's own analysis of Hurston seems to shift ground as it progresses. Although he begins with an almost Romantic conception of the writer as inheritor of an overlooked folklore, he concludes with discussion of Hurston's 'dialogical diction' (*Signifying Monkey*, p. 215), suggesting a position closer to the one I have outlined. For another discussion of these manoeuvres 'between and among black and white territories' see Elaine Neil Orr, *Subject to Negotiation*, pp. 46–66.

13. Richard Wright, 'Between Tears and Laughter', *New Masses* (5 October 1937), excerpted in Harold Bloom (ed.), *American Women Fiction Writers, 1900–1960*, vol. 2 (Philadelphia, Penn.: Chelsea House, 1997), p. 15.

14. Robert Hemenway, *Zora Neale Hurston: A Literary Biography*, p. 242. Hemenway discusses the responses of Locke and Wright to *Their Eyes Were Watching God*, pp. 240–3. Hurston's interest in the 'folk' and the 'folkloric' continues to be seen as an escape from 'history'. See Hazel Carby's contrast of Hurston to the urban realist, Ann Petry: *Reconstructing Womanhood: The Emergence of the Afro-American Woman Novelist* (New York and Oxford: Oxford University Press, 1987), pp. 164–6, 175. Carla Kaplan's 'The Erotics of Talk: "That Oldest Human Longing" in *Their Eyes Were Watching God*', *American Literature*, **67** (1995), pp. 115–42 refutes Carby by reading Hurston's folkloric interest in voice and desire within an historical context provided by the Harlem Renaissance.

15. Nella Larsen, *Quicksand* and *Passing* (1928 and 1929; London: Serpent's Tail, 1989), p. 18. Future references in the text are to this edition (which combines Larsen's two novels in one volume).

16. Claudia Tate summarises these arguments about the 'tragic mulatta' in 'Desire and Death in *Quicksand*, by Nella Larsen', *American Literary History*, **7** (1995), pp. 234–60 at pp. 238–9. Tate herself sets up a psychoanalytical reading: 'The desire of the text is to achieve Helga's black identity and to displace her abjected body' (p. 256).

17. Houston A. Baker, Jr, *Modernism and the Harlem Renaissance* (Chicago, Ill.: University of Chicago Press, 1987), pp. 31–2.

18. W. DuBois, 'The Talented Tenth' (1903), *Writings* (New York: Library of America, 1986), pp. 842–61 at p. 842.

19. For another reading of Larsen's commentary on black identity politics see Carla Kaplan, 'Undesirable Desire: Citizenship and Romance in Modern American Fiction', *Modern Fiction Studies*, **43** (1997), pp. 144–69. She interprets *Passing* in terms of a subliminal lesbian desire that is bound up with a search for racial and national belonging. 'Through Clare's desire for Irene and for blackness, Larsen is able to represent a complex play of possible – but incompatible and irreconcilable – understandings of race, identity politics, and the politics of recognition' (p. 162). Kaplan's acknowledgement of an 'incompatible and irreconcilable' range of political options is in keeping with my own sense of Larsen's sobering view of the talented tenth.

20. Commentary on the careers of American women writers, and what they might tell us about the economic and psychological shaping of creativity, is hampered by the lack of significant research in this area. There are many individual biographies, but very few synoptic accounts of what, *in toto*, the role of novelist meant to American women in the first half of this century.

21. Jessie Fauset, excerpts from her March 1922 column in *The Crisis*, reprinted in *The Chinaberry Tree: A Novel of American Life and Selected Writings* (1931; Boston, Mass.: Northeastern University Press, 1995), p. 348. Future page references to this novel and Fauset's essays are to this edition and are placed in the text.

22. For a discussion of Fauset and Larsen as radical explorers of black female desire see Ann duCille, 'The Bourgeois, Wedding Bell Blues of Jessie Fauset and Nella Larsen', *The Coupling Convention: Sex, Text, and Tradition in Black Women's Fiction* (New York: Oxford University Press, 1993), pp .86–109.

23. Jessie Fauset, *Plum Bun: A Novel without a Moral* (1929; Boston, Mass.: Beacon Press, 1990), p. 14. Future references in the text are to this edition.

24. See the discussion of the critical reception in Deborah McDowell's 'Introduction' to *Plum Bun*, pp. ix–xxxiii.

25. Laura Hapke, *Daughters of the Great Depression: Women, Work, and Fiction in the American 1930s* (Athens, Ga., and London: University of Georgia Press, 1995).

26. Constance Coiner, *Better Red: The Writing and Resistance of Tillie Olsen and Meridel Le Sueur* (New York and Oxford: Oxford University Press, 1995), p. 27.

27. Agnes Smedley, *Daughter of Earth* (New York: Feminist Press, 1973), p. 8. Future quotations in the text are to this edition.

5 'There are So Many Horrible Examples of Regional Writers'

1. 'An Interview with Flannery O'Connor and Robert Penn Warren', *Vagabond* (Vanderbilt University), 4 (February 1960), pp. 9–17 at p. 17.

2. Louis D. Rubin and Robert D. Jacobs, 'Introduction' to *South: Modern Southern Literature in its Cultural Setting* (1961; Westport, Conn.: Greenwood Press, 1974), p. 12.
3. Two important accounts of the field: C. Hugh Holman, *The Roots of Southern Writing: Essays on the Literature of the American South* (Athens, Ga.: University of Georgia Press, 1972); Richard Gray, *The Literature of Memory* (London: Edward Arnold, 1977).
4. Carla Kaplan, 'Reading Feminist Readings: Recuperative Reading and the Silent Heroine of Feminist Criticism', in Elaine Hedges and Shelley Fisher Fishkin (eds), *Listening to Silences: New Essays in Feminist Criticism* (New York and Oxford: Oxford University Press, 1994), pp. 168–94. As the title suggests, this volume is a prime example of a feminist criticism rooted in the idea of 'silence'.
5. Lorna Scott Fox, review of Paul Binding's, *The Still Moment, London Review of Books*, vol. 16, no.18 (22 September 1994).
6. Eudora Welty, *One Time, One Place: Mississippi in the Depression – A Snapshot Album* (New York: Random House, 1971), p. 3
7. Ibid., p. 6.
8. Interview with Bill Ferris in *Images of the South: Visits with Eudora Welty and Walker Evans*, Southern Folklore Reports no. 1 (Memphis, Tenn.: Center for Southern Folklore, 1977), p. 23.
9. *One Time, One Place*, p. 8.
10. Eudora Welty, 'Preface' to *The Collected Stories of Eudora Welty* (London: Penguin, 1983), p. x. Subsequent references in the text are to stories reprinted in this volume.
11. Eudora Welty, *One Writer's Beginnings* (Cambridge, Mass.: Harvard University Press, 1984), pp. 68–9.
12. Patricia S. Yaeger, ' "Because a Fire Was in My Head": Eudora Welty and the Dialogic Imagination', *PMLA*, **99** (1984), pp. 955–73. Yaeger's is a relatively rare instance of the application of theoretical reading to Welty; the extent of Welty's complexity has continually been underestimated by literary scholars.
13. Harold Bloom, 'Introduction', *Modern Critical Views: Eudora Welty* (New York: Chelsea House, 1986), p. 6.
14. Eudora Welty, *Losing Battles* (1970; London: Virago, 1986), p. 155.
15. Willa Cather, *Death Comes for the Archbishop* (1927; London: Virago, 1981), p. 199.
16. Eudora Welty, *Delta Wedding* (1945; London: Virago, 1982), p. 30. Future references in the text are to this edition.
17. Charles Taylor, *Multiculturalism and the 'Politics of Recognition'* (Princeton, NJ: Princeton University Press, 1992), p. 25.
18. Katherine Anne Porter, *The Days Before* (New York: Harcourt, Brace, 1952), p. 110.
19. Joan Givner, *Katherine Anne Porter: A Life* (New York: Simon & Schuster, 1982), pp. 360, 450–3; Janis P. Stout, *Katherine Anne Porter: A Sense of the Times* (Charlottesville, Va.: University Press of Virginia, 1995), p. 130.
20. Katherine Anne Porter, *The Days Before*, p. 188.
21. Katherine Anne Porter, 'Pale Horse, Pale Rider', in *The Collected*

Stories (London: Jonathan Cape, 1964), p. 306. Future references to this story are placed in the text and are to this edition.

22. On this subject see Nina Baym, 'The Myth of the Myth of Southern Womanhood', *Feminism and American Literary History* (New Brunswick, NJ: Rutgers University Press, 1992), pp. 183–96.

23. Eudora Welty, 'The Eye of the Story' (1965) in R. P. Warren (ed.), *Katherine Anne Porter: A Collection of Critical Essays* (Englewood Cliffs, NJ: Prentice-Hall, 1979), pp. 72–80.

24. Katherine Anne Porter, 'Flowering Judas', in *Flowering Judas and Other Stories* (London: Jonathan Cape, 1936), pp. 148, 152, 167.

25. Caroline Gordon, *None Shall Look Back* (1937; New York: Cooper Square, 1971), pp. 102–3. Future quotations in the text are to this edition.

26. Frederick Hoffman, 'Caroline Gordon: The Special Yield', *Critique* , 1 (1956), pp. 29–35 at p. 31.

27. Caroline Gordon, 'Flannery O'Connor's Wise Blood', *Critique*, 2 (1958), pp. 3–10 at p. 9.

28. Joyce Carol Oates, 'The Action of Mercy', *The Kenyon Review*, 20 (1998), pp. 157–60 at p. 158.

29. Flannery O'Connor, letters to Miss Cecil Dawkins: 19 May 1957, in *The Habit of Being: Letters*, ed. Sally Fitzgerald (New York: Farrar, Straus & Giroux, 1979), p. 221; 12 September 1958, in the O'Connor material, Special Collections, McFarlin Library, University of Tulsa, Oklahoma.

30. Flannery O'Connor, *The Complete Stories of Flannery O'Connor* (1971; London: Faber & Faber, 1990), p. 508. Future references to this collection of stories are placed in the text.

31. Jon Lance Bacon, *Flannery O'Connor and Cold War Culture* (Cambridge: Cambridge University Press, 1993), pp. 3, 156. The problem with Bacon's argument is that Catholics as often as not were super-patriots within the US of the 1950s. Senator Joe McCarthy's appeal was, in part, to Catholics keen to demonstrate their nationalism by attacks on 'reds' and horrifed by 'atheistic communism'. The account of the sorority awards was in the *Atlanta Journal* (24 April 1960), p. 156 (amongst the O'Connor material, McFarlin Library).

32. Letter to Miss Cecil Dawkins, 9 October 1958, *The Habit of Being: Letters*, p. 298.

33. Letter to Miss Cecil Dawkins, 28 May 1961, McFarlin Library. This letter is not collected in *The Habit of Being*; certain other political statements are either edited in Fitzgerald's volume, or not collected at all.

34. Flannery O'Connor, *The Habit of Being: Letters*, pp. 78, 101.

6 Dysfunctional Realism

1. Elaine Tyler May, *Homeward Bound: American Families in the Cold War Era* (New York: Basic Books, 1988), p. 135.

2. Carl Degler, *At Odds: Women and the Family in America from the*

Revolution to the Present (New York and Oxford: Oxford University Press, 1980), p. 439.

3. Marynia Farnham and Ferdinand Lundberg, *The Modern Woman: The Last Sex* (New York: Harper & Brothers, 1947). For a trenchant account of this work, see William H. Chafe, *The American Woman: Her Changing Social, Economic, and Political Roles, 1920–1970* (Oxford and New York: Oxford University Press, 1972), pp. 202–6.

4. Chester Eisinger, *Fiction of the Forties* (Chicago, Ill., and London: University of Chicago Press, 1963), p. 4.

5. See Thomas Hill Schaub's dissection of Mailer, 'Rebel without a Cause: Mailer's White Negro and Consensus Liberalism', in *American Fiction in the Cold War* (Madison, Wis.: University of Wisconsin Press, 1991), pp. 137–62.

6. Barbara Ehrenreich, *The Hearts of Men: American Dreams and the Flight from Commitment* (London: Pluto Press, 1983), pp. 30, 53.

7. Ibid., pp. 54–6 discusses *On the Road*.

8. Elizabeth Hardwick, *The Ghostly Lover* (1945; New York: Ecco Press, 1989), p. 312. Future references in the text are to this edition.

9. Ann Petry, *The Street* (1946; London: Virago, 1986). Future references in the text are to this edition.

10. Jean Stafford, *The Mountain Lion* (1947; Austin, Tex.: University of Texas Press, 1992), p. 231. Future references in the text are to this edition.

11. This piece and others written for the *New York Times* in the early 1970s are discussed by Shelley Ratcliffe Rogers, ' "A Heady Refreshment": Secrecy and Horror in the Writing of Jean Stafford', *Literature and History*, 3rd series, **3** (1994), pp. 31–63.

12. Ibid., p. 34.

13. 'Ann Petry talks about First Novel' (*Crisis*, **53**, January 1946), cited and discussed by Keith Clark, 'A Distaff Dream Deferred? Ann Petry and the Art of Subversion', *African American Review*, **26** (1992), pp. 495–505. Clark argues that Lutie might be seen as a subversive rather than a tragic heroine (a good example of the 'progressive' critical readings mentioned in earlier chapters).

14. Robert Bone, *The Negro Novel in America*, rev. edn (New Haven, Conn.: Yale University Press, 1965), p. 180.

15. Bucklin Moon, 'Both Sides of the Street', *New Republic* (11 February 1946); reprinted in Harold Bloom (ed.), *American Women Fiction Writers, 1900–60*, vol. 2 (Philadelphia, Penn.: Chelsea House, 1997), pp. 162–4.

16. Jane Bowles, *Two Serious Ladies* (1943), in *The Collected Works of Jane Bowles* (London: Peter Owen, 1984), p. 128. Future references in the text are to this edition.

17. John Ashbery, *New York Times Book Review* (29 January 1967); reprinted in Harold Bloom (ed.), *American Women Fiction Writers, 1900–60*, vol. 1 (Philadelphia, Penn.: Chelsea House, 1997), pp. 26–7 at p. 27.

18. Susan Rosowski, 'Molly's Truthtelling, or, Jean Stafford Rewrites the Western', in Michael Kowalewski, *Reading the West: New Essays on the*

Literature of the American West (Cambridge: Cambridge University Press, 1996), pp. 157–76 at p. 158.

19. Russell Reising, 'Making the World Safe for Symbolism: Charles Feidelson, Jr', in *Unusable Past: Theory and the Study of American Literature* (New York and London: Methuen, 1986), pp. 173–87.
20. Jean Stafford, *A Mother in History* (London: Chatto & Windus, 1966), pp. 3, 71.
21. Terry Caesar suggests that to place Stafford's portrait of the mother alongside male, postmodern representations of the mother (for example, in novels by Doctorow and DeLillo) would make 'intriguing reading': 'Motherhood and Postmodernism', *American Literary History*, 7 (1995), pp. 120–40 at p. 137.
22. Rosalind Rosenberg, *Divided Lives: American Women in the Twentieth Century* (London: Penguin, 1993), p. 147.
23. Elizabeth Hardwick, 'The Art of Fiction, 87', interview with Darryl Pinckney, *Paris Review*, 96 (1985), pp. 21–51 at p. 38.
24. Elizabeth Hardwick, *A View of My Own: Essays in Literature and Society* (London: Heinemann, 1964), p. 170.
25. Ibid., pp. 172–4. In the *Paris Review* interview Hardwick admitted that she no longer stood by this review, and acknowledged that she had been criticised for it. 'The Art of Fiction, 87', p. 42.
26. *A View of My Own*, p. 35.
27. Elizabeth Hardwick, *Sleepless Nights* (New York: Random House, 1979), p. 46. Future references in the text are to this edition.
28. Hazel Rowley, 'Poetic Justice: Elizabeth Hardwick's *Sleepless Nights*', *Texas Studies in Literature and Language*, 39 (1997), pp. 399–421. Rowley cites Hardwick's 'The Cost of Living' from the *New York Review of Books*, 18 October 1973.

7 'What's Happening in America'

1. Betty Friedan, *The Feminine Mystique* (1963; New York: W. W. Norton, 1974), pp. 19–20.
2. Christopher Lasch, *The Culture of Narcissism* (New York: W. W. Norton, 1978), p. 5.
3. *Radical Feminism*, ed. Anne Koedt, Ellen Levine and Anita Rapone (New York: Quadrangle Books, 1973), p. 280.
4. Two important surveys of the period illustrate the assumption that this experimentalism was masculine: Malcolm Bradbury, *The Modern American Novel* (Oxford and New York: Oxford University Press, 1984), and Tony Tanner, *City of Words* (London: Jonathan Cape, 1971). Oates is omitted from each study. Tanner deals with Sontag and Plath; Bradbury with neither.
5. Elaine Tyler May, 'Cold War – Warm Hearth: Politics and the Family in Postwar America', in Steve Fraser and Gary Gerstle (eds), *The Rise and Fall of the New Deal Order* (Princeton, N.J.: Princeton University Press, 1989), pp. 153–81. See also May's indispensable *Homeward*

Bound: American Families in the Cold War Era (New York: Basic Books, 1988).

6. Feminist articulations of postmodern theory encompass a vast terrain of argument. For a brief but illuminating selection see the texts collected in 'Epistemologies' in *Feminisms*, ed. Sandra Kemp and Judith Squires (Oxford and New York: Oxford University Press, 1997), pp. 142–215, especially the extracts from Jane Flax, Elizabeth Wright and Patricia Waugh.

7. Walter Benjamin, 'The Storyteller', in *Illuminations*, trans. Harry Zohn (London: Fontana, 1992), pp. 83–107 at p. 86, 89, 107.

8. *The Bell Jar* is another of those texts (cf. *The Awakening* or *Passing*) where critics have sought political progressivism amidst the ruins of the heroine's life. Thus Teresa De Lauretis's 1976 essay, 'Rebirth in *The Bell Jar*', reprinted in Linda W. Wagner (ed.), *Sylvia Plath: The Critical Heritage* (London and New York: Routledge, 1988), pp. 124–34.

9. Cited by Jacqueline Rose, *The Haunting of Sylvia Plath* (London: Virago, 1991), p. 107. Rose's study investigates the 'haunting' of Plath's *oeuvre* by 'real life', especially in the aftermath of her suicide.

10. Sylvia Plath, *The Bell Jar* (1963; London: Faber & Faber, 1966), p. 25. Future references in the text are to this edition.

11. Jacqueline Rose suggests, however, that the novel's adoption of the *New Yorker* style (punchy, epigrammatic, hip) represents a kind of wish-fulfilment for Esther: if she were a writer this Salinger-like prose would be the result (and therefore, in voicing this tale, Esther also enters the male world of writing which otherwise has excluded her) (*The Haunting of Sylvia Plath*, pp. 187–8).

12. bell hooks, *Feminist Theory: From Margin to Center* (Boston, Mass.: South End Press, 1984), pp. 1–15.

13. Susan Sontag, interview with Edward Hirsch, *The Paris Review*, **137** (1995), pp. 176–208 at p. 185.

14. Susan Sontag, 'The Aesthetics of Silence', *Styles of Radical Will* (1969; London: Vintage, 1994), p. 28.

15. *The Paris Review*, **137**, p. 190.

16. Susan Sontag, *The Benefactor* (1963; London: Vintage, 1994), p. 1.

17. *The Paris Review*, **137**, p. 187.

18. Liam Kennedy, *Susan Sontag: Mind as Passion* (Manchester: Manchester University Press, 1995), pp. 54–5.

19. Susan Sontag, *Death Kit* (1967; London: Vintage, 1994), p. 2. Future references in the text are to this edition.

20. George Dekker's *The American Historical Romance* (Cambridge: Cambridge University Press, 1990) remains the most comprehensive discussion of this form, and is particularly important for its discussion of the philosophical and historiographical roots of the genre.

21. Susan Sontag, *The Volcano Lover* (1992; London: Vintage, 1993), p. 236. Future references in the text are to this edition.

22. Georg Lukács, *The Historical Novel*, trans. Hannah and Stanley Mitchell (English edition; Harmondsworth: Penguin, 1962), pp. 32–3.

23. *The Paris Review*, **137**, p. 207.

24. Ibid., p. 195.

25. Sally Robinson, review essay on Oates, *Michigan Quarterly Review*, **31** (1992), pp. 400–14 at p. 411.

26. Joyce Carol Oates, *On Boxing* (1987; London: Bloomsbury, 1997), pp. 53–4.

27. Ibid., pp. 169–70, 33, 72.

28. Ibid., pp.167–8.

29. Joyce Carol Oates, 'Notes on Failure', *The Hudson Review*, **35** (1982), pp. 231–45 at pp. 231, 237.

30. Joyce Carol Oates, 'Frankenstein's Fallen Angel', *Critical Inquiry*, **10** (1984), pp. 543–54; 'Jekyll/Hyde', *The Hudson Review*, **40** (1988), pp. 603–8.

31. Joyce Carol Oates, 'Afterword', *Expensive People* (1968; Princeton, N.J.: Ontario Review Press, 1990), p. 242.

32. Joyce Carol Oates, 'How I Contemplated the World from the Detroit House of Correction and Began My Life over Again', in *The Wheel of Love* (New York: Vanguard Press, 1970), p. 170. Future references in the text are to this edition.

33. Philip Roth, *Reading Myself and Others* (London: Jonathan Cape, 1975), pp. 117–35 at p.120.

34. Joyce Carol Oates, *(Woman) Writer* (1988), cited by Tony Hilfer, *American Fiction since 1940* (London and New York: Longman, 1992), p. 190.

35. Joyce Carol Oates, *The Rise of Life on Earth* (New York: New Directions, 1991), pp. 109–10.

36. Robert Scholes, *The Fabulators* (New York: Oxford University Press, 1967), p. 12. Scholes has revised and expanded this book as *Fabulation and Metafiction* (Urbana, Ill.: University of Illinois Press, 1979).

8   Fictions for the Village

1. See, for example, Rafael Pérez-Torres, 'Knitting and Knotting the Narrative Thread – *Beloved* as Postmodern Novel', *Modern Fiction Studies*, **39** (1993), pp. 689–707.

2. Caroline Rody, 'Toni Morrison's *Beloved*: History, "Rememory," and a "Clamor for a Kiss" ', *American Literary History*, **7** (1995), 92–119 at p. 94.

3. Toni Morrison, interview with Tom LeClair, in Leclair and Larry McCaffery (eds), *Anything Can Happen: Interviews with Contemporary American Novelists* (Urbana, Ill.: University of Illinois Press, 1983), pp. 252–61 at p. 253.

4. Toni Morrison, *The Bluest Eye* (1970; London: Picador, 1990), pp. 1–2. Future quotations in the text are to this edition.

5. Susan Willis, 'Eruptions of Funk: Historicizing Toni Morrison', in Henry Louis Gates, Jr (ed.), *Black Literature and Literary Theory* (1984; New York and London: Methuen, 1987), pp. 263–83 at p. 265.

6. Toni Morrison, *Beloved* (1987; London: Picador, 1988), p. 3. Future references in the text are to this edition.

7. Frances E. W. Harper, *Iola Leroy*, p. 64.
8. Ashraf H. A. Rushdy, 'Daughters Signifyin(g) History: the Example of Toni Morrison's *Beloved*', *American Literature*, **64** (1992), pp. 567–97. Rushdy summarises the Garner story, and argues that Morrison's novel 'is about the establishment of a communal narrative' (p. 591).
9. 'Talking cure' and 'poetics of absence' are phrases used by Caroline Rody in her aforementioned essay, 'Toni Morrison's *Beloved*: History, "Rememory," and a "Clamor for a Kiss" ', pp. 99–100.
10. Peter Kolchin, *American Slavery, 1619–1877* (1993; London: Penguin, 1995), pp. 50, 126, 138.
11. Bessie W. Jones and Audrey Vinson, 'An Interview with Toni Morrison' (1985), reprinted in Danille Taylor-Guthrie (ed.), *Conversations with Toni Morrison* (Jackson, Miss.: University Press of Mississippi, 1994), pp. 171–87 at pp. 176–7.
12. My reading here is an Aristotelian one; but it might be argued that Morrison's enfolding of controlled, rational, reflective meditations and wild chaos (both erotic and violent) is equally indebted to Nietzsche's analysis of the Apollonian and Dionysian polarity within Greek tragedy.
13. Jones and Vinson, 'An Interview with Toni Morrison', p. 177.
14. Toni Morrison, cited by David Cowart, 'Faulkner and Joyce in Morrison's *Song of Solomon*', *American Literature*, **62** (1990), pp. 87–100 at p. 88. Cowart's piece is a typical example of an intertextual approach to Morrison; he locates stylistic similarities and thematic analogies, but fails to advance an embracing theory of why intertextuality is important to her.
15. Henry Louis Gates, Jr, 'Harlem on Our Minds', *Critical Inquiry*, **24** (1997), pp. 1–12 at p. 9.
16. Zora Neale Hurston, *Their Eyes Were Watching God*, pp. 23–4.
17. Elaine Showalter, *Sister's Choice*, p. 7.
18. Maxine Hong Kingston, *The Woman Warrior* (1977; London: Picador, 1981), p. 148. Future references in the text are to this edition.
19. 'A *MELUS* Interview: Maxine Hong Kingston', with Marilyn Chin, *MELUS*, **16** (1989), pp. 57–74 at p. 70.
20. Sau-ling Cynthia Wong, 'Necessity and Extravagance in Maxine Hong Kingston's *The Woman Warrior*: Art and the Ethnic Experience', *MELUS*, **15** (1988), pp. 3–26 discusses (and refutes) attacks on Kingston for the 'inauthenticity' of her fiction.
21. 'A *MELUS* Interview', p. 71.
22. Cynthia Ozick, 'What Literature Means', *Partisan Review*, **49** (1982), 294–7.
23. Janet Handler Burstein, 'Cynthia Ozick and the Transgressions of Art', *American Literature*, **59** (1987), 85–101. Burstein argues that stories such as 'Usurpation' expose the heretical self-aggrandisement of the artist.
24. Interview with Cynthia Ozick, conducted by Elaine M. Kauvar, *Contemporary Literature*, **34** (1993), pp. 359–94.
25. Cynthia Ozick, 'The Question of Our Speech: the Return to Aural Culture', *Partisan Review*, **51** (1984), pp. 755–73.

26. Cynthia Ozick, 'Levitation', in *Levitation: Five Fictions* (1976; Syracuse, NY: Syracuse University Press, 1995), p. 3. Future references in the text are to this edition.
27. Cynthia Ozick, *The Messiah of Stockholm* (New York: Alfred A. Knopf, 1987), p. 104.
28. Interview with Christina Davis (1986), reprinted in *Conversations with Toni Morrison*, pp. 223–33 at pp. 226–7.

Bibliography

The following bibliography is designed to suggest a series of varied routes into the study of American women's fiction. The material under the first four bibliographical headings will be of interest primarily to the more general reader in search of initial guidance; the last section, which collates articles on specific authors, is aimed at a more specialist readership. The emphasis there is on recent or current work in major research journals. In the first section, of primary texts by the authors themselves, I have followed the convention of listing the fictions themselves (by date of publication), followed by non-fiction works (essays, letters, etc.).

1. Primary Literary Sources

Antin, Mary, *The Promised Land* (1912; New York and London: Penguin, 1997).

Barnes, Djuna, *Nightwood* ('The Original Version and Related Drafts', Norman, Ill.: Dalkey Archive Press, 1995).

Bowles, Jane, *The Collected Works of Jane Bowles* (London: Peter Owen, 1984).

Brontë, Charlotte, *Villette* (1853; Oxford: Oxford University Press, 1984).

Cather , Willa, *Alexander's Bridge* (1912; London: Virago, 1990).

——, *O Pioneers!* (1913; London: Virago, 1983).

——, *The Song of the Lark* (1915, revised edition 1937; London: Virago, 1982).

——, *My Ántonia* (1918; London: Virago, 1980).

——, *One of Ours* (1922; London: Virago, 1987).

——, *The Professor's House* (1925; London: Virago, 1981).

——, *My Mortal Enemy* (1926; London: Virago, 1982).

——, *Death Comes for the Archbishop* (1927; London: Virago, 1981).

——, *Shadows on the Rock* (1931; London, Virago, 1984).

——, *Sapphira and the Slave Girl* (1940; London: Virago, 1986).

——, *Not under Forty* (London: Cassell, 1936).

——, *On Writing*, with a Foreword by Stephen Tennant (1949; New York: Alfred A. Knopf, 1968).

——, *Willa Cather in Person: Interviews, Speeches and Letters*, ed. L. Brent Bohlke (Lincoln: University of Nebraska Press, 1986).

Chopin, Kate, *The Awakening* (1899; New York and London: W. W. Norton, 1994).

Crane, Stephen, *Maggie: A Girl of the Streets* (*A Story of New York*), ed. Thomas A. Gullason (1893; New York and London: W. W. Norton, 1979).

Dreiser, Theodore, *Jennie Gerhardt*, ed. James L. W. West III (1911; Philadelphia, Pa.: University of Pennsylvania Press, 1992).

Ellison, Ralph, *Invisible Man* (1952; London: Gollancz, 1953).

Fauset, Jessie, *Plum Bun: A Novel without a Moral* (1929; Boston, Mass.: Beacon Press, 1990).

——, *The Chinaberry Tree: A Novel of American Life and Selected Writings* (1931; Boston, Mass.: Northeastern University Press, 1995).

Ferber, Edna, *So Big* (New York: Doubleday, 1924).

Fitzgerald, F. Scott, *The Great Gatsby* (1926; London: Penguin, 1990).

——, *Tender is the Night* (1934, revised edition 1951; London: Penguin, 1986).

Gaskell, Elizabeth, *The Life of Charlotte Brontë* (1857; London: Penguin, 1985).

Gilman, Charlotte Perkins, *The Yellow Wallpaper and Other Stories*, ed. Robert Shulman (Oxford: Oxford University Press, 1995).

——, *Women and Economics: A Study of the Economic Relation between Men and Women as a Factor in Social Evolution*, ed. Carl N. Degler (1898; New York: Harper Torchbooks, 1966).

——, *The Home* (New York: McClure, Phillips, 1903).

——, *Herland* (1915; New York: Pantheon, 1979).

Gordon, Caroline, *Penhally* (1931; New York: Cooper Square, 1971).

——, *None Shall Look Back* (1937; New York: Cooper Square, 1971).

Hardwick, Elizabeth, *The Ghostly Lover* (1945; New York: Ecco Press, 1989).

——, *Sleepless Nights* (New York: Random House, 1979).

——, *A View of My Own: Essays in Literature and Society* (London: Heinemann, 1964).

Harper, Frances E. W., *Iola Leroy or Shadows Uplifted* (1892; London: X Press, 1997).

Heller, Joseph, *Something Happened* (London: Jonathan Cape, 1974).

Hemingway, Ernest, *The Essential Hemingway* (1947; London: Grafton, 1977).

——, *Selected Letters, 1917–1961*, ed. Carlos Baker (New York: Scribner's, 1981).

Hopkins, Pauline E., *Contending Forces: A Romance Illustrative of Negro Life North and South* (1900; New York and Oxford: Oxford University Press, 1988).

——, *Of One Blood: Or, the Hidden Self* in *The Magazine Novels of Pauline Hopkins* (1902–3; New York: Oxford University Press, 1988), pp. 440–621.

Hurston, Zora Neale, *Their Eyes Were Watching God* (1937; London: Virago, 1986).

——, *Novels and Stories* (New York: Library of America, 1995).

——, *I Love Myself when I am Laughing: A Zora Neale Hurston Reader*, ed. Alice Walker (New York: Feminist Press, 1979).

——, *The Sanctified Church* (Berkeley, Cal.: Turtle Island, 1981).

James, Alice, *The Diary of Alice James*, ed. and with an Introduction by Leon Edel (1894; Harmondsworth: Penguin, 1964).

Jewett, Sarah Orne, *The Country of the Pointed Firs and Other Stories* (London: Penguin, 1995).

Kesey, Ken, *One Flew over the Cuckoo's Nest* (1962; London: Picador, 1973).

Kingston, Maxine Hong, *The Woman Warrior* (1977; London: Picador, 1981).

——, *China Men* (1980; London: Picador, 1981).

——, *Tripmaster Monkey: His Fake Book* (London: Picador, 1989).

Larsen, Nella, *Quicksand and Passing* (1928, 1929; London: Serpent's Tail, 1989); this volume contains Larsen's two novels in one edition.

Lowell, Robert, *The Dolphin* (London: Faber, 1973).

——, *History* (London: Faber, 1973).

——, *For Lizzie and Harriet* (London: Faber, 1973).

Mailer, Norman, *An American Dream* (London: André Deutsch, 1965).

Miller, Arthur, *The Crucible* (1953; London: Penguin, 1968).

Morrison, Toni, *The Bluest Eye* (1970; London: Picador, 1990).

——, *Beloved* (1987; London: Picador, 1988).

——, *Jazz* (1992; London: Picador, 1993).

——, *Paradise* (1997; London: Chatto & Windus, 1998).

——, *Conversations with Toni Morrison*, ed. Danille Taylor-Guthrie (Jackson, Miss.: University Press of Mississippi, 1994).

O'Connor, Flannery, *Wise Blood* (1952; London: Faber & Faber, 1968).

——, *The Complete Stories of Flannery O'Connor* (1971; London: Faber & Faber, 1990).

——, *The Habit of Being: Letters*, ed. Sally Fitzgerald (New York: Farrar, Straus & Giroux, 1979).

——, 'An Interview with Flannery O'Connor and Robert Penn Warren', *Vagabond* (Vanderbilt University), 4 (February 1960), pp. 9–17.

Oates, Joyce Carol, *Expensive People* (1968; Princeton, N.J.: Ontario Review Press, 1990).

——, *The Wheel of Love* (New York: Vanguard Press, 1970).

——, *The Rise of Life on Earth* (New York: New Directions, 1991).

——, *Heat and Other Stories* (1991; New York: Plume, 1992).

——, *On Boxing* (1987; London: Bloomsbury, 1997).

——, 'Notes on Failure', *The Hudson Review*, 35 (1982), pp. 231–45.

——, 'Frankenstein's Fallen Angel', *Critical Inquiry*, 10 (1984), pp. 543–54.

——, 'Jekyll/Hyde', *The Hudson Reviw*, 40 (1988), pp. 603–8.

Olsen, Tillie, *Silences* (London: Virago, 1978).

Ozick, Cynthia, *Levitation: Five Fictions* (1976; Syracuse, N.Y.: Syracuse University Press, 1995).

——, *The Messiah of Stockholm* (New York: Alfred A. Knopf, 1987).

——, 'What Literature Means', *Partisan Review*, 49 (1982), pp. 294–7.

——, 'The Question of our Speech: The Return to Aural Culture', *Partisan Review*, 51 (1984), pp. 755–73.

Petry, Ann, *The Street* (1946; London: Virago, 1986).

Plath, Sylvia, *The Bell Jar* (1963; London: Faber & Faber, 1966).

Porter, Katherine Anne, *Flowering Judas and Other Stories* (London: Jonathan Cape, 1936).

——, *The Days Before* (New York: Harcourt, Brace, 1952).

——, *The Collected Stories* (London: Jonathan Cape, 1964).

Roth, Philip, *Reading Myself and Others* (London: Jonathan Cape, 1975).

Salinger, J. D., *The Catcher in the Rye* (1951; London: Penguin, 1994).

Smedley, Agnes, *Daughter of Earth* (1929; New York: Feminist Press, 1973).

——, *Battle Hymn of China* (New York: Alfred A. Knopf, 1943).

Sontag, Susan, *The Benefactor* (1963; London: Vintage, 1994).

——, *Death Kit* (1967; London: Vintage, 1994).

——, *The Volcano Lover* (1992; London: Vintage, 1993).

——, *Alice in Bed* (New York: Farrar, Straus & Giroux, 1993).

——, *Styles of Radical Will* (1969; London: Vintage, 1994).

——, *On Photography* (1977; London: Allen Lane, 1978).

——, *Illness as Metaphor* (New York: Farrar, Straus & Giroux, 1978).

Stafford, Jean, *The Mountain Lion* (1947; Austin, Tex.: University of Texas Press, 1992).

——, *A Mother in History* (London: Chatto & Windus, 1966).

Stein, Gertrude, *Three Lives* (1909; Harmondsworth: Penguin, 1979).

——, *Look at Me Now and Here I Am: Writings and Lectures, 1909–45* (London: Penguin, 1971).

——, *Geography and Plays* (Boston: Four Seas Company, 1922).

——, 'Pink Melon Joy' (1915) and 'Geography', (1923) in *A Gertrude Stein Reader*, ed. and with an Introduction by Ulla E. Dydo (Evanston, Ill.: Northwestern University Press, 1993), pp. 280–305, 467–70.

——, *The Autobiography of Alice B. Toklas* (1933; London: Penguin, 1966).

——, *Narration: Four Lectures*, with an Introduction by Thornton Wilder (Chicago: University of Chicago Press, 1935).

——, *Gertrude Stein's America*, ed. Gilbert A. Harrison (Washington, D.C.: Robert B. Luce, 1965).

Stein, Gertrude, and Leon M. Solomons, *Motor Automatism* (1896; New York: Phoenix Book Shop, 1969).

Steinbeck, John, *The Grapes of Wrath* (1939; London: Pan, 1975).

Stowe, Harriet Beecher, *Uncle Tom's Cabin* (1852; Oxford: Oxford University Press, 1998).

Tyler, Ann, *Saint Maybe* (1991; London: Vintage, 1992).

——, *Ladder of Years* (1995; London: Vintage, 1996).

Updike, John, *Rabbit, Run* (1960; London: André Deutsch, 1961).

Walcott, Derek, *Omeros* (London: Faber, 1990).

Welty, Eudora, *Delta Wedding* (1945; London: Virago, 1982).

——, *Losing Battles* (1970; London: Virago, 1986).

——, *The Collected Stories of Eudora Welty* (London: Penguin, 1983).

——, *One Time, One Place: Mississippi in the Depression – A Snapshot Album* (New York: Random House, 1971).

——, *One Writer's Beginnings* (Cambridge, Mass.: Harvard University Press, 1984).

Wharton, Edith, *The Touchstone* (1900) in *Madame de Treymes and Others: Four Short Novels* (London: Virago, 1984).

——, *Ethan Frome* (1911; London: Everyman, 1993).

——, *The Custom of the Country* (1913; London: Everyman, 1993).

——, *Summer* (1917; London: Penguin, 1993).

——, *The Age of Innocence* (1920; London: Everyman, 1993).

——, *French Ways and their Meaning* (New York: Appleton, 1919).

Wharton, Edith, and Ogden Codman, Jr, *The Decoration of Houses* (1897; New York: W. W. Norton, 1978).

2. The Historical and Cultural Context

DeBeauvoir, Simone, *The Second Sex*, trans. H. M. Parshley (1949; London: Jonathan Cape, 1953).

Bok, Edward, *The Americanization of Edward Bok* (New York: Scribner's, 1920).

Bourne, Randolph, 'Trans-National America', *Atlantic Monthly*, 118 (1916) 86–97.

Chafe, William H., *The American Woman: Her Changing Social, Economic, and Political Roles, 1920–1970* (Oxford and New York: Oxford University Press, 1972).

Cunard, Nancy (ed.), *Negro Anthology* (London: Wishart, 1934).

Degler, Carl, *At Odds: Women and the Family in America from the Revolution to the Present* (New York and Oxford: Oxford University Press, 1980).

Douglas, Ann, *The Feminization of American Culture* (1977; London: Macmillan, 1996).

DuBois, W., 'The Talented Tenth' (1903), in *Writings* (New York: Library of America, 1986), pp. 842–61.

Ehrenreich, Barbara, *The Hearts of Men: American Dreams and the Flight from Commitment* (London: Pluto Press, 1983).

Farnham, Marynia and Ferdinand Lundberg, *The Modern Woman: The Last Sex* (New York: Harper and Brothers, 1947).

Fox, Richard Wightman and T. J. Jackson Lears (eds), *The Culture of Consumption: Critical Essays in American History, 1880–1980* (New York: Pantheon Books, 1983).

Friedan, Betty, *The Feminine Mystique* (1963; New York: W. W. Norton, 1974).

Goodman, Paul, *Growing up Absurd* (1960; London: Gollancz, 1961).

hooks, bell, *Feminist Theory: From Margin to Center* (Boston, Mass.: South End Press, 1984).

Koedt, Anne, with Ellen Levine and Anita Rapone (eds), *Radical Feminism* (New York: Quadrangle, 1973).

Kolchin, Peter, *American Slavery, 1619–1877* (London: Penguin 1995).

Kolodny, Annette, *The Lay of the Land: Metaphor as Experience and History in American Life and Letters* (Chapel Hill, N.C.: University of North Carolina Press, 1975).

——, *The Land before Her: Fantasy and Experience of the American Frontiers, 1630–1860* (Chapel Hill, N.C.: University of North Carolina, 1984).

Laing, R. D., *The Divided Self: An Existential Study in Sanity and Madness* (Harmondsworth: Penguin, 1965).

Lasch, Christopher, *The Culture of Narcissism: American Life in an Age of Diminishing Expectations* (New York: W. W. Norton, 1978).

May, Elaine Tyler, *Homeward Bound: American Families in the Cold War Era* (New York: Basic Books, 1988).

——, 'Cold War – Warm Hearth: Politics and the Family in Postwar America', in Steve Fraser and Gary Gerstle (eds), *The Rise and Fall of the New Deal Order, 1930–1980* (Princeton, N.J.: Princeton University Press, 1989), pp. 153–81.

Mencken, H. L., *In Defence of Women* (1918; London: Jonathan Cape, 1927).

Raban, Jonathan, *Bad Land: An American Romance* (London: Picador, 1996).

Riesman, David, *The Lonely Crowd: A Study of the Changing American Character* (New Haven, Conn.: Yale University Press, 1950).

Rosenberg, Rosalind, *Divided Lives: American Women in the Twentieth Century* (London: Penguin, 1993).

Skolnick, Arlene, *Embattled Paradise: The American Family in an Age of Uncertainty* (New York: Basic Books, 1991).

Stearns, Harold E. (ed.), *Civilization in the United States: An Inquiry by Thirty Americans* (1922; Westport, Conn.: Greenwood Press, 1971).

Taylor, Charles, *Multiculturalism and the 'Politics of Recognition'* (Princeton, N.J.: Princeton University Press, 1992).

Veblen, Thorstein, *The Theory of the Leisure Class* (1899; New York: B. W. Huebsch, 1918).

West, Rebecca, *The Strange Necessity* (1928; London: Virago, 1987).

Whyte, William H., *The Organization Man* (New York: Simon & Schuster, 1956).

Wilson, Sloan, *The Man in the Gray Flannel Suit* (New York: Simon & Schuster, 1955).

Woolf, Virginia, *Three Guineas* (1938; London: Hogarth Press, 1986).

3. General Literary Studies and Literary History

Ammons, Elizabeth, *Contending Stories: American Woman Writers at the Turn into the Twentieth Century* (New York and Oxford: Oxford University Press, 1992).

Baker, Jr., Houston A., *Modernism and the Harlem Renaissance* (Chicago and London: University of Chicago Press, 1987).

——, *Blues, Ideology, and Afro-American Literature: A Vernacular Theory* (Chicago and London: University of Chicago Press, 1987).

Baym, Nina, *Feminism and American Literary History* (New Brunswick, N.J.: Rutgers University Press, 1992).

Bell, William Davitt, *The Problem of American Realism: Studies in the Cultural History of a Literary Idea* (Chicago and London: University of Chicago Press, 1993).

Benjamin, Walter, *Illuminations*, trans. Harry Zohn (1955; London: Fontana, 1992).

Benstock, Shari, *Women of the Left Bank: Paris, 1900–1940* (London: Virago, 1987).

Bloom, Harold (ed.), *American Women Fiction Writers, 1900–1960*, 3 vols (Philadelphia: Chelsea House, 1997).

Bone, Robert, *The Negro Novel in America*, rev. edn (New Haven, Conn.: Yale University Press, 1965).

Bradbury, Malcolm, *The Modern American Novel* (Oxford and New York: Oxford University Press, 1983).

Braidotti, Rosa, *Nomadic Subjects: Embodiment and Sexual Difference in Contemporary Feminist Theory* (New York: Columbia University Press, 1994).

Carby, Hazel, *Reconstructing Womanhood: The Emergence of the Afro-American Woman Novelist* (New York and Oxford: Oxford University Press, 1987).

Coiner, Constance, *Better Red: The Writing and Resistance of Tillie Olsen and Meridel Le Sueur* (New York and Oxford: Oxford University Press, 1995).

Daly, Brenda O., and Maureen T. Reddy, *Narrating Mothers: Theorizing Maternal Subjectivities* (Knoxville, Tenn.: University of Tennessee Press, 1991).

Dekker, George, *The American Historical Romance* (Cambridge: Cambridge University Press, 1990).

DuCille, Ann, *The Coupling Convention: Sex, Text, and Tradition in Black Women's Fiction* (New York: Oxford University Press, 1993).

DuPlessis, Rachel Blau, *The Pink Guitar: Writing as Feminist Practice* (New York and London: Routledge, 1990).

Edmond, Rod, *Affairs of the Hearth: Victorian Poetry and Domestic Narrative* (London: Routledge, 1988).

Eisinger, Chester, *Fiction of the Forties* (Chicago and London: University of Chicago Press, 1963).

Feidelson, Charles, *Symbolism and American Literature* (Chicago: University of Chicago Press, 1953).

Fiedler, Leslie A., *Love and Death in the American Novel* (New York: Criterion Books, 1960).

Gallagher, Catherine, *The Industrial Reformation of English Fiction: Social Discourse and Narrative Form, 1832–1867* (Chicago and London: University of Chicago Press, 1985).

Gates, Henry Louis, Jr, *The Signifying Monkey: A Theory of African–American Literary Criticism* (New York and Oxford: Oxford University Press, 1988).

—— (ed.), *Black Literature and Literary Theory* (1984; New York and London: Methuen, 1987).

Gelfant, Blanche, *The American City Novel* (Norman, Okl.: University of Oklahoma Press, 1954).

Gray, Richard, *The Literature of Memory* (London: Edward Arnold, 1977).

Hapke, Laura, *Daughters of the Great Depression: Women, Work and Fiction in the American 1930s* (Athens and London: University of Georgia Press, 1995).

Hilfer, Tony, *American Fiction since 1940* (London and New York: Longman, 1992).

Holman, C. Hugh, *The Roots of Southern Writing: Essays on the Literature of the American South* (Athens, Ga.: University of Georgia Press, 1972).

Kemp, Sandra, and Judith Squires (eds), *Feminisms* (Oxford and New York: Oxford University Press, 1997).

LeClair, Tom and Larry McCaffery (eds), *Anything Can Happen: Interviews with Contemporary American Novelists* (Urbana, Ill.: University of Illinois Press, 1983).

Lukács, Georg, *The Historical Novel*, trans. Hannah and Stanley Mitchell (Harmondsworth: Penguin, 1962).

Moers, Ellen, *Literary Women* (London: Women's Press, 1978).

Orr, Elaine Neil, *Subject to Negotiation: Reading Feminist Criticism and American Women's Fictions* (Charlottesville and London: University Press of Virginia, 1997).

Reising, Russell, *Unusable Past: Theory and the Study of American Literature* (New York and London: Methuen, 1986).

Rubin, Louis D., and Robert D. Jacobs (eds), *South: Modern Southern*

Literature in its Cultural Setting (1961; Westport, Conn.: Greenwood Press, 1974).

Schaub, Thomas Hill, *American Fiction in the Cold War* (Madison: University of Wisconsin Press, 1991).

Scholes, Robert, *Fabulation and Metafiction* (Urbana, Ill.: University of Illinois Press, 1979).

Showalter, Elaine, *Sister's Choice: Tradition and Change in American Women's Writing* (Oxford and New York: Oxford University Press, 1994).

Smith, Henry Nash, *Virgin Land: The American West as Symbol and Myth* (Cambridge, Mass.: Harvard University Press, 1950).

Tanner, Tony, *City of Words: American Fiction, 1950–1970* (London: Jonathan Cape, 1971).

Tichi, Cecelia, *Shifting Gears: Technology, Literature, Culture in Modernist America* (Chapel Hill, N.C.: University of North Carolina, 1987).

Tompkins, Jane, *Sensational Designs: The Cultural Work of American Fiction, 1790–1860* (New York and Oxford: Oxford University Press, 1985).

Williams, Raymond, *Culture and Society* (1958; London: Hogarth Press, 1987).

4. Books: Single-Author Studies

Allen, Carolyn, *Following Djuna: Women Lovers and the Erotics of Loss* (Bloomington, Ind.: Indiana University Press, 1996).

Bacon, Jon Lance, *Flannery O'Connor and Cold War Culture* (Cambridge: Cambridge University Press, 1993).

Bauer, Dale M., *Edith Wharton's Brave New Politics* (Madison: University of Wisconsin Press, 1994).

Beer, Gillian, *Virginia Woolf: The Common Ground* (Edinburgh: Edinburgh University Press, 1996).

Bell, Millicent (ed.), *The Cambridge Companion to Edith Wharton* (Cambridge: Cambridge University Press, 1995).

Bloom, Harold (ed.), *Modern Critical Views: Zora Neale Hurston* (New York and Philadelphia: Chelsea House, 1986).

——, *Modern Critical Views: Eudora Welty* (New York and Philadelphia: Chelsea House, 1986).

Ferris, Bill, *Images of the South: Visits with Eudora Welty and Walker Evans*, Southern Folklore Reports no. 1 (Memphis, Tenn.: Center for Southern Folklore, 1977).

Givner, Joan, *Katherine Anne Porter: A Life* (New York: Simon and Schuster, 1982).

Hemenway, Robert E., *Zora Neale Hurston: A Literary Biography* (1977; London: Camden Press, 1986).

Kennedy, Liam, *Susan Sontag: Mind as Passion* (Manchester: Manchester University Press, 1995).

Mobley, Marilyn Sanders, *Folk Roots and Mythic Wings in Sarah Orne Jewett and Toni Morrison* (Baton Rouge and London: Louisiana State University Press, 1991).

O'Brien, Sharon, *Willa Cather: The Emerging Voice* (New York and Oxford: Oxford University Press, 1987).

Reynolds, Guy, *Willa Cather in Context: Progress, Race, Empire* (Basingstoke: Macmillan, 1996).

Rose, Jacqueline, *The Haunting of Sylvia Plath* (London: Virago, 1991).

Schroeter, James (ed.), *Willa Cather and her Critics* (Ithaca, N.Y.: Cornell University Press, 1967).

Seyersted, Per, *Kate Chopin: A Critical Biography* (Oslo: Universitetsforlaget, 1969).

Slote, Bernice, and Virginia Faulkner (eds), *The Art of Willa Cather* (Lincoln: University of Nebraska Press, 1974).

Stout, Janis P., *Katherine Anne Porter: A Sense of the Times* (Charlottesville, Va.: University Press of Virginia, 1995).

Taylor-Guthrie, Danille (ed.), *Conversations with Toni Morrison* (Jackson, Miss.: University Press of Mississippi, 1994).

Wagner, Linda W. (ed.), *Sylvia Plath: The Critical Heritage* (London, and New York: Routledge, 1988).

Walker, Jayne L., *The Making of a Modernist: Gertrude Stein from 'Three Lives' to 'Tender Buttons'* (Amherst: University of Massachusetts Press, 1984).

Warren, Robert Penn (ed.), *Katherine Anne Porter: A Collection of Critical Essays* (Englewood Cliffs, N.J.: Prentice-Hall, 1979).

Wolff, Cynthia Griffin, *A Feast of Words: The Triumph of Edith Wharton* (New York: Oxford University Press, 1977).

5. Critical Articles

Baym, Nina, 'Melodramas of Beset Manhood – How Theories of American Fiction Exclude Women Authors', in Elaine Showalter (ed.), *The New Feminist Criticism* (London: Virgo, 1986), pp. 63–80.

Bloom, Edward, A. and Lillian Bloom, 'The Genesis of *Death Comes for the Archbishop*', *American Literature*, 26 (1955), pp. 479–506.

Boudreau, Kristin, ' "A Barnum Monstrosity", Alice James and the Spectacle of Sympathy', *American Literature*, 65 (1993), pp. 53–67.

Burstein, Janet Handler, 'Cynthia Ozick and the Transgressions of Art', *American Literature*, 59 (1987), pp. 85–101.

Caesar, Terry, 'Motherhood and Postmodernism', *American Literary History*, 7 (1995), pp. 120–40.

Cappello, Mary, 'Alice James: "Neither Dead nor Alive" ', *American Imago*, 45 (1988), pp. 127–62.

Chin, Marilyn, 'A *Melus* interview: Maxine Hong Kingston', *MELUS*, 16 (1989), pp. 57–74.

Chisholm, Dianne, 'Obscene Modernism: *Eros Noir* and the Profane Illumination of Djuna Barnes', *American Literature*, 69 (1997), pp. 167–206.

Clark, Keith, 'A Distaff Dream Deferred? Ann Petry and the Art of Subversion', *African American Review*, 26 (1992), pp. 495–505.

Cowart, David, 'Faulkner and Joyce in Morrison's *Song of Solomon*', *American Literature*, 62 (1990), pp. 87–100.

Dalgarno, Emily, ' "Words Walking without Masters": Ethnography and the Creative Process in *Their Eyes Were Watching God*', *American Literature*, 64 (1992), pp. 519–41.

Dock, Julie Bates, ' "But one Expects That": Charlotte Perkins Gilman's *The Yellow Wallpaper* and the Shifting Light of Scholarship', *PMLA*, 111 (1996), pp. 52–63.

Douglas, Ann, 'The Literature of Impoverishment: The Women Local Colorists in America, 1865–1914', *Women's Studies*, 1 (1972), pp. 2–40.

Ernest, John, 'From Mysteries to Histories: Cultural Pedagogy in Frances E. W. Harper's *Iola Leroy*', *American Literature*, 64 (1992), pp. 497–518.

Fisher, Philip, 'American Literary and Cultural Studies since the Civil War', in Stephen Greenblatt and Giles Gunn (eds), *Redrawing the Boundaries: The Transformation of English and American Literary Studies* (New York: MLA, 1992), pp. 232–50.

Gates, Jr, Henry Louis, 'Harlem on our Minds', *Critical Inquiry*, 24 (1997), pp. 1–12.

Gillman, Susan, 'Pauline Hopkins and the Occult: African–American Revisions of Nineteenth-Century Sciences', *American Literary History*, 8 (1996), pp. 57–82.

Hirsch, Edward, Interview with Susan Sontag, *Paris Review*, 137 (1995), pp. 176–208.

Hoffman, Frederick, 'Caroline Gordon: The Special Yield', *Critique*, 1 (1956), pp. 29–35.

Howard, June, 'Unraveling Regions, Unsettling Periods: Sarah Orne Jewett and American Literary History', *American Literature*, 68 (1996), pp. 365–84.

Hutchinson, Stuart, 'From *Daniel Deronda* to *The House of Mirth*', *Essays in Criticism*, 47 (1997), pp. 315–31.

Kaplan, Carla, 'Reading Feminist Readings: Recuperative Reading and the Silent Heroine of Feminist Criticism', in Elaine Hedges and Shelley Fisher Fishkin (eds), *Listening to Silences: New Essays in Feminist Criticism* (New York and Oxford: Oxford University Press, 1994), pp. 168–94.

——, 'The Erotics of Talk: "That Oldest Human Longing" in *Their Eyes Were Watching God*', *American Literature*, 67 (1995), pp. 115–42.

——, 'Undesirable Desire: Citizenship and Romance in Modern American Fiction', *Modern Fiction Studies*, 43 (1997), pp. 144–69.

Kauver, Elaine, M., interview with Cynthia Ozick, *Contemporary Literature*, 34 (1993), pp. 359–94.

Koestenbaum, Wayne, 'Stein is Nice', *Parnassus*, 20 (1995), pp. 297–319.

Kolodny, Annette, 'A Map for Rereading: Or, Gender and the Interpretation of Literary Texts', *New Literary History*, 11 (1980), pp. 451–67.

Lanser, Susan, S., 'Feminist Criticism, "The Yellow Wallpaper", and the Politics of Color in America', *Feminist Studies*, 15 (1989), pp. 415–41.

Little, Jonathan, 'Nella Larsen's *Passing*: Irony and the Critics', *African American Review*, 26 (1992), pp. 173–82.

McDowell, Deborah, ' "The Changing Same": Generational Connections and Black Women Novelists', *New Literary History*, 18 (1987), pp. 281–302.

Nealon, Christopher, 'Affect-Genealogy: Feeling and Affiliation in Willa Cather', *American Literature*, 69 (1997), pp. 5–37.

Pérez-Torres, Rafael, 'Knitting and Knotting the Narrative Thread – *Beloved* as Postmodern Novel', *Modern Fiction Studies*, 39 (1993), pp. 689–707.

Pinckney, Darryl, 'The Art of Fiction, 87', Interview with Elizabeth Hardwick, *Paris Review*, 96 (1985), pp. 21–51.

Roddy, Caroline, 'Toni Morrison's *Beloved*: History, "Rememory," and a "Clamor for a Kiss" ', *American Literary History*, 7 (1995), pp. 92–119.

Rogers, Shelley Ratcliffe, ' "A Heady Refreshment": Secrecy and Horror in the Writing of Jean Stafford', *Literature and History*, 3rd series, 3 (1994), pp. 31–63.

Rosowski, Susan, 'Molly's Truthtelling, or, Jean Stafford Rewrites the Western', in Michael Kowalewski (ed.), *Reading the West: New Essays on the Literature of the American West* (Cambridge: Cambridge University Press, 1996), pp. 157–76.

Rowley, Hazel, 'Poetic Justice: Elizabeth Hardwick's *Sleepless Nights*', *Texas Studies in Literature and Language*, 39 (1997), pp. 399–421.

Rushdy, Ashraf H. A., 'Daughters Signifyin(g) History: the Example of Toni Morrison's *Beloved*', *American Literature*, 64 (1992), pp. 567–97.

Singal, Daniel Joseph, 'Towards a Definition of American Modernism' *American Quarterly*, 39 (1987), pp. 7–26.

Smith-Rosenberg, Carroll, 'The Female World of Love and Ritual: Relations between Women in Nineteenth-Century America', *Signs*, 1 (1975), pp. 1–29.

Somerville, Siobhan, 'Passing Through the Closet in Pauline E. Hopkins's *Contending Forces*', *American Literature*, 69 (1997), pp. 139–66.

Tate, Claudia, 'Desire and Death in *Quicksand*, by Nella Larsen', *American Literary History*, 7 (1995), pp. 234–60.

Taylor, Helen, 'Walking through New Orleans: Kate Chopin and the Female Flâneur', *Symbiosis*, 1 (1997), pp. 69–85.

Wong, Sau-ling Cynthia, 'Necessity and Extravagance in Maxine Hong Kingston's *The Woman Warrior*: Art and the Ethnic Experience', *MELUS*, 15 (1988), pp. 3–26.

Yaeger, Patricia S., ' "Because a Fire was in my Head": Eudora Welty and the Dialogic Imagination', *PMLA*, 99 (1984), pp. 955–73.

Young, Elizabeth, 'Warring Factions: *Iola Leroy* and the Color of Gender', *American Literature*, 64 (1992), pp. 273–97.

Index

Major discussion of a particular author is indicated in **bold** type.